The Furious Passage of James Baldwin

The Furious Passage of James Baldwin

FERN MARJA ECKMAN

M Evans
Lanham • New York • Boulder • Toronto • Plymouth, UK

M. Evans
An imprint of The Rowman & Littlefield Publishing Group, Inc.
4501 Forbes Boulevard, Suite 200, Lanham, Maryland 20706
http://www.rlpgtrade.com

10 Thornbury Road, Plymouth PL6 7PP, United Kingdom

Distributed by National Book Network

British Library Cataloguing in Publication Information Available

Library of Congress Cataloging-in-Publication Data Available

ISBN 13· 978-1-59077-320-8 (pbk· alk paper)

♾™ The paper used in this publication meets the minimum requirements of American National Standard for Information Sciences—Permanence of Paper for Printed Library Materials, ANSI/NISO Z39.48-1992.

For Irv, my love

Acknowledgements

I would like to express my appreciation to James Baldwin for his unstinting cooperation on those occasions when he kept his appointments with me.

I am deeply grateful to all those—named and unnamed—who, by sharing with me their memories and experiences, helped me trace Mr. Baldwin's passage from Harlem to the present. To say that this book could not have been written without their assistance may seem like the conventional, pale tribute, but in this case represents no less than the truth.

I am indebted to Dorothy Schiff of the NEW YORK POST, who initially pointed the way; Marcy Elias Rothman and Nora Ephron for their research in Los Angeles and Puerto Rico, respectively; Jean Steinberg for her editorial suggestions; Art Simmons and Joseph A. Barry for their reports from Paris; Mollie Parkes and Dr. Leon Drusine for their many discussions with me on interpretation. To my friend and colleague, Ted Poston, and most of all to my husband, Irving Eckman, I offer affectionate thanks for their unfailingly patient criticism and counsel.

Fern Marja Eckman

New York City
June 21, 1966

All of James Baldwin's quoted comments, unless otherwise specified in the text or in the notes, were taken from transcripts of interviews I had with him over a period of twenty-nine months. The bulk of our talks took place in his New York residence (first in a friend's apartment, then in his own), but several were held under less formal circumstances in schools, a backyard, the lobby of the building in which he lived, the Overseas Press Club, a car, two bars and a station wagon.

F.M.E.

"Make this clear in your story. I do *not* hate white people. I can't afford to. Just because I want to live. And I haven't got enough emotional energy. There's some *people* I hate—but some of them are black. I think people mistake my vehemence—and, you know, this becomes so sad. I'm vehement and indignant. That's not the same thing as hatred. Or even the same thing as bitterness. Y'know?"

One

James Arthur Baldwin was born in 1924 in Harlem, which is geographically part of the United States but sociologically an island surrounded by the rest of the country. He was born a Negro. And to some extent this accidental conjunction of time and place has dictated his course. But it does not define who he is.

This slight, dark man is salt rubbed in the wounds of the nation's conscience. He is the shriek of the lynched. He is an accusing finger thrust in the face of white America. He is a fierce, brilliant light illuminating the unspeakable and the shameful. Gadfly and bogey man, triumphant and despairing, he has been an impassioned spokesman for the ranks of unheard Negroes, a spokesman initially appointed—and anointed—by the whites.

But first and foremost he is a writer, an American phenomenon, one of the nation's great creative artists. Like every creative artist, Baldwin mirrors the mountains, valleys and plains of his environment. In his frail person, he embodies the paradoxes and the potentials of the integration battle in the United States.

In his oratory, and sometimes in his prose, there are apt to be passages clouded by confusion; and his political innocence has made a number of his allies apprehensive. But his emotional impact is uncompromising: harsh, violent and beautiful.

Three times now his books have secured a niche on the bestseller list, confirming his commercial attractions and enhancing his literary prestige. His old-young features with their medieval cast have been exposed frequently enough in photographs, interviews and lectures to have seemed ubiquitous. Luminaries on several continents clamor to meet him.

But all of this is part of the glittering panoply of the public Baldwin. And: "The James Baldwin the public knows is not the Jimmy I know," says his sister and secretary, Mrs. Gloria Davis Karefa-Smart.

Jimmy Baldwin, jagged as a sliver, belongs to a generation of angry, middle-aged men. He is a nonconformist, a partially reconstructed expatriate, a flagrant individualist disavowed by the bulk of middle-class Negroes, who recoil from his unorthodox conduct and even less orthodox standards. A champion of first-class citizenship for Negroes, Baldwin failed to vote in the 1964 Presidential election because—somehow—he never quite got around to registering. Yet to many of his countrymen his name is a synonym for his entire race.

"I'm small and I have big eyes," says Jimmy Baldwin, "and I come on, you know, kind of dramatic. But there's something very misleading about my manner. I'm not *entirely* what I look like . . ."

He looks like a wood carving in a Gothic cathedral (not Notre

Dame, which he doesn't care for, but perhaps Chartres, which he loves). He is economically built, even stingily, tiny and narrow, so thin it is hard to believe he casts a shadow.

But there is a nervous vitality in him that is self-perpetuating, a delight that not infrequently spills over, submerging the grief. Still, he could often say, as he did in a letter to an editor several years ago: "I have been way down yonder in the valley by myself, where I couldn't hear nobody pray. Except, occasionally, me."

He moves swiftly, constantly, like a flickering light. "I hate using a nineteenth-century word like mercurial," says novelist Norman Mailer, "but Jimmy is one person I'd apply that to. He's sensitive, like an exposed nerve. His affirmations are always full of little denials, his denials always full of little reservations."

White supremacists shrill that Negroes really want to usurp their place in the sun: their titles, their prestige, their women and their jobs. That is not Jimmy Baldwin's ambition. "I don't want to be fitted into this society," he says. "I would rather be *dead*. In fact, there's no difference between being fitted into this society and *dying*."

Baldwin is a member of a disadvantaged minority who benefits more than most of his fellow Americans from this country's affluence and upward mobility. Burdened only by his periodic bouts of melancholy, yet buoyed up by his infinite capacity for gaiety, he swings around the globe, from Rome to Monrovia to Berlin to San Juan to Corsica to Tel Aviv to Cannes, governed only by his own restless impulses.

Intuitive, rash, impractical, lonely, frightened, witty, rebellious and superlatively gifted, he manages within a short span of time to convert each new locale into a perambulating court. Gathering around him a variegated collection of companions and freeloaders, Baldwin moves among them with financial indulgence and royal caprice.

In an effusive mood, he hugs his followers, kisses them or merely touches them lightly with the tips of his long, narrow fingers. "The laying-on of hands," says a former associate, nodding. "Sometimes it's an act of affection and sometimes an act of hostility. Sometimes he's pushing people *away*, actually. Sometimes it's an effort to get in touch emotionally through physical contact."

At first Baldwin is charmed and comforted by the demands for his favor: for a share, if only a token share, of his influence, his reputation, his achievements, his attention and his material resources. Gradually the pressures multiply. As they converge upon him, his skin turns ash-gray, his extravagant eyes expand, his angular frame contracts and he grows drunk, almost feverish, with anxiety.

At this point, staggering with weariness, terrified that he is on the verge of a crackup, he allows himself to be induced to flee. Sanctuary is any other corner of the world that permits him to escape the avaricious pack. Arriving at his destination (usually Paris or Istanbul, but often Fire Island or Westchester or Connecticut), he settles down to a relatively sensible regimen in what passes with him for seclusion.

Eating a little more, drinking a little less and sleeping a bit more regularly, he recuperates. As his spirits revive, he chaffs at the monotony of his self-imposed restrictions and eventually shoots up flares that signal the end of his isolation. By telephone, word of mouth and just possibly extrasensory perception, he dispatches bulletins announcing his latitude, longitude and receptive state. Soon visitors flock to him.

Baldwin welcomes them indiscriminately. Then, by stages as predictable as the symptomology of a well-charted disease, he is crowded and jostled into irritability and despair. Hounded by his retinue, blind with exhaustion, his work at a standstill, his appetite gone, he complains that the dependence he nurtured is robbing him of his life-rhythm. Even his sense of humor deserts him: "I'm sick and tired of people with no beat of their own using *my* beat," he snaps.

As he whirls through this cycle, at once pilot and passenger, he is universally greeted with recognition. For Baldwin, alternately gratified and exasperated by his fame, brimming with love and fury so inextricably intermingled that he frequently confuses one with the other, has emerged in the second half of the twentieth century as a major American writer and an international symbol of the Negro revolution.

Perhaps more than any other American, the author of GO TELL IT ON THE MOUNTAIN, NOTES OF A NATIVE SON, THE AMEN CORNER, GIOVANNI'S ROOM, NOBODY KNOWS MY NAME, ANOTHER COUNTRY, THE FIRE NEXT TIME, BLUES FOR MISTER CHARLIE and GOING TO

MEET THE MAN has compelled his white contemporaries to acknowledge that shining their shoes and scrubbing their floors and harvesting their crops do not spark joy in black citizens. He has made it embarrassingly clear that he finds the North, liberal as well as conservative, no less guilty of bigotry than the South. Moreover, he regards it as impertinent for white people to assume they must accept the Negro. "The really terrible thing...," he wrote in an open letter to a nephew, "is that *you* must accept *them.*"

Whatever the form in which Baldwin chooses to preach his sermons—novel, essay, play, short story or speech—his message is delivered with a blend of eloquence, bluntness and Biblical wrath (the fruit of an adolescent career in the pulpit) that mesmerizes his audiences and sends them forth half convinced fire and smoke issue from his nostrils.

He says out loud, furiously, unapologetically, what his race has been thinking for a century. His words are at once a release for the inarticulate Negro and a warning to what Baldwin habitually refers to as "the Southern oli-*garch*-y," the consonantal diphthong pronounced as if he were biting into it, as in cheetah and chill and cheat, with ominous effect.

"I picked the cotton," he said, addressing some twelve hundred students at Cambridge University. "I carried it to market. I built the railways under someone else's whip—for nothing, for nothing! The Southern oligarchy was created by *my* labor, *my* sweat, the violation of *my* children—all this in the land of the free and the home of the brave."

It was one of innumerable variations on a favorite theme but the fervent rhetoric of this New York bachelor, who first crossed the Mason-Dixon line on a journalist's mission and is best acquainted with cotton in its manufactured form, drew from the young Englishmen and women wild applause, climaxed by a two-minute standing ovation. The contrast between Baldwin's titanic ire and childlike dimensions, no less than the power of his jeremiads and the sense of terrible justice underlying them, almost invariably ignites such demonstrations of enthusiasm, even when his listeners are themselves the target of his recriminations. In his excoriation they seek the solace of expiation.

There is a violence in Baldwin, even while he counsels peace, that creates its own lines of communication in an age that laments its absence. ("I am not by temperament nonviolent," he asserts. And, with even more vehemence: "I'll bet in all your lives—and I know in mine—that the only time you heard nonviolence admired was when black men preached it.") His hostility is like an elemental force; it sets up a subterranean current, operating on a primitive—even visceral—level, for a dialogue of the unconscious between the two races.

The charges he flings at white America generally find their mark in the literate and the vulnerable. What they hear with their nerves and respond to with their blood is a scream of pain from a man who insists he is at least their equal and always their victim. It is an authentic challenge from the ghetto-jungle Baldwin inhabited during his early days, but it is phrased with a poet's grace.

The river of resentment surging through Jimmy Baldwin never begins to run dry. Perhaps to provide an outlet for this turbulence, he deliberately lives on the edge of disaster, the way some communities live in the shadow of a volcano. Any incident might conceivably topple him over the brink. He views his continued existence with perpetual surprise; each twenty-four hours impresses him as a temporary reprieve from the grave.

If the cumulative shock of his accelerated pace and frenetic routine should fail to carry him off prematurely, Baldwin anticipates still another short cut to Golgotha: assassination. Long before the ambush death of Medgar Evers and the treachery that struck down President Kennedy in Texas, Baldwin was prophesying that he himself would probably be slain by white fanatics in the South; or even, he footnoted, "right here in the North."

More than most human beings, Baldwin is acutely conscious of his own fear. "All I know of my own life," he declares, "is that I've been scared to death since I was born and I'll be scared until I die. But, if you're scared to death, walk *toward* it." Baldwin, sheathed in his own kind of valor, has walked toward it often.

On Sunday, October 6, 1963, with the opening guns blazing in the civil rights crusade, Jimmy Baldwin—with his brother David —flew down to Selma, Alabama, on a few hours notice to help James Forman, executive secretary of the Student Nonviolent Coordinating Committee (SNCC), launch a Negro-voter registration drive. Shortly after midnight, Forman was briefing the Baldwins.

"We were sitting around talking," Jimmy Baldwin says. Stalked by memories of cruelty and frustration, still shaken by them, he relives the expedition in recounting it. "You would be aware of—" He breaks off and starts again. "Sudden silences fell. And then you'd realize that a car was coming. And that everyone was listening. And, of course, you did *too*, then. Y'know?

"And the car would—you'd see the lights of the car pass the window. In this total silence. And you'd be aware that everyone, including you, was waiting for bullets. Or a *bomb*. And the car would pass and you'd go to the blinds and look out. And then we'd start again . . ."

And so the night passed. Early Monday morning, the heat was already oppressive. Baldwin, who rarely rises before noon, was posted outside the Dallas County Courthouse, watching the lines of Negro applicants, three hundred and seventy-five of them, each risking reprisal and retaliatory unemployment.

The strategy of Selma's white opposition was to stall the registration process inside the building and intimidate the Negroes waiting outside. The press, scenting a story of national importance, trailed Baldwin.

"It was very peaceful in the beginning," he says. "We could talk to the people on the line, which was stretched around the corner. There was no real hassle. There was only a very faint harbinger of what was to come in the fact that the posse was out by about eleven-thirty, and the men with helmets kept saying to us, 'You're blocking the sidewalk—move along, move along.' No matter where we stood, these men would stick behind us and say we were blocking the sidewalk. No matter *where* we were.

"Their manner was a hard thing to describe. It was—the only word I can find for it was that it was mindless, y'know? They sounded like—they sounded like *parrots*. This was the only phrase they'd ever learned, the only phrase they ever used: 'Move along—you're blocking the sidewalk.' No matter where you *were*: 'Move along—you're blocking the sidewalk.'

"And *also*, I must say, when I finally looked into their faces, they were terrified, you know. *With* their guns and their helmets. And terrified in a very strange way. Terrified as the mindless are terrified. Because the only way they could react to any pressure, you know, was a rock or bullet or gun. And they don't have *any* other defenses at all!

"And this is—this is the police force the Southern oligarchy has used—and *created*—to protect their interests. Because the people are as capable of responsibility as I am of—of *flying*. With my own *arms*."

Big Jim Clark, the Dallas County sheriff, patrolling the scene with his deputies, decreed that any Negro who dropped out of line—to drink at the segregated fountain, to visit the segregated lavatory, to buy a sandwich at the segregated counter—would not be permitted to return.

"Finally," says Baldwin, "we started to go into the courthouse. And it's a *County* courthouse. And the two helmeted men at the door said we couldn't come in. And Jim Forman said: 'We have to go upstairs to the courthouse. What do you mean we can't come in?' And they said (*again*, you know; it's very striking; they just repeated the same phrase), 'You can't come in.'

"When we said, 'Why can't we come in?'—you know: 'You can't come in.' And Jim Forman said, 'Do you mean you're forbidding us to enter a County Courthouse?' And the guard said, 'You have to ask *him* about that.' To the *other* guard, who had looked away. And the first guard finally said that we had to go in through the *front* door.

"So we went around to the front door, where the line was, and the sheriff said we couldn't get in *there*—we had to go around to the *side* door. So we went around to the side door again and the man said we couldn't get *in*. And then, you know, we were standing there, trying to figure out what to do next, and he said, 'You're blocking the door.'"

Baldwin laughs aloud, but his laughter has mayhem in it. "So we moved to the side. And all this is happening, by the way, under the eyes of the Justice Department and the FBI. Who are taking *pictures* and making *phone* calls."

The Baldwins decided about then that they had to have a drink. They bought a bottle of whiskey and retired to the SNCC office. Jimmy Baldwin jotted down some notes. Then, together with local leaders, laden with piles of sandwiches for the Negroes waiting to register, they resumed their battle stations.

The climate had altered. State troopers were in evidence, their cars deployed bumper to bumper. Guns, clubs and cattle prodders were now prominently displayed.

"And there was a gang of—I can only say *hoodlums*," says Baldwin. "The white—you know, hangers-on. I was *furious*. The thing is you get—you're so scared. I was scared in the *morning*, before it all began, you know. And I was scared the *first* time I walked around there. But, later on, I wasn't scared at all. I got— that's exactly what happens, y'know: your fear *is* swallowed up by—*fury*. Yah. What you *really* want to do is *kill* all those people. And, you know, you feel *that* so strongly that—that you haven't got the time to be *afraid*.

"And those *faces*. My God. You know? The face of the poor white in the South is a—is a real *blasphemy*. A *real blasphemy*. Anyway, we started trying to feed the people. But the sheriff was not allowing anybody to talk to anyone on the line. You couldn't *talk* to them. You were not allowed to *talk* to them. And the food issue then began to be crucial. Because if you couldn't talk to them, you couldn't *feed* them, you know.

"And it was *very* hot. And there they stood, the people on line. Leaning on one another's shoulders, sort of. And they took off their *shoes*. And then somebody figured out we could put all the sandwiches in a shopping bag and carry it to the *end* of the line and have, you know, those sandwiches passed up by the people on the *line*. Kind of a bucket-brigade thing.

"And I walked over to the sheriff and Jim Forman was saying, you know, that the people had been standing there for a *long* time and it was hot and they were hungry. And that we had to feed them. And the sheriff said, 'I'll not have them molested in any way.' He said it four times, you know. *Four times*, no matter what anybody said. They told him, 'We don't want to *molest* them; we want to *feed* them.' And he said, 'I will not have them molested in any way.'

"And finally Jim said: 'Are you *really* forbidding us to talk to these people and feed these people? Don't you know that's against the law?' And the sheriff said: 'I don't care if it is against the law. That's my *order*.' And he turned away . . . Big Jim Clark. I wish to God that somebody'd blow his head off! It would help. It *would help!*

"Anyway, there was nothing—so we walked back across the street. There was nothing—you had a *feeling* about these people. One of the reasons—one of the things I mean when I say that it would [help], you know—there are some people whose only reason to be, whose only human *use*, is that they should come to a *violent death*," says Jimmy Baldwin. "Their *only* human use . . ."

"I don't think—I *really* don't think that—I'm beginning to *suspect* that, in all my misadventures with *myself* and other *people*, that people don't really *change*. You know? They become whatever they were—or they fail to become whatever they *might* have become. But they don't *change*. I'm not so sure that I've *changed* at all. Do y'know?"

Two

Applause flares, sudden, excited, like the popping of firecrackers, as the miniature figure in tan corduroy trots out on the platform of the Community Church of New York.

Baldwin, a guest speaker this evening, moves briskly to a chair in the rear, crosses his legs, whips out from an inner pocket a pen and a folded sheet of paper and starts to write (with his left hand), completely absorbed in thought, frowning a little so that the neat parentheses between his peaked brows are even more deeply incised than usual.

It is a few minutes after eight and every inch of standing and sitting room in the severely handsome auditorium has been occupied for more than a quarter of an hour. The spectators, intent, solemn, almost all of college age, predominantly Caucasian, dressed for the most part in the elaborately sloppy fashion endorsed by their generation, focus their expectant gaze upon him, as though hoping to catch some glimmer of his fire.

Oblivious, Baldwin scribbles away, pressing a thumb to his mouth and gnawing at the inside of his lip. Occasionally he glances up, his mourning eyes probing the far corners of the hall. In the second row center, his mother, Mrs. Emma Berdis Baldwin, a trim woman in black, her glasses gleaming, blows him a kiss. David Baldwin, less fortunate in his position, lolls against a pillar.

Dr. Donald S. Harrington, minister of the non-sectarian institution, radiating satisfaction, announces that all one thousand seats are filled, with two hundred and fifty guests downstairs in a room equipped with a loudspeaker, two hundred more massed in the side aisles and two thousand outside—a gasp, half startled, half congratulatory, swells and fades—in a queue winding "all around the block."

This tribute will please Baldwin later. Right now it falls on deaf ears; suffering from the stagefright that afflicts him on such occasions, he wipes his slender, beautiful (and perspiring) hands on the knees of his trousers.

Harrington introduces him ("There is no one in the country better able to reach the conscience of America, black or white, than James Baldwin") and he advances to the lectern Baldwin has a player's infallible timing. For five seconds, ten, fifteen, he stands there motionless, staring out at the audience, taking its measure, encouraging it to take his. Dwarfed by the massive architecture, he looks like a gnome, his head too weighty for his body.

"I hope nobody will think I'm copping a plea if I say I'm a little tired," he says quietly. "I've said arbitrarily I've set us the common task of discussing our common trouble." No one here has to be told the nature of that trouble. "Perhaps we can establish a dialogue here tonight. And perhaps, with passion and morality, we will be able to rock that rock that is Washington."

The low-keyed prologue is not entirely contrived. Baldwin is unquestionably weary. But his leashed fervor builds suspense. "I am going to say some very reckless things tonight," he is saying. "So I want to make it absolutely clear I represent only myself. I am talking to you tonight as Jimmy Baldwin, born in Harlem, and I am speaking to you not as a leader, but as one of the poets you produced."

There is a faint stir—of admiration? of pride? "Whether we like it or not," says Baldwin, "we have reached a point in this country where, black or white, all methods of communication have become unusable." The ready reservoir of sympathy he is even now tapping disproves this argument; and no one knows it better than Baldwin.

He leans on the lectern, a former evangelist returned to the pulpit, at ease now as he always is once his speech is under way. Over and over again, he stresses the economic motives behind segregation: the commercial benefits white America derives from maintaining black America as a source of cheap labor.

"People who came to America, contrary to the myths of TV, radio and Hollywood," he declares, still on a low-pitched note, but now it is tinged with irony, "were neither saints nor sinners nor pilgrims. They were people who weren't able to *make* it where they were . . ." His listeners are gratified; this is what they came to hear. "I represent the *on-ly* man who *nev-er* wanted to come here." There is a groundswell of laughter.

"But, if I had not come under the double coercion of the Bible and the gun, we'd never have all those railroads. And cotton would never have become king. And our economic situation would be en-*tirely* different."

He is chanting a familiar litany, altering the order of invocation, but not its content. Baldwin long ago acquired the habit of referring to himself as though he were the personification of his race, incorporating within his own fragile shell the history, the attributes and—above all—the tragedy of American Negroes. In a man of impressive physique, this might seem pretentious. But Baldwin's diminutive size imbues his metaphors with the purity of abstraction; he arouses only compassion and consent when he slips into the role of a versatile John Henry, plowing fields, baling cotton, laying tracks, leveling timber, driving steel with a mighty, twelve-pound hammer.

What he says is now drenched with the naked intensity that is

Baldwin's style—in writing, in talking, in living. His words are delivered at an uneven pace, sometimes with a rush, sometimes with long, brooding intervals. His voice, resonant, a bit theatrical, with a hint of the vaulted intonation good English actors often have, slurs a little when he reaches a climax, compressing a phrase into a single, vibrant syllable.

In the course of the next half hour, he unfurls the broad canvas of inequity that is the Negro's lot in the United States. He calls for a rent moratorium to prod Harlem's landlords into repairing slum tenements. He advocates the use of America's industrial and commercial power—the power generated by the sweat of black men—"for ourselves and the liberation of this country." He says, "We are responsible for our own freedom; we are not *begging* for it . . ."

It is Baldwin's conviction that none of us in the United States, regardless of individual attitude and the blamelessness of our deeds, can really be judged innocent. We have all of us, he re-iterates, contributed in some degree to the subjugation of a people, passively or actively, overtly or covertly, consciously or unconsciously. And it is this thesis that makes so many squirm. For who among us can deny his silence at some moment when he should have bellowed? And who can suppress the suspicion that he has too often avoided commitment, substituting the luxury of indignation for involvement? Baldwin's ferocity strips from his best-intentioned countrymen their cloak of complacency and plucks at weaknesses they would rather forget—or never knew they had.

"The only thing worse than being a black man in America is being a white man in America," he says. "Segregation doesn't mean *I* am segregated. *You* are. We *all* are!"

The white population of the United States, he notes scornfully, has professed admiration for Negroes and Dr. Martin Luther King: "It has admired them—and has done nothing whatever to help them. And, what is worse, intends to go *on* admiring them and doing *noth*-ing what-*ever* to help them—but let them go to *jail.*"

The white faces crane forward. "It's only when the *black* man buys a gun," Baldwin says, "that the country becomes *moral.* And *Christian.*" His mouth twists. "I don't want to see any more blood —*any*one's blood," he exclaims. "My God!"

23

Racial stereotypes outrage Baldwin and he has always countered them, sometimes naïvely by refraining from eating watermelon, sometimes deftly with satiric parries. "It is not true I came here tonight carrying a knife," he says now. "And, in fact, I very *rarely* carry a knife ..." There is a ripple of amusement, followed by a round of clapping; his mother courteously abstains.

In rapid succession, he swipes at the police ("they know who they're working for"), evaluates the national economy ("it's absolutely impossible for any Negro, no matter who he is, to fit into the economic structure of this country as it is") and furnishes a formula ("we must make—shall I say The Establishment?—afraid of *us*").

His glare is baleful. His fingers dart admonition. Now abruptly he subsides. He seems to shrink, to shrivel. "It is very hard," he says softly, "to be black and grow up in this country. A friend of mine says it is a very dangerous pursuit. But I beg you to believe it is also dangerous for the white man."

His tone is somber: "The terms of our revolution—the *American* revolution—are these: not that I drive you out or that you drive me out, but that we learn to live *together*."

Baldwin steps to the side of the reading desk and scrutinizes the faces before him. "I am not an exotic rarity," he reminds them. "I am not a stranger. I am none of these things. On the contrary: for all you know, I may be your uncle, your brother" —his possible nieces, nephews, brothers and sisters cheer this kinship vociferously—"among *other* things!" For the first time he smiles, his cheeks creasing into multiple folds. The audience roars its appreciation.

"I am no longer black. Maybe I'd *like* to be. Maybe I'd like to go back to *Sierra Leone*. That's where I *came* from." (Actually, of course, Baldwin has no idea from what part of Africa his ancestors departed, but he has friends in Sierra Leone and some portion of America's twenty million Negroes undoubtedly originated there. His license with such details may provoke cynicism, but through these minor deviations from fact he often manages to ram home a fundamental reality.) "But I've been here a long time," he says now. "I'm part of you, and you're part of me ..."

Thunderous applause accompanies him off stage. Above the blurred, pounding palms, the faces are flushed and exultant. Some of Baldwin's glory has rubbed off on them. Hearing, they have gained the illusion that they are even now marching forward with him—pioneers all—to that brave, new world where ignorance is banished and men can be different, yet truly free.

Harrington reappears to urge Baldwin to address the overflow crowd outside. A cordon of brown, young men, impassive and steely-eyed, springs up around Baldwin ("street arabs," he comments later; "probably neo-Muslims; I never saw them before") and skillfully maneuvers him through a side door, barring anyone from getting within touching or speaking range. There is something in their arrogance, something impersonal and menacing, reminiscent of the ruthless efficiency of an elite corps in a totalitarian state.

The night is warm. Baldwin's coat is slung over his shoulders like a cape. The hundreds still waiting for him now press close. Baldwin leaps up on a bench and his self-assigned guards align themselves horizontally in front of him, their chins jutting forward, their stiff backs toward the celebrity their aggression shields and cages.

Jimmy Baldwin, who abhors military ritual and is even offended by the pageantry of parades, cannot resist the drama of this moment. He bends forward, arms outstretched, Henry V at Agincourt, Wellington at Waterloo, and places his hands on the shoulders of two lieutenants. "I would like to say what I said inside," he announces.

His summary is crisp. "There are several things we Negro people can do for *themselves*," he says with the obscure syntax that may fog his speeches but never his writing. "We don't have to *ask* Mr. Charlie for favors." The light from a street lamp glints on his gold ring. "We can make *him* come to *us*."

Several boys and girls who might conceivably qualify as Mr. Charlies and Miss Annes bob their heads. Baldwin, swayed by emotion, is apt to belabor a Negro audience as though it were white, exhort a white group as though it were Negro. "No one of you who are white can go back to Poland or Ireland or England, any more than I can go back to Africa," he says. "I'm not a stranger dancing on the levee. I was never a happy darkie. I *suffered* . . ."

Once again the applause booms out, bouncing back from the surrounding buildings, reverberating down Manhattan's sidestreets. Baldwin, his fatigue dissipated, is bustled back into the auditorium. The response he has twice evoked has recharged his flagging energy, and the tightness that pinched his features a little more than an hour ago has been washed away by a wave of exhilaration.

Building a bridge from one human island to another, spanning the void between his personality and the next, is instinctive with Baldwin. His need for communion, for its reassurance and its balm, is urgent; it cannot be contained by his books. Even encounters with autograph hunters kindle warmth in him and he confers upon each of them a sense of intimacy reserved by others for less casual confrontations.

He deliberately leaves himself wide open to life, erecting none —or few—of the usual barriers behind which most of us huddle. Those who connect with him, struggling to pin down this unfamiliar quality, flounderingly describe Baldwin as a saint, or as one uncorrupted finally in the really important areas.

He himself offers an alternate interpretation. "I'm suggesting that one try to listen to one's heart," he says. "And tell the truth. In my own experience, the only thing which is really frightening is the effort one makes to avoid it—to avoid the truth. Nothing—*nothing*—has ever happened to me as bad as what I *thought* it would be. And the worst things that ever happened to me in my life have *always* been—on this level, anyway—when I was trying, in one way or another, to convince myself of something which I knew wasn't true. Because I was afraid to face it."

Truth obsesses Baldwin. He turns its merciless rays upon himself as well as upon America. "Jimmy is terrifying," says Dr. Kenneth B. Clark, the psychologist whose studies provided the foundation for the Supreme Court's historic school desegregation decision. "Because he demands of anybody who comes in contact with him a look at some aspect of truth. How the hell do I say this?—Jimmy confronts you, not just racially, but with the human predicament."

This does not alleviate Baldwin's own predicament. His alienation is much more than skin-deep; it pervades every crevice of his being. He has explored the world and himself, and claims to have accepted both, but is at bottom reconciled to neither. When he is alone, he wages unending war against what he has termed "one's ghastly inadequacy," and in these struggles he is eternally defeated, his ego shattered on the battlefield, his wounds "awake and throbbing." It is then, he has written, that death beckons "like the only light on a high, dark, mountain road, where one has, forever and forever! lost one's way."

Jimmy Baldwin has traveled that high, dark mountain road often. His journeys there are journeys into anguish. In the opinion of his Freud-oriented friends (an opinion they circumspectly conceal, since the subject of their diagnosis dismisses psychoanalysis with the acid comment, "No one's navel is worth that much attention"), Baldwin has a compulsive death wish that compels him to seek out situations where he can flirt with extinction. There are moments when he himself is pierced with fatalism. At a dinner party, an editor cited the automobile accident that killed Camus as "a form of suicide." Baldwin, stung, cried out, "But that's *me!*"

He consistently pursues peril. It lends substance to the unnamed terror that has preyed upon him since childhood. Growing up, it was his experience that the act of breathing—of surviving, really—involves danger.

Initially it confronted him in the guise of his stepfather, David Baldwin, a dour clergyman who indicted the entire white world for oppressing the black. But this attitude camouflaged a more desperate condition: sustaining the bitterness that ultimately consumed him, constantly feeding it, was his agonized acceptance of the myth of racial inferiority.

David Baldwin was twice a victim: victimized by the economic and social ramifications of the white man's theory and victimized again, even more brutally, by his unwilling belief in it. It was years before Jimmy Baldwin began to understand the nature of his stepfather's dilemma.

The rage that dominated David Baldwin and tyrannized his family was not buried with him. It was passed on, only intellectually diluted, to the boy whose virtues the older man regarded as offenses. Jimmy Baldwin today is the guardian of David Baldwin's anger; it burns steadily, like a sacred flame.

Whether Baldwin's estrangement from the American community stems, as he himself suggests, wholly from his tribulations as a Negro or whether its roots can more directly be traced back to his almost unendurable childhood plight is a problem that must trouble anyone who reads him.

Even if the seeds of his desolation were implanted in his

earliest years by his stepfather, the torment then inflicted upon Baldwin has been exacerbated by his treatment at the hands of white America. And this knowledge, festering in him, prevents him from purging himself of the poisons of hate as he sporadically —and quite sincerely—thinks he has.

He says he isn't sure that he has changed at all But his attitude toward the late David Baldwin has mellowed considerably. Jimmy Baldwin, rarely charitable toward the United States, never forgiving, but beginning on occasion to be both charitable and forgiving toward the despot of his youth, reasons that his stepfather, like himself, was after all a sacrifice on the altar of white hypocrisy.

There is, of course, ample justification to bolster up this conclusion. There is also a central weakness: few American men of any race are cast in the unloving, flagellating mold of the senior David Baldwin. But the tide of history has deflected Jimmy Baldwin's ancient grievances from his punitive stepfather to his punitive nation, a displacement by no means uncommon; and perhaps this burden is easier for him to bear.

"The reason I never will hate anybody again," Jimmy Baldwin testifies, "is that it's—it's *too*—too *demeaning* a confession, you know, on your *own* part, if you *need* to hate somebody. It means that you're *afraid* of the *other* thing, y'know—which is to *love* and be *loved*, which is *another* confession."

He is lounging on a couch in the living room of a renovated brownstone in lower Manhattan, not far from the East River, where for several months he has been the intermittent guest of a German-born lawyer. His favorite brother, David, a younger, taller, huskier, better-looking version of Baldwin himself, straddles a chair near the door. Lucien Happersberger, a handsome Swiss salesman and painter who often doubles as Baldwin's secretary, is screening telephone calls.

The décor is insistently modern, with the angular, sawed-off look popular in the 'thirties. One pair of men's shoes stands pigeon-toed on the gray-blue rug; another pair is lined up in front of a bookcase stocked with French, German and English titles. A shirt and a tie are draped around the back of a chair.

It is afternoon but the Venetian blinds are drawn to bar the glare of the sun—and perhaps to simulate twilight, a time of day Baldwin finds congenial. He is wearing a white sweatshirt with three red stripes daubed on the back ("a joke—it means I'm a member of the United States Olympic Drinking Team"), black chinos and sandals purchased in Puerto Rico. As the day progresses, he swings through his regular daily cycle of liquid nourishment, sipping first coffee (his breakfast), then beer from a can (his lunch) and, finally, scotch. It will be growing dark before he starts to nibble at eggs and toast.

"Y'know, you simply cannot—I can be all kinds of *people* in public," Baldwin says. "Or to myself, in front of my *mirror*. But in relation to someone who loves me or someone I *love*, you know, all these masks have to *go*. And everyone's *afraid* of that. Afraid of being seen as he is or she is. But that's the *price*, you know. That's why love is so *frightening*, I'm *sure*.

"Because you really *have* to come down *front* and be who*ever* you are. And you don't *know* who you *are*, y'know. You discover that partly—you discover that *really* through somebody *else*. And everybody's *afraid* of this *revelation*. You know, it isn't done in a *day*. Once you've done it, it isn't so terrifying—though the hangover remains. Once you meet the *barrier*, I think—once you've made some crucial *turning* point, then, hopefully, you can handle it from then on out, y'know. Because you *know* you *can*."

He is reclining now, the back of his neck resting on a turquoise pillow, one leg extended, the heel braced against the top of the coffee table. He flexes his ankle, left, right, left, peering at it contemplatively.

"When I have a fight with—who*ever*," he says, "or they with me, I—we *both* know that something in one's self or in the other person—or equally in *both*, which both people are *clinging* to, in one way or another, has been *touched*. Something that has been *struck—hurts*. And, you know, the organism *rushes* to *protect* it. Whatever it *is*. What*ever* it is, you know.

"I suppose it's possible, even now, you know, to—maybe *a* person in the *world* can *hurt* me by saying, 'You're pop-eyed.' And, you know, it isn't the physical state of being *pop-eyed*. It's what all those things—it's what it *meant* to me. All those things I've evolved to protect myself against—a certain *judgment* of *myself*, when I was *younger*, y'know. And when this is—*hit*, then, y'know, you *react* as you did when you were a *kid*.

"And in every crisis in my *own* life, in a way, I discover that what really comes to the *fore*, what really comes *up*, is where you were in the *first* place. You know, you have to deal with it all over *again*, as though you hadn't *already*. In that sense, it's never *done*. I don't mean to be simplistic about it. But I do mean that, in some *essential* way, that I think the *core* of *you* is kind of *unchangeable*, you know.

"It's kind of depressing." As he speaks, he slips down to the floor and perches there, his back resting against the couch. "But, on the other hand, it could be *marvelous*, too. You know, I think there is something very impressive about being *able* to get *through* the world—and still be able to be *hurt*. Because most people seem to give that *up* so *soon* . . .

"I think that *if* one—I don't know how to put this: if you don't manage to strike some kind of connecting—*real connection* with yourself, which is *always* a connection with everybody else, then you *perish*. I really think that this is the way that *goes*.

"You know, I never understood the whole art-for-art's-sake, for example. Because it seems to me that's pure *bullshit*. It's not even an *argument*. The connection you've got to make has to be rooted *deep* in *you*. And that is really deep in something else.

"Most people learn how to *protect* themselves against life— very quickly. In my own case, if I learned how to protect myself, as I obviously *should* have, I'd have had to do it so soon that I would have to *die*. I'd—I would have to *die* then, you know, in effect. Since I couldn't do that, I had to turn my back on that and go to the opposite *extreme*, really. Which is to do my best to keep myself *open*. Really to work at *that*.

"Because, you know, if any person closes himself up, then he just ceases to grow. If a *writer* does it, then he just doesn't become a *writer*, y'know. In a way, the best and the worst things *about* me are connected with that *necessity* . . ."

That necessity—to keep himself unarmored and unguarded— hurls him repeatedly into "misadventures" where he risks too much for too little; but it is also the foundation of his life and his art. In Paris, during eight years of self-exile from the United States, Baldwin fought to bare himself to "whole *areas* of life— which I would never have *dared* to deal with in America."

What Paris disclosed to him and what he dared to deal with is the material he ultimately wove into his novels:

GO TELL IT ON THE MOUNTAIN, a story of Harlem adolescence in which, according to its author, homosexuality is "implicit in the boy's situation" and "made almost explicit" in his tentative gropings toward a seventeen-year-old Sunday School teacher; GIOVANNI'S ROOM, which deals with a love affair between two white men; and ANOTHER COUNTRY, a dissection—almost a vivisection—of eight characters, Negro and white, and their interlocking intimacies, heterosexual, homosexual and bisexual.

Baldwin, unflinchingly candid in self-appraisal, his honesty impeded only by the limitations of perspective inherent in being inside looking out, is not inclined to post "No Trespassing" signs on any aspect of his life or career to indicate that beyond this point lies forbidden territory.

Indeed he is certain that what is wrong with the United States —and his list is formidable—is that precisely too much is forbidden, love above all, with crippling consequences for the populace; and that this, in turn, has swerved white America from sexual health to the frantic sexual exploitation of the Negro, who has been conveniently metamorphosed into a phallic fetish.

Unhesitatingly, but with mounting agitation, Baldwin explains why homosexuality, a form of love legally banned in the United States, is a recurrent motif in his fiction. "There are two reasons for it, I think," he says. "Which are the same reason."

Using his elbow as a lever, he lifts himself to his feet, raises his shirt an inch or two and absentmindedly scratches his belly. Then he sits down on the couch again. Propping up his knees, he loops his arms around his jackknifed legs, chainsmoking, imbibing a double scotch on the rocks at the slow, steady tempo he maintains throughout his waking hours.

"The most brutal aspect of it, which is why people make such a fuss about the homosexuality in my novels—the real reason behind the fuss is that, no matter what they—I mean white people —say, I was once a Negro adolescent in this country.

"And, for example, when I hit Greenwich Village, one of the reasons why my years there were so terrifying was not only because of white women, but also because of white *men*. Who looked just like *Eisenhower*." He slaps his glass on the table, "And I was a kid," he says furiously. "I didn't know any of the things I've since had to find out.

"People got mad at ANOTHER COUNTRY. And the reason they got mad is because it's *true*. And it's much worse than that. One of the reasons that homosexuality, for example, occupies so large a place in ANOTHER COUNTRY is because it's an *American* phenomenon in that book—and in my experience. It would not *ever* happen that way in any other country of the world—except, possibly, Germany.

"And, in this country, what we call homosexuality is a grotesque kind of—of *waxworks*. You know? Which is the other side of what we call *heterosexuality* here." His eyes burn with contempt. "*Nobody* makes any connections! So naturally you get, you know, you get this truncated, de-balled, galvanized activity which thinks of itself as *sex*.

"It's not sex at *all*. It's pure desperation. It's *clinical*. D'you know? It comes out of the effort to tell one's self a lie about what human life is like. It comes out of the attempt to cling to definitions which cannot contain *any*body's life.

"American homosexuality is a waste primarily because, if people were not so *frightened* of it—if it wouldn't, you know—it really would cease in effect, as it exists in this country now, to *exist*. I mean the same way the Negro problem would disappear. People wouldn't have to spend so much time being defensive—if they weren't *endlessly* being *condemned*. I know a whole lot of people who aren't homosexual at *all*—who *think* they are. That's *true*. I know a lot of people who turn into junkies because they're *afraid* they might be *queer*.

"The only people who *talk* about homosexuality, you know, the way—in this *terrible* way—are Americans. And Englishmen and French and Germans. The Anglo-Saxons. The *Puritans*. In Italy, you know, men kiss each other and boys go to bed with each other. And no one is marked for life. No one imagines that—and they grow up, you know, and they have children and raise them. And no one ends up going to a *psychiatrist* or turning into a junkie because he's afraid of being *touched*.

"You know, *that's* the root of the whole—of the *American* thing. It's not fear of—it's not a fear of men going to bed with men. It's a fear of anybody touching anybody! That's what it comes to. And that's what's so horrible about it.

"If you're a Negro, you're in the center of that *peculiar* affliction because *anybody* can touch *you*—when the sun goes down. You know, you're the target for everybody's fantasies. If you're a Negro female whore, he comes to you and asks you do for him what he wouldn't ask his wife to do—nor any other *white* woman. But you're a *black* woman! So you can do it—because you know how to do *dirty things!*"

Baldwin's posture is rigid. Only his eyes and his mouth are alive. "And if you're a *black boy*," he says, hate, deadly, undisguised, seething in his voice, "you wouldn't be-*lieve* the holocaust that opens over your head—with all these despicable—*males* —looking for somebody to act out their fantasies on. And it happens in this case—if you're sixteen years old—to be *you!*"

The final word explodes, leaving Baldwin panting. No one speaks. No one is capable of speaking. He remains bolt upright, immobilized by the high-voltage arc of tension still crackling through the room. His pain is almost a tangible presence. The silence crescendoes. Finally someone stammers. "But, in Italy, they . . ."

"They understand," says Baldwin, cutting in, "that people were born to *touch* each other."

"My mother used to say I was just like him. Whenever she said that, she looked very worried: 'Just like him—just like your father.' That was when she would, you know, slap me—or something. And it frightened the shit out of me, too! I must say. I thought, in those days—I thought (and I also knew that she didn't mean that)—I thought, taking it at its face value, that she meant I was like, you know—Mr. Baldwin. But I knew very well—somewhere—that that was not what she meant. You know, it was—I didn't know —you know it's horrible to be a child! Because you know more as a child than you do as a grownup and you can't—you can't—you can't cope with it."

Three

Looking back, looking far back into the aching past, back to "some things really *so* painful that I really have not thought about them *since*—literally not thought about them *since*," this is the first thing Jimmy Baldwin remembers:

"I don't know if this actually happened to me or I *dreamed* it. It must have been when I was between two and three. I seem to be on my mother's shoulder, in the kitchen. She was taking me somewhere. It was winter time. I was dressed up in one of those woolen things"—he pretends to tie a bow under his chin. "Caps and things. Y'know? And my father was washing dishes. He was *smiling*. I think he *liked* me, in a *way*. Maybe it's a fantasy. But that's my earliest memory. The very first thing I remember. The *very first* thing I remember—saying goodby to my father . . ."

Dream or fantasy or memory, it is an oasis in time, this fragment of the past retrieved by Jimmy Baldwin. In the nightmare that was his childhood, there were few interludes as pleasant.

Only when he was "very, *very* little" could he imagine his stepfather liking him—not demonstratively, of course, not even then; but at least "in a way." "And then," Baldwin says flatly, "I didn't think so any *more*." The malignity directed at him was too overwhelming to be misconstrued. That first memory he retains is almost his last of David Baldwin smiling—smiling at him, at the boy, Jimmy.

The stern, implacable, pathologically malevolent deacon detected little cause to smile in the bleakness that enveloped him. A Sunday preacher who labored in a bottling plant, he never earned more than a marginal income, frequently less. Remote, majestic, much older than his wife, he carried with him from New Orleans to Harlem, from early manhood to the tomb, an unlimited capacity for introspection and rancor. He knew almost no happiness of his own, and had none at all to spare for his family. David Baldwin's vision of life was as black as himself, but far less beautiful.

Vengeance—although he did not call it that—absorbed him totally: vengeance against the sinners who rejected his blackness; vengeance against a society that condemned him and his children after him to the periphery of life here on earth; and perhaps, in his heaviest hours, vengeance even against the unkind God who had stained his skin and made him despise himself, and Who now could only even matters by relegating all His alabaster children to eternal hellfire and damnation.

All of this David Baldwin, pledged to sanctity, artfully concealed from himself, but not from the uninhibited gaze of the young. "The church for him was almost literally a way of getting back at white people," Jimmy Baldwin has said. "He had God. And God would judge them. God would punish them. He wanted to kill them, and he couldn't kill them. So he hoped God would. And he hoped that all his life . . ."

Such was the father whose paranoia distorted Jimmy Baldwin's childhood and destroyed it. Such was the man who taught the boy he was ugly, the ugliest child ever seen, ugly as the Devil's son (his peaked hairline ugly, his peaked eyebrows ugly, his protuberant eyes ugly, his faintly cleft chin ugly)—so ugly that he must relinquish all hope of achieving salvation through love. Such was the man who estranged Jimmy Baldwin from himself, divesting him of tenderness and self-esteem, until he believed that his very flesh and bone proclaimed him "a worthless human being." ("How," he was to query at forty, "is it possible for the child to grow up if the child is not loved?")

Restating a principle learned long ago under the scourge and often reviewed since, so that the words as he says them are devoid of inflection, Baldwin explains, "I was little and I was ugly." Slowly feeling filters back into his voice: "You take your estimate of yourself from what the world says about you. You know, I was always told that I was ugly. My *father* told me that. And everybody else. But mostly my father. So I believed it. Naturally. Until *today* I believed it . . ."

Naturally? Not quite. The lesson literally had to be pounded into him, whipped into him. And still, helplessly, he kept trying to woo David Baldwin and convert his vindictiveness into love. "I'm *sure* I did," Jimmy Baldwin says. "Because I wouldn't have *hated* him so much if I hadn't. You know, *inevitably* I would. You know, he was—he was my *father*."

From this monolithic presence, as much an object of veneration as of hate, the boy took his image of himself. He had no other. He lacked, he says now, even proof of his existence. The vicious and castrating discrimination he strikes back at so vehemently today is indivisible from the discrimination he first experienced at home. "I did not have any human identity," Baldwin explains.

It was then he was dispossessed. It was then he set out on that dreary road "where one has forever and forever! lost one's way." Black or white, male or female, he would have been doomed to wander there, sentenced to it by David Baldwin's cruelty. ("Children can survive without money or security or things,"

Jimmy Baldwin was to write with his blood, again at forty, "but they are lost if they cannot find a loving example, for only this example can give them a touchstone for their lives.")

Through the circuitous process of ascribing David Baldwin's psychological deformities (as well as the nerve-deep trauma they induced in himself) to the deprivations and humiliations both endured as Negroes, Jimmy Baldwin may eventually reclaim his father. "I yearned for him all my life," Baldwin has said, "and this is a terrible thing for a man to face."

The eldest of nine children in a family always uncertain of the next meal ("it's my melancholy conviction that I've scarcely ever had enough to eat"), he was inescapably assigned the responsibility of looking after his brothers and sisters. Any failure in this area, real or fancied, drew swift retibution from David Baldwin.

"I guess the one thing my father *did* do for me was that he taught me how to *fight*," Jimmy Baldwin says. "I had to know how to fight because I *fought* him so hard. He taught me—what my real *weapons* were. Which were patience and a kind of ruthless determination. Because I had to endure whatever it was; to *endure* it; to go under and come back *up;* to *wait*. He taught me everything I *know* about hate. Which means he taught me everything I know about *love*, too. When he died, I realized what I really wanted was for him to *love* me. For me to be able to *prove* myself to him."

David Baldwin's antagonism was stamped with respect. "There was a very funny kind of knowledge that he had of me," Jimmy Baldwin says. "In some ways, I think my fight *pleased* him. That he liked it, you know. Because *he* was very *complex,* too. And he was somewhere—unwillingly—very *proud* of me.

"I think it *hurt* him—because I was not actually his son—to *feel* that way. But still—it showed in very small things. Very *minor* things. I guess it mainly showed in—especially as we got older—in a certain *dependence* on me. There were some things he knew I would do. He would have liked to have been pleased. And he *would* have been pleased—if I had been his son."

But Jimmy Baldwin wasn't. The boy discovered that (he uncovered it, really, then quickly recovered it before he could know what he knew) shortly after he had deciphered by himself the intricacies of reading: when he was still too young for school, probably not yet five. He was just high enough to reach "the bottom of the bookshelf."

It was, he recalls, lined with something like red velvet and filled with dusty, old volumes—"no *books*, really"—and the Bible: "It was a family Bible. And the date of my birth"—August 2, 1924, in Harlem Hospital—"was in it. No"—his concentration is almost trance-like—"*not* the date of my birth. The date of my mother's marriage. And she was married in 1927. And I knew that I was born in 1924. And I didn't know what this *meant*.

"I remember—I'm reconstructing this—I know it was 1927, anyway. I didn't make any—I was bewildered by it. But I didn't know what it meant. I was small enough—I remember my mother was at the sink. And I was small enough to be looking *up* at her. And I asked her, you know, if she'd ever been *married* before. Which is a kind of cunning child's question. And I watched her face. Which is what a child does. And I realized I'd asked a dangerous question. And she didn't answer me.

"She said, 'Why do you ask me that, son?' And I said something like, 'Oh, nothing,' y'know. And I didn't think about it any more. Because there was nothing to think *about*, y'know. But I was —obscurely—uh—upset. Somewhere . . ."

David Baldwin, the son of a slave, himself enslaved by his fanatic adherence to the outward forms of churchly canon, imposed his own rigorous code on his offspring. He prohibited even such mild diversions as shooting marbles, going to movies, playing jazz.

Invading the white community, even tentatively fraternizing with it, was a serious infringement. The punishment he meted out was both physical and verbal. "My father was a rough cat," comments his irreverent namesake, David Baldwin, Jr. "When he beat you, you were *beat*. He was a minister, but my mother was more religious."

The constantly expanding household included the youngest son of his first marriage, Sam, on whom the clergyman lavished all his affection. It was not reciprocated. Samuel Baldwin bolted when he was seventeen, forever severing communication with his father, leaving eight-year-old Jimmy heir to a strange and unrelenting battle.

The boy was precocious, sensitive, quiet, reliable. These were virtues David Baldwin would have prized in Sam. In Jimmy, their possession amounted to betrayal—and was chastised as such. Thus all his assets of intellect and character were transformed into liabilities. Each time he distinguished himself in another bid for his father's approval, he merely succeeded in firing his father's rage. It was a murderous relationship.

Jimmy Baldwin, who has excavated almost every level of his life, mining it for the raw materials that have enriched his books, has never delved into his childhood. "Well," he said, "I think it's one of the things that I've avoided looking at." Perhaps only a masochist would have done otherwise. Baldwin's earliest years were a period of such unrelieved anguish that survival preoccupied him completely, delaying even recognition of the racial problem that eventually drove him from the United States for almost a decade.

"My childhood was *awful*," Baldwin says now, "but it was awful in another way. It wasn't awful, so far as I knew *then*—I hadn't made any clear connection between the fact of my color and the fact of my childhood. My childhood was awful in the way *many* childhoods are. Because we were *poor*, y'know. There were too many of us.

"And, you know, I think the whole issue with my father, and with the kids, and *Harlem*, made the whole concept of color come into my life somewhat *late*. You know, I was *aware* of it—I was not *un*aware of it. But it hadn't affected me—so to speak—*directly*. Because the struggle of just keeping alive in Harlem was too great for such *abstractions*, even."

He had to muster all his defenses for that struggle, in which he was pitted not just against Harlem ("the only *human* part of New York," he remarks now with that ambivalence so many of us exhibit toward the neighborhoods that bred us), but primarily against the triple threat of paternal enmity, poverty and the procession of infant rivals his mother brought back from the maternity ward: George in 1927, Barbara in 1929, Wilmer in 1930, David in 1931, Gloria in 1933, Ruth in 1935, Elizabeth in 1937 and Paula Maria in 1943.

Mrs. Emma Berdis Jones Baldwin had arrived in New York from Deals Island, Maryland, a wisp of iron with vague aspirations for acting, an indestructible graciousness and the great, dark eyes with which she endowed each of her four sons and five daughters. Her first born never got accustomed to what he has described as her "exasperating and mysterious habit of having babies."

Each of her pregnancies alarmed him. "I remember being frightened," he says. "Each time. Yeah. I was afraid she wouldn't come *back*. I don't remember resenting the baby. And it's possible that I wouldn't have, y'know—in such a setting. But, after a *while*, anyway, I think I probably resented *very* much my brother George. Who's the *first* one. And I may have resented Barbara—she was born when I was five.

"But I think I got, relatively speaking, *used* to it. I think I got fascinated by the—by the mechanism of the baby itself, sort of. Maybe I took out a lot—y'know, of what I *felt*—a lot of *need* for *love* (I'm sure that's true)—by loving *them*. Because I still *do* that. Yah. I'm sure that's one of the—the compensations that I invented, y'know, for *myself* . . ."

Mrs. Baldwin, unable to stand up to her husband, constantly tried to appease him. Craving peace, always on the defensive, she persuaded her children to follow her own policy of submission. She functioned as a kind of underground.

But David Baldwin was very much above ground, bigger than life, obtrusive, abrasive, omnipresent. Jimmy Baldwin couldn't budge without colliding with some manifestation of his father's malice. So ingrained was this pattern that in every rebuke he encountered, in every frown, he reconstructed David Baldwin. There was nowhere the boy could hide. Engulfed by his stepfather's personality, sunk in it, like a fossil fixed in amber, Jimmy Baldwin never really came to terms with what was to be his lifelong imprisonment.

Once his half brother Sam had quit the field, vowing to return only for his father's funeral, David Baldwin's impartial hostility united his family against him. "You know," says Jimmy Baldwin, "if he had been a little more *astute*"—and here he laughs a little—"then maybe one of us—maybe he would have created a great dissension in our lives.

"But, as a matter of fact, his pressure was so absolute that he really *welded* us to-*geth*-er. We couldn't afford, you know, to—we didn't *have* anybody but each other. We couldn't have had our *mother*, y'know. Because she was too busy dealing with *him* and too busy, you know, washing dishes and scrubbing floors and having *babies*.

"What she *did* was mainly a kind of *contraband*, y'know. She did things for us behind his back. We always *knew* it was behind his back. We also knew what he would do to her if he found out—what he *did* do to her if he found out. She was our ally, but she was, y'know—it was part of our common situation not to impose too great a burden on her."

Faithfully he supervised his charges: he walked the toddlers two at a time in a stroller; he shepherded the older children across the Harlem River to the Bronx (sometimes the Madison Avenue Bridge would pivot to let a tall ship go by, and that was ecstasy) on hazardous excursions to the Bond plant, where he would buy at a discount six loaves of day-old bread and—with luck—rush them home before prowling gangs of kids could hijack them.

"He was my right arm," says Mrs. Baldwin, gentle but indomitable. "He took care of them all. Of course, he wasn't a girl, but he was very dependable. He'd get them to bed and then say, 'Is there anything else I could do for you, mama?' He's been like a second father. I can't say he really was sickly, but he was on the delicate side. He never had the vitality most boys have in growing up. He never got into trouble with other boys—he was too shy.

"He was very easy to raise. He lived in books. He'd sit at a table with a child in one arm and a book in the other. The first book he ever read through was UNCLE TOM'S CABIN. I think it came to us from a friend. Jimmy was about eight. There was something about that book. I couldn't understand it. He just read it over and over and over again. I even hid it away up in a closet. But he rambled around and found it again. And, after that, I stopped hiding it."

Possibly the "something" that magnetized him was that stock comedy figure, Topsy, who must have struck the boy as his feminine counterpart. She was exactly his age and, like him, a misfit, isolated, ridiculed, repugnant to those around her. She had his own round eyes, his own solemnity, his own quickness and keenness (she even learned to read, as he had, with magical speed), his own generosity and his own misery.

The descriptions of her must have reminded him irresistibly of his stepfather's taunts: "wicked," "odd and goblin-like," "a gnome from the land of Diablerie," "so ugly, and always will be." And the comparatively happy ending (the adult Topsy, now cherished for her grace and favor, is serving with dedication as a missionary in Africa) must have seemed to him then as much as he could pray for.

(In 1949, more critical, Baldwin indulged in a venomous assault on "the self-righteous, virtuous sentimentality" of Mrs. Stowe's novel. His gibes at the excessive violence in her tale, then ninety-seven years old, are themselves rather excessively violent. Against this background, it is interesting to note the remarkable similarity in context and Old Testament foreboding between the final paragraphs of Harriet Beecher Stowe's anti-slavery tale and Baldwin's own anti-segregation essay, "Down at the Cross," in THE FIRE NEXT TIME.)

After UNCLE TOM'S CABIN, the boy steeped himself in literature, commuting to the library on 135th Street three and four times a week, reading "everything there," devouring books as though they were "some weird kind of food." And, for him, they were. He had thought his pain and heartbreak unprecedented. Now he began to realize, however dimly, that his lacerations were the stigmata of mankind.

School, where Jimmy Baldwin scored a series of notable successes, was just another torment for him. "I was physically a target," he says. "It worked *against* me, y'know, to be the brightest boy in class and the smallest boy in class. And I suffered. So I really *loathed* it."

But it was there at Public School 24 that Jimmy Baldwin acquired some inkling of his superior resources. "I can't say it gave me *confidence*," he says. "But it gave me a weapon. I knew I was smart." He was still unsure how he would use that advantage, or even if he could. But he was aware that it would help him attain his goal, whatever that might be: even revenge.

The nation's racial cleavage was not yet clear in his mind. When he came home from school one afternoon, his shirt snowy as always ("to prove again you were not a nigger"), his mother asked his teacher's color. She was, the boy said after reflection, "a little bit colored and a little bit white," a genetic allusion science might be tempted to apply to much of America.

Yet, with hindsight, Baldwin feels he was fortified, if even unwittingly, by the knowledge that his principal, Mrs. Gertrude Ayer, was a Negro (then the only one of that rank in the entire city). For Jimmy Baldwin, who lived on Park Avenue—upper Park Avenue, where the trains clack by en route to greener pastures—and played in garbage dumps and assumed that these were the boundaries of his future as well as his present, Mrs. Ayer's status was a rainbow conveying unspecified promise.

Moreover, the principal liked him, and he sensed that she did. "I remember him," observes Mrs. Ayer, now retired, "as a very slim, small boy with that haunted look he has still." She proved to him, Baldwin says, that he didn't have to be "entirely defined" by his circumstances.

No less significant was Orilla Miller, a young midwestern substitute with an open, guileless face, who rejoiced in the talent she discerned in her diffident pupil. "She was very, *very* nice to me," Baldwin says. "She was marvelous. In a way, maybe, you know, she helped me later when I *did* meet white people who—were not so nice. Well, at that point in my life, I didn't *hate* white people. I didn't even know anything *about* them. You know? They weren't even a different color. It didn't have any *weight*, the different color . . ."

It had crushing weight, however, for his stepfather, who never ceased to regard the drama coach with distrust. During the next four or five years, Miss Miller influenced Jimmy Baldwin and encouraged him. It may be she even saved him. It was Orilla Miller who took him to his first play—"a real play on a real stage." Under her guidance, he perceived there was a way out of the trap: "The world she showed me seemed very far away, but it was real. It was there."

When David Baldwin was laid off from his job, Miss Miller steadfastly buttressed the family. Mrs. Baldwin, grateful as her husband was not, called the teacher "a Christian," a tribute Jimmy Baldwin's mother did not bestow lightly.

The 1939 World's Fair tantalized the junior Baldwins. Jimmy, who was receiving carfare and lunch money at school, systematically skimped until he had saved enough to treat his brothers and sisters to a foray into "The World of Tomorrow." Then, in the midst of their jubilant planning, their father fell ill and required medication.

"Jimmy told me, 'Mama, take the money and get the prescription filled,'" Mrs. Baldwin explains. "I said, 'No, you'll lose your chance to go to the World's Fair.' It was the last week. Jimmy said, 'Mama, I don't mind.' The next day, in the morning mail, there was a whole envelope of tickets from Miss Miller. Her friend had gotten sick and couldn't use them. So Jimmy took the kids to the World's Fair after all."

Mrs. Baldwin sought in vain to modify the magnitude of her husband's inadequacies. It was she who sent the notes to Jimmy's teachers ("She had the gift of using language beautifully," Mrs. Ayer recalls; "I remember her above all other mothers"), and earnestly checked on his progress. "They'd praise him to the highest," Mrs. Baldwin comments, "and one of them said to me: 'How dare you come and ask me how Jimmy is doing? He's doing fine!'"

It is Jimmy Baldwin's impression that his mother "worked somewhere all day and half the night" as a domestic. With his three brothers, he would meet her at the subway exit at midnight. "Usually we hadn't eaten," he says. "Mother was paid daily, so we'd stop off at a grocery store and she'd buy some food and we'd go home and eat supper. The time didn't matter. We were all pretty hungry."

Summer and winter, Mrs. Baldwin diligently brushed and combed and vaselined the children's hair (it was "shameful" for it to be nappy). In cold weather, their arms and legs and faces were greased so they wouldn't look ashy. Jimmy Baldwin, "mercilessly scrubbed and polished," used to wonder if his mother thought she could wash away the mahogany, or possibly bleach it.

At Frederick Douglass Junior High School, he continued to roll up excellent grades. He had composed the lyrics of the farewell song at Public School 24 and now, at JHS 139, he had an opportunity to savor again the honey-sweet taste of victory when he was elevated to editor of The Douglass Pilot. But his elation was momentary.

"With whom could I *share* it?" he inquires. "You can't share *those* things with your teacher. And I didn't have a very strong sense of myself. When I told my mother, she was *frightened* because my *father* didn't like it. I simply exposed myself more."

He rarely mingled with his classmates. "He was small and funny-looking," sums up a fellow student at Douglass, "and the kids picked on him cruelly." They screeched "Bug eyes!" at him, jeered him as a sissy, sneered at the praise heaped on him by English teachers.

For Jimmy Baldwin, who was to be honored a quarter of a century later as alumnus of the year (with his name inscribed on a plaque commemorating outstanding graduates), JHS 139 was a Roman circus where, five times a week, from September through June, he had to compete in the arena against scores of bigger, stronger, scrappier youngsters, each of them a paralyzing duplication of his stepfather.

But the boy had one refuge. It was a hill in Central Park. He would run up the slope and, racing toward the top, toward the boundless canopy of the sky, he would be flooded with exultation and the fierce, untrammeled power known only to the very young and the very solitary and the very ambitious. From the summit, he could see the sweep of New York, black Harlem uptown, the white city downtown. And it was there, he vowed, there in that shining, white citadel, that he would some day make himself heard.

As he grew older, he would drift across the frontiers into the rich, clean, unfriendly metropolis beyond Harlem, sometimes a timid tourist, sometimes a salesman peddling shopping bags, sometimes a potential conqueror surveying new terrain. His reception however was invariably icy, just as it was at home. Once, as an adolescent, he was winging toward 42nd Street and the main branch of New York's public library, whose stone lions enthralled him, when a policeman directing traffic in the middle of Fifth Avenue muttered, "Why don't you niggers stay uptown where you belong?" He could not know that Jimmy Baldwin, belonging nowhere and to no one, resided in limbo.

Moreover, the police had already started bullying him even within Harlem's walls. There was something about him that provoked assault by the men in uniform: perhaps it was merely his size that made him so vulnerable; but it may be that they glimpsed in the depths of this civil, law-abiding youth an interior resistance impervious to their brand of authority.

He was about ten, and puny for his age, when two Harlem patrolmen stopped him in an empty lot. Smug in their bias, snug in it, they amused themselves with speculation on his ancestry and probable sexual prowess while they frisked him. They left him flat on his back. "And I wished," says Jimmy Baldwin, "I had a machine gun to kill them . . ."

Instead he began to translate what he felt, everything he felt, his hate and his fear and his terrifying loneliness, into words: "the agony way." And he scrawled those words on paper, even on paper bags. He wrote all the time, plays and poetry and short stories.

"And writing was my great consolation," he says. Writing, he was invisible. Writing, he was invincible. Writing, he was at last safe, because "nobody cares" what a writer looks like: "I could write to be eighty and be as grotesque as a dwarf, and that wouldn't matter.

"For me, writing was an act of love. It was an attempt—not to get the world's attention—it was an attempt to be loved. It seemed a way to save myself and to save my family. It came out of despair. And it seemed the only way to another world."

"It's unexpectedly hard to talk about myself. You see, *really*—I feel very—this is the kind of thing which I do at the desk. But I never *talk* about these things. I really never *do*. I must really one day go back and deal with the whole figure of my father—in another way . . ."

Four

Writing was Jimmy Baldwin's consolation but the rewards he derived from it very early in his boyhood fell so far short of what he really wanted that he seems to have blocked them out altogether. Rubbed raw by his stepfather's sadism, he was all the more susceptible to the badgering that plagued him in school.

"I was just as small and just as thin as Jimmy in those days," says Randolph Douglas, valedictorian of Baldwin's class at 139, now chairman of the science department at another Manhattan junior high school. "We were the 'smart' ones. But I guess Jimmy was the scapegoat. They used to joke at him because his hair looked as though it had been cut with a bowl. We sat on opposite sides of the aisle in our ninth year. He was very, very quiet. Pensive. Apart from the rest of us. Standoffish or lonely: I didn't know which it was—then. He didn't smile much. But there wasn't much to smile about in those days."

Ragging is a schoolboy tradition and Jimmy Baldwin wasn't the only butt at 139. But his contemporaries weren't content to dub him "Froggy" and "Popeyes" and let it go at that. Some of them ridiculed him with cruder epithets that must have made him writhe in panic, knotting his stomach and jellying his knees. Inevitably he must have interpreted such gibes as proof that his father was not lying: he really was uglier and more sinful than all his fellows.

No wonder he loathed school. No wonder the bullying to which he was subjected finally extinguished the brighter (but fewer) episodes. Hounded and bedeviled though he was, a target at home and in class, he was still "the best writer" at 139. "Oh, yes," says Randy Douglas. "We knew it then. Everyone accepted that as a fact. Jimmy was our writer. I remember that he wrote all the time. And I remember how much I admired him . . ."

From the beginning, Baldwin was outstanding in English ("Yeah, yeah," he concedes). From the beginning, the ability he was born with, flatteringly evident to his instructors, flourished under their tutelage. Whatever dreams he had were supported, if not inspired, by the compliments that festooned his compositions and book reports.

Baldwin's years at Douglass were punctuated with experiences that should have been—must have been—some kind of compensation, even if they have since plummeted to the bottom of his recollection, lost to him there in the silt of time.

"It was clear to me when I was very, very young," he now insists, "that I could either live or die, and it was entirely up to me. Because no one—because *no* one was going to *help* me . . ."

But at thirteen he had been sufficiently heartened by the help of others to have commented, ". . . Everyone seems to think I have talent." That admission, part of a short story published in The Douglass Pilot in 1938, appeared under the byline of "James Baldwin, 9B1."

It appears then that, at the very time he now feels he was

bereft of help, his teachers were fanning his creativity (or, at the very least, his confidence in it) with sufficient skill to persuade the apprehensive adolescent that he was a talented writer. "I knew *that* when I was very young," he says. "Oh, I guess by the time I was—I must have known that by the time I was ten or twelve. I always wrote the class plays and all that jazz."

Yet that is not what he remembers but what he has to be nudged to remember. Perhaps it is because he was denied the one factor he deemed essential as a child, his stepfather's love, that Jimmy Baldwin deprecates the faculty approval beamed on him in school. It is as though he has had to blot out every trace of the good to focus all the more fiercely on the bad.

Junior High School 139, like the elementary school he attended, was less dismal than most of their counterparts in Harlem today. For one thing, what Kenneth Clark (himself a graduate of 139) describes derisively as "the cult of we-can't-teach-Harlem-pupils-because-they're-so-poor-and-so-culturally-deprived" had not yet sprung up. Moreover, the pathology of the ghetto was somewhat less marked than it is now. Many of the teachers, both Negro and white, demanded the best of their classes; and often got it.

But Baldwin's memory plays tricks on him. It is oddly selective, almost evasive. Of the late Countee Cullen he says, "He taught me French." And of Herman W. Porter, Baldwin observes, "He tried to teach me math—he didn't succeed, but I thought he was a very nice man." But Cullen, already renowned as a poet, was in charge of Douglass' literary club, of which young Jimmy was a prominent member. And Porter doubled as faculty adviser to The Douglass Pilot, in which capacity he was frequently consulted by Editor Baldwin.

Years later, in Paris, he was to acknowledge his debt to Cullen in a message to his widow. And at fourteen Baldwin voluntarily expressed his appreciation of the assistance Porter had rendered. That Jimmy Baldwin now overlooks the connection of these two men with his writing, linking them only with the French and the math in which he displayed neither interest nor competence, has impressed a former classmate as "rather peculiar."

Cullen, author of COLOR and COPPER SUN and BALLAD OF A BROWN GIRL, chubby but brisk, always carrying a briefcase stuffed with books and papers, had given his allegiance to France during extended stays there. He once explained to a friend, precisely as

Baldwin would do a couple of decades later, that he was not treated as a stranger in Paris as he was in the United States whenever he left the confines of Harlem. He was, for most of the boys in his elite writing group, a memorable figure.

"We were very proud of Cullen," says Edward F. Carpenter, Baldwin's schoolmate at Douglass, later a guidance counsellor there. "Many of us belonged to the Salem Methodist Church, where his father was the minister. We knew he was a poet and that he'd been to France. He was aware of the racial problem, but he didn't beat a drum. He talked to us about Paris. He tried to show us Harlem wasn't the whole world—he tried to broaden our horizons. He was very important to all of us.

"We kind of looked up to this man, who had published books and who laughed easily and talked without an accent. He introduced us to the works of Negro authors I'd never heard of before. And he wasn't afraid to touch a boy. He'd put an arm around a boy's shoulders—boys like that; I've learned to do the same thing myself now, as a teacher. And I've consciously imitated the way Cullen walked so rapidly through the corridors.

"The boys in our group didn't pick on Jimmy. He was intense, sharp-minded—on the ball, as we say now. He wrote things that were much more meaningful than the rest of us did."

Baldwin has effaced all of this. "If he says so, it must be so," he says of Carpenter's recollection. "Carpenter," he repeats thoughtfully. "Carpenter . . ." He shakes his head and says without conviction, "That name sounds familiar . . ."

Yet it is inconceivable that Baldwin was neglected by Cullen ("I think Cullen showed a special interest in everybody in his club," Carpenter says). Or that the boy could have failed to have identified himself with this poet who was, like himself, a Negro and the son of a minister, yet had carved out a reputation as a man of letters.

Herman W. Porter, then a newcomer to the school system, was no less conspicuous a landmark at Douglass. Tall, lean, handsome, with military carriage and the glowing bronze skin Caucasians pride themselves on acquiring after judicious exposure to the sun, Porter was affable but formal. "I was Mr. Discipline," he confides cheerfully.

The son of a Terra Haute janitor, Bill Porter worked his way through Harvard ("there were nine Negroes in my class, more than Harvard had ever had before, and we were just tolerated; but Cambridge is very dear to me"), only to discover that there was no place in the United States for a chemist a shade or two darker than the spectrum classified as white.

He served in World War I as a second lieutenant in the all-Negro Ninety-Second Division, heading an intelligence unit in the Argonne and acting as unofficial interpreter for his outfit. But, when peace came, Washington hemmed, hawed and rejected his application for the regular Army ("they didn't know what to do with colored officers").

For a year he ran a butcher shop in Manhattan with two partners who had been similarly discarded by the Army (both had studied a year at Harvard Law School and one was to be the first Negro to sit on the New York bench as City Court Judge Francis Ellis Rivers). When that enterprise collapsed, Porter spent more than a decade clerking in the Post Office until he could complete the requirements for teaching.

Porter was—and is—something of a stoic. But his generation is not that of the Negro revolution, and his outlook differs radically from that of today's Negroes. Bill Porter, whose grandparents were slaves ("my father missed it by only three years"), remarks philosophically: "I was telling my wife the other day—and she didn't think too highly of it—that I thought I was lucky to have been born free."

The ambiance at Douglass Junior High School was altered by Porter's coming. Into its classrooms (and, eventually, its offices), he injected something of his own tough-fibred morale. "You wanted Mr. Porter to think the best of you," says a former student. "You wanted to do right because he felt you could. He was a father image. My God, yes! A father who would love you, as well as set limits."

Baldwin, so urgently in need of a father, seems to have responded to this quality. He may now recall Porter only as a math teacher; but Porter's memory is undimmed. "Running a school magazine was outside my field," Porter reminisces, still straight, still handsome, his crew-cut hair now white. "But I remember it as one of the finest experiences I had—because I had Jimmy Baldwin as my editor-in-chief.

"He was a tiny, little fellow. He'd sit on the couch that used to be right there"—Porter gestures at the exact spot in the scrupu-

lously tidy apartment he and his wife have occupied since 1930—
"and his feet didn't touch the floor. Maybe they still wouldn't!

"He was writing short stories that he wanted me to see. They
were lurid, I must say. And I guess I told him so. He'd come here,
bringing all his material up to me to correct. He could write
better than anyone in the school—from the principal on down, in
my opinion. He was very shy. And apparently he lived for one
thing: to write. Yah. To write."

In the fall of 1937, when both were embarking on their final
year at 139, Baldwin and Randy Douglas were teamed as The
Pilot's associate editors. The issue that semester, in compliance
with an official "suggestion," was to be dedicated to "The School
and The Community," a topic on which Porter, the Hoosier, regarded himself as less than authoritative. "But I knew where to
go," he says with satisfaction.

On a Saturday morning he strode from Lenox Avenue and the
immaculate order of his childless flat to 2171 Fifth Avenue, where
Jimmy Baldwin lived. The streets that day were as gray as the
threatening skies. But Porter did not find his walk depressing.
Automatically matching his long steps to martial music heard
only by him, the mathematics teacher reveled in the permutations
and combinations of Harlem's non-seasonal vitality.

His pleasure subsided rapidly under the shock of "the unbe-
lievably poverty-stricken" Baldwin menage. The noise and the
clutter and the crowding overwhelmed him. Mrs. Baldwin, a
gaggle of youngsters underfoot, remained in the background. It
was David Baldwin who dominated the next half hour.

Wrapped in a tattered bathrobe and his customary hauteur, he
did not bother to conceal from the caller that his presence was an
intrusion. Porter outlined his mission, explaining that he wanted
Jimmy to accompany him to the Forty-Second Street Public Library and research Harlem's early history. David Baldwin's consent was unspoken and obviously reluctant. He said very little but
he made Porter realize he was distinctly unwelcome. The teacher
felt relieved when Jimmy was ready and they could depart.

But the strain had been harder on the boy, who had been given
no opportunity to brace himself for the unexpected encounter
between the two men. For the teen-ager, their confrontation must
have been harrowing. On the bus downtown, Baldwin was visibly
nervous. Even today, whenever his emotional equilibrium is

rocked, he gets sick to his stomach. At thirteen, he fought his nausea manfully.

Porter, noticing the boy's symptoms, leaned over and opened the window. Baldwin restrained himself until they descended from the bus. Then—"right there in the middle of Fifth Avenue," Porter relates with a grin—the boy vomited. But a few minutes in the fresh air soon revived him.

Porter steered his protégé to a librarian and informed her why they were there. Then, handing Baldwin enough money for carfare, certain he would carry out his task with distinction, the teacher returned home.

On his own in the vastness and complexity of the block-long building, with its belligerently utilitarian décor, hooded lamps that resembled weaving cobras and no less forbidding patrons, Jimmy Baldwin may have flinched but he did not flee. Fear had been by then too long his familiar; he had trained himself to withstand its assaults.

"You know," Porter marvels, "I'm sure that was the first time he'd ever seen that library and yet he turned in a superb job—really, a superb job."

From his afternoon of reading, the boy pieced together a smoothly flowing chronicle, avoiding the overelaborate detail and the too-rigid adherence to source material that often blight the efforts of much older historians. Here and there the digest, subsequently featured in The Pilot, achieved an almost professional élan:

HARLEM—Then and Now

By James Baldwin, 9A1

I wonder how many of us have ever stopped to think what Harlem was two or three centuries ago? Or how it came to be as it is today? Not many of us. Most of us know in a vague way that the Dutch lived in Harlem "a long time ago," and let it go at that. We don't think about how the Indians were driven out, how the Dutch and English fought, or how finally Harlem grew into what it is today. Now I am going to tell you a little about this. Listen:

17th Century

In 1636, inspired by glowing accounts of Harlem, a Dr. Johannes de la Montagne, his family and a handful of settlers landed at 125th Street and the Harlem River. They landed when Harlem was a wilderness. Nature reigned supreme.

Courageously these people set about making a home out of this wilderness. They chopped down trees, they built their homes, and tried to make something out of the land. It was tough going at first. The houses were hard to heat, the crops refused to grow. They were often cold, hungry, and frightened, a feeling not lessened by the sight of Indians running around in the forest. But they stayed because they couldn't and wouldn't go back.

And one day, in the beginning of Spring, a Dutch housewife discovered a little green shoot growing. "Look!" she cried. "Corn is growing!" And it grew. All over, it grew. Farms that before had been thought barren yielded up corn by the bushel. People enlarged their farms, planted more seed. A Danish capitalist, Jochem Pieter, had a farm that extended from 125th to 150th Streets, along the Harlem River. All over people were jubilant. They had nothing to fear. This was "good earth."

But the Indians did not like it. The squeak of cart wheels and swish of scythes warned them that their "happy hunting grounds" would soon be taken away from them.

18th Century

The 18th Century found Harlem in English hands. She had been conquered in 1664.

Harlem had improved a great deal. The farms were more pretentious. Many people had slaves. All in all, Harlem was a very proper little village. At that time, of course, Seventh Avenue was a mere dirt road, St. Nicholas Park was old "Breakneck Hill" (a very appropriate title), Mt. Morris Park was "Old Snake Hill" and the place where the family went for picnics. There was no Madison Avenue, no Lenox Avenue, and no tenements. There were no sidewalks, no asphalt streets, no large churches and schools, etc. In fact, the schools were just little one-room buildings.

That was Harlem in the 18th century.

19th Century

Harlem had changed greatly. Now there were streets, or at least public roads. Seventh Avenue was still dirt, though, and people drove up and down in carriages, and in the winter time in sleighs. Men and women on horseback were a common sight. One hundred and twenty-ninth and one hundred and thirtieth streets were residential sections of stately beauty. There were many very fine mansions throughout the section. Where 131st Street playground is now, there once stood an elegant mansion, only recently torn down. Ere a decade had passed, tenements had sprung up. Smooth, dependable asphalt streets replaced rough, muddy roads, and farms and all that goes with them gradually disappeared.

20th Century

Today, as we all know, Harlem is a large, thickly populated urban community—a city within a city, with fine streets and avenues, parks, playgrounds, churches, schools, apartment houses, theatres, etc.

However, there is still great room for improvement. The tenements people were once so proud of are now rather dangerous firetraps and should be rebuilt. There has been some effort on the part of the Housing Authorities to improve them, but as yet they have only operated in a very small field.

Now we, who are interested in Harlem, hope that the future will bring a steady growth and improvement.

Only three years after this expression of optimism, Jimmy Baldwin was to denounce America's social institutions with almost as much passion as he does today. But at thirteen he was still relying heavily on the attitudes prescribed in his civics course and the daily newspapers. After touring the $4,000,000 Harlem River Housing Project with other members of The Pilot Club late in November, Baldwin submitted a solidly factual report; in its preface, he again parroted the conventional editorial views of the ghetto.

"Everyone knows that, excepting the lower East Side," he wrote, "Harlem is the worst slum section in the city. Harlem has more delinquency, disease, and a higher death rate than any other portion of our 'Great Unfinished City.' That is one reason why we hear so much about shooting brawls, stabbings, and other such things in Harlem. To help correct these and other conditions, the New York City Housing Authority selected Harlem as the base of its new experiments."

His detachment could have stemmed from boredom. But in his analysis of movies he displayed a precocious sophistication. His screengoing must have been sadly hampered by his family's chronically depleted economy and his father's tirades against the motion picture as a device of the devil. Nevertheless the young critic could appraise filmmaking techniques with a cool and calculating eye.

After viewing A CHRISTMAS CAROL on a double bill in Douglass' auditorium one Wednesday afternoon, he judged the "Our Gang" comedy "by far the best" of the two, the superlative establishing the decisiveness of his choice if not his mastery of grammar. With noteworthy aplomb, Baldwin assured his readers he was something of a Dickens specialist, then hailed Hal Roach's THE SUNDOWN LIMITED as "a most refreshing relief from the dark, gloomy and unconvincing Dickensonian movie that preceded it."

During his last term at Douglass, Baldwin was The Pilot's chief executive. The position was a jab of adrenalin: he wrote incessantly, conferring with Porter two and three times a week. But the teacher declines even a measure of credit for his pupil's literary career.

"I would never be one to say that I had an influence there," Porter says firmly. "You obviously feel good when someone you've been in contact with turns out well. But I can't claim any credit for it—any more than I think that those other students of mine who went to the electric chair (and there were some) did so because I was derelict in my duties. I doubt very much that I influenced Baldwin's writing. In the first place, he wrote so well that he didn't need much help."

That is undoubtedly true. But what was indispensable to him was someone who believed in him. And Porter did. Years after Jimmy Baldwin graduated from Douglass (and years before he streaked across the American scene as a new and promising essayist), Porter would remind his colleagues:

"Remember Baldwin? Oh, you must remember him. That boy could *write*."

"There really *is* a level on which, you know, *everybody* finds himself—*dictated* to—by his *time* and his *place*. By the fact that you're born in 1924, in a certain country, a certain color—and, you know, sharing certain assumptions—dictates a certain *course*. Dictates, in some way, what you will *do*."

Five

In the June issue of The Douglass Pilot, the lead editorial revealed Editor Baldwin in pontifical mood. The style, prissy and inspirational, suited the upbeat theme, "Be the Best." But tucked away in the awkward, little exercise in self-conscious virtue was the author's manifesto:

"If I am a playwright, I should try to improve a troubled world, and try to be numbered among the great artists of my race."

This declaration was dropped into the piece almost casually to illustrate the hypothesis that: "It's not what you do that counts, but how you do it." Just a few pages on, however, in a sketch called "One Sunday Afternoon," Jimmy Baldwin spelled out his intentions with a resolution and a clarity that signified he would be deterred by neither bulky obstacles nor balky soothsayers. The sentimentality of the editorialist lingered on but now it was expressed in terms of his weakness for melodrama, leavened by wry pokes at the author.

On a Sunday stroll, he spies a tramp sinister enough to be "in disguise" and tails him to a restaurant. There the suspect presses his nose against the showcase and the tyro detective abandons hope of ferreting out a criminal:

For he was not looking into the restaurant as though he wanted to hold up the cashier; he simply looked as though he were hungry and wanted a square meal.

I had a quarter which I had kept in my pocket for two weeks. I toyed with the idea of sticking it into his pocket and running . . .

But the tramp straightened up and began to walk again . . . and the detective in me overcame the humanitarian and forced me on.

We walked straight over to St. Nicholas Park and entered. I followed him to a more or less secluded section, and once there he turned on me so savagely that I nearly jumped out of my skin.

"What are you following me for?" he demanded. So! It seemed I wasn't such a good sleuth after all. He had known all along that I was following him.

"Want to make fun of a poor bum?" he went on bitterly. "Want to laugh at him, jeer at him? Nice, isn't it? To laugh at a guy that hasn't had any decent food for three days?"

Suddenly his voice rose on a furious note, verging on hysteria —"Get out of here, you little fool! Get out."

"I will not get out," I retorted. "It's not my fault you're a bum. I guess it's nobody's fault but your own." We glared at each other. He laughed bitterly.

"That's where you're wrong, sonny." He was suddenly quite calm. "I'm a bum—but it's not my fault."

"Then whose . . . ?"

"Sit down and listen," he said; and so while the sun slowly sank in the west, Pete, the tramp told me the story of his life.

"I was born," he said, "in New England. My parents were true New Englanders—bleak and cold. So when I told them I wanted to be an actor they were, to put it mildly, shocked. What? Their son enter a theatre and act on a stage? Never! I pleaded with them. I tried to show them that acting was a job, just like any other job, but they refused to listen.

"They wanted me to be an undertaker, a doctor, or a minister. In vain, I protested that I had no aptitude for undertaking, that I did not like medicine or surgery, and that the ministry was out of my line. I wanted to fly in another direction but my mother clipped my wings.

She became ill. And now she no longer ordered me to fulfill her wishes; she begged me. Well, I gave up my hopes of being an actor and settled down to being a country doctor. I was not a brilliant student in college and the medical course was very difficult for me. From the first, I was a failure. I didn't have inside of me the spark that makes a man a doctor. Everything in me wanted to be an actor. I made mistake after mistake and the people lost confidence in me.

"Soon nobody at all came to me. I sank lower and lower and I was deep in debt, so one day I tried to get away from it all and hitchhiked my way here to New York.

"Here it was even worse. I lived from hand to mouth; when I was lucky at getting odd jobs, I ate; when I wasn't, I didn't. I lived in the streets and I slept in parks. I was no good, a tramp—a failure."

He got up.

"So you see, kid, it wasn't my fault? I just wanted you to know that."

"Why don't you try to get a job acting?" I demanded.

"No, son, it's too late now. I'm too old. I've wasted too much time. All these years when I should have been building myself up in my profession I've been bumming around."

He paused as though he were weighing something in his mind. Then, he shrugged his shoulders, a gesture of defeat.

"No," he said shortly, "it's too late now."

I looked at him, at his threadbare suit, his shabby shoes. Yes, it was too late for Pete, now.

There was a long, long silence. Finally he said,

"Say, kid, what's your name?"

"Jimmy," I said.

"What do you want to be when you grow up?" he asked.

"A writer," I said.

"Plays?" he asked.

"Yes," I answered.

He looked at me. "How do you know you can do it?"

"Well, I'm very good in English, and I've written quite a number of plays in school, and everyone seems to think I have talent. I'm willing to work very hard in order to succeed."

"Good for you," he said softly. Then he took me by the shoulders and said, "Listen, kid, don't you ever—ever—let anybody else live your life for you. You do the work that you're best fitted for, as well as you can do it, and you'll be successful at it. That's the most important thing in life, doing what you can do well, the way you ought to do it. Don't you ever forget what I've said. You see before you a man who is a failure in life because he wasn't courageous enough to stare opposition in the face and stare it down."

He paused and looked at me. "My parents would have gotten over my being an actor. They'd have been proud of it sometime." He grinned and held out his hand. "Goodbye, Jimmy!" I took it. "Goodbye, Pete," I said.

He smiled at me, and ambled off, his back bent, his hands in his pockets, and the legs of his trousers flapping slightly in the wind.

But in my heart, I was happy. For—while he was not looking—I had slipped the quarter in his pocket!

The structure of this parable was evidently designed to externalize the argument Baldwin must have been silently conducting with his scoffing parents. Although he transposed them from Southern Negroes to Northern whites, he kept them in a minor key. Possibly he could not imagine them any other way: they remained "bleak and cold," like David Baldwin.

The dénouement in "One Sunday Afternoon" amounted to a proclamation that James Baldwin was determined to "go for broke," regardless of the cost. That is still his credo today. But the thirteen-year-old, a bit tremulous under his bravado, soothed himself by hinting broadly that the tribulations involved in living his own life would be transitory; success and parental pride would "sometime" vindicate him—heaven, in short, was just around the corner.

A four-page newspaper, The Bulletin, was founded at Douglass that spring. Porter promptly dispatched the crack editor of The Pilot on his first journalistic assignment. The cub reporter, neat, punctual as he was never to be as an adult, arrived one evening during Open School Week to cover a parents' conference. He was quivering with eagerness and bristling with freshly sharpened pencils. The story he later turned in was an imitation of a popular gossip column and Porter cleared it without hesitation.

"I thought it was exceedingly well written," he says. "Jimmy described what a teacher wore and then added a little comment. He mentioned Miss A and then Miss B, who was dressed in such-and-such a way—very complimentary, actually. But then he inserted the phrase, 'stern as always.'"

Porter's lips quirk. "Absolutely innocent, you know. The woman was very hard-working but rather elderly. The boys didn't like her—although many of them later wrote her that they were just beginning to appreciate how much she'd done for them. She used to show me the letters.

"Well: the principal called me over after that edition of The Bulletin came out. He asked me if I'd proofread the copy. I said, 'Sure.' He said: 'Miss B doesn't like this. She's hysterical.' She kept crying and crying. You know what we had to do? We had to burn that whole issue! And I'm so sorry I didn't keep a copy. I knew I had something special in Baldwin, even if I didn't know just how special . . ."

And so Jimmy Baldwin went forth from Douglass, his objectives formulated, his course unwavering. His abhorrent associations with the school had not yet obscured his more agreeable moments there; or perhaps his relationship with Porter held more significance for him then than the furtive needling of his classmates.

"I saw him just once more," Porter says. "He came back to Douglass to see me almost a year later. He was in high school. We chatted a bit. I said, 'Baldwin, give me something to put in The Bulletin.' He sat right down and dashed it off. It didn't take him more then ten minutes. I have it still."

The old man clicks his tongue. "I used to have it in Baldwin's own writing," he says. "But that disappeared. Well, I didn't read it that day until after he'd left. Otherwise I might have asked him to change one word. But I think it's remarkable, when I reread it now, that a kid that age could produce anything this mature."

Porter's judgment was sound. In the eulogy the boy tossed off to please Bill Porter, there were flashes—almost a preview—of the subtle cadence that is Jimmy Baldwin's today. The adolescent who had been known as a goody-goody had few pranks of which he could boast to Douglass' current student crop. But he made the most of feeble material by blowing up his single—and entirely involuntary—clash with the school authorities into a lively exploit that supplied the appropriate touch of swagger:

I graduated from Douglass in the spring term of 1938. That is to say, I was neither hopelessly bad nor exceptionally good. I crammed for tests, even as you have been doing this term, and as students have done from time immemorial. I did no more work than I thought necessary, played more than I should have, exasperated most of my patient teachers, and in general behaved like a schoolboy.

I was interested in the literary life before I came to Douglass, and my interests found a great stimulus in The Pilot. Mr. Porter was in charge in those dear, bygone days, and it was he who guided me from the sentimental, over-written horrors I began with to something approaching an intelligent style. His interest sprang, I believe, from the fact that I was at that time the only student in Douglass who had absolutely no comprehension of anything concerning mathematics.

In those days, I was comfortably supposed by all to have one foot in the grave, and I staggered about looking like a cross between the Ancient Mariner and Bette Davis in the last reel of OF HUMAN BONDAGE. Miss Smith, under whose jurisdiction we all were, took one look at me, and promptly bought a gallon of cod liver oil and poured it down my throat. It was mixed in some sort of malt solution, which kept the taste down, and it brought me back from the pearly gates—which puts me (and mankind) in Miss Smith's eternal debt.

I remember my period of editorship with that speechless pride and joy of which only a junior high school graduate is capable. It was at that same time that the paper The Bulletin was born, and between the birth cries of the one and the growing pains of the other, yours truly and the entire Pilot staff had their hands full.

I shall never be able to forget the noisy Pilot meetings in an abandoned gym on the third floor, where promises flowed like honey, but where work stood still. And the hardly more sedate conferences in Miss Smith's office where contributions received final judgment, and where my gossip columns (outlawed by an irate teacher after reading an unflattering column) were laughed over and summarily burned.

It is a fact that has struck me forcefully, whenever I pause to consider it, that whatever activity I was engaged in at Douglass— newspaper, magazine, play-acting—that no matter how flippantly we attacked it, our job was completed on schedule. We might play a bit too often and laugh a bit too much, but we were always there for the starting plug.

It is this spirit of good will and friendship which makes Douglass one of the greatest junior high schools in the country. Long may she stand!

Beaming, Porter again scans the pages of Baldwin's paean. "The 'Miss Smith' he referred to is Dora Smith," the teacher explains. "She was the assistant principal and she used to give him cod liver oil every day—even though we weren't supposed to medicate the students. And I wouldn't be surprised if that didn't make the difference—he was that close to the line.

"You know what I would have asked him to change? 'Yours truly.' That's the only thing I didn't care for. The rest of it is just fine."

Twenty-five years were to elapse before Baldwin revisited 139. During that long hiatus, his "speechless pride and joy" were eclipsed and he remembered Douglass only with unadulterated horror. "I never want to see it again," he said repeatedly. "Never." When this was reported to Porter, he was upset. "Boys can be cruel," he says now. "I wish I'd known how they heckled Baldwin. I'd have stopped it."

It was in the spring of 1963 that the student body voted Jimmy Baldwin "alumnus of the year." Lionel E. McMurren, an assistant principal who had been at Douglass with Baldwin, wrote a letter notifying his former schoolmate of this honor and suggesting his acceptance could improve the Harlem child's self-image.

Baldwin's resistance melted, a process probably hastened by the knowledge that one of those balloting for him was his nephew, James Mitchell, to whom the writer had addressed an open letter, "My Dungeon Shook" (the prologue to the longer essay in THE FIRE NEXT TIME). On June 22nd, with his "baby sister" Paula Maria, Jimmy Baldwin trekked back to Harlem and his alma mater, an unrepentant but good-humored prodigal, holding before Douglass' pupils his own impeccably tailored image—in a charcoal, mohair suit—as a partial reflection of their own.

James Mitchell, a ninth-year man and appropriately nonchalant, but clasping an inscribed copy of THE FIRE NEXT TIME, was sitting in the back. Spotting him, Baldwin hurried to the rear, took his towering namesake by the hand and led him down the aisle to a chair on the platform.

Bill Porter, in retirement a year, was too ill to be present. But McMurren read aloud to the assembly the essay Porter had preserved from Baldwin's last visit, tactfully deleting the allusion to the incendiary column and its even more incendiary end (but fellow alumnus Ed Carpenter privately reminded the guest of honor of this scandalous episode and he shouted with glee).

Then, standing on the stage of JHS 139, flanked by two bas reliefs of Washington Crossing the Delaware, Jimmy Baldwin looked into the tiered faces—just as scrubbed and polished as his had been—and told them: "White people have convinced themselves the Negro is happy in his place. It's your job not to believe it one moment longer . . ."

Some ten blocks away, Alice Porter was bustling about her kitchen. At McMurren's request, Baldwin had promised to call on his old adviser at the close of the ceremony. "McMurren telephoned me in the morning and said he and Jimmy would be coming over," Porter remembers. "Well, we had no liquor in the house. So my wife went out and bought a bottle." Mrs. Porter nods. "I prepared a big spread for lunch, too," she says. "But Baldwin never came . . ."

"McMurren telephoned again," Porter says, not reproachful, just regretful. "He told me Jimmy's agent wouldn't let him come. That he had an appointment downtown. I guess Baldwin's very busy. He can't be everywhere. And I understand that . . ."

The morning after he received his award, Baldwin was in Riverside Church to watch his nephew receive his diploma at a joint graduation exercise conducted by Douglass and another junior high school. Baldwin's avuncular role could not mask his fame. Whispers and craning heads heralded his arrival. Within minutes, James Mitchell's uncle had been ushered to the podium. When the keynote speech had been delivered and the annual rites of passage were almost at an end, Baldwin was brought forward.

The youngsters of both schools, forsaking decorum, cheered and whistled and applauded. Old enough himself now to be the father of a Douglass graduate, Jimmy Baldwin smiled down at them. It was a sunburst of a smile, and its incandescence intensified the din before quiet could be restored. Baldwin leaned toward the microphone. Then, his voice glistening with emotion, he conferred on those boys and girls the paternal blessing he had longed for but never heard.

"You're beautiful and I love you," Jimmy Baldwin said.

"The peculiar quality of Harlem is that it has no reference to any other place, no other country. If you go into another ghetto, Eastern Jew or Pole or whatever, it is essentially part of the old world brought over here, which has not yet been assimilated into the new world. But that is not the case in Harlem. Harlem has not come from any of those places. It was created here. And no one has any *intention* of assimilating it . . ."

Six

The catalyst called puberty overstimulated Jimmy Baldwin's awareness of the evil within and without. Everything he felt, everything he thought, everything he dreamed and everything he saw during the summer of his fourteenth birthday convinced him of his own depravity.

Raised in a Holy Roller household that adhered to biblical injunction with zealous literalness, he was a thorough Puritan whose conscience clanged with guilt at any deviation he detected in himself from his father's narrow ethical code.

"I was kept off the streets almost completely," Baldwin says now, "because I was so busy taking care of—keeping the *kids* off the street. So, from a social point of view, I was entirely unequipped for school."

From a psychological point of view, he was even less equipped for the normal but bewildering physical developments that transmuted all the ingredients of his life, some of them good, most of them bad, but all of them at least familiar. He no longer knew what to anticipate from his body, his voice, his mind. Their declaration of independence, alarming in itself, was interpreted by him as conclusive proof of his innate wickedness.

He was sure he read corroboration in the faces of the racketeers, prostitutes, pushers, hustlers and bookies parading along Lenox Avenue. In the past their eyes had always slid over and beyond him, unseeing. But they saw him now. He had shed invisibility along with innocence. "Whose little boy are you?" they asked him, men and women, leering, only half in jest. His certainty that they were soliciting his participation in every variety of crime and sin filled him with dread.

The girls he knew had abruptly acquired the curves and the complex urgency of physiological maturity. And from the boys there now emanated a wariness and a despair as though biology, stripping them of illusion, had forced them to realize they would never—could never—climb above the barren level inhabited by their fathers.

Higher education, even the highest education, too seldom succeeded in scaling the ramparts that sealed off Harlem's residents. "There is no other ghetto like Harlem," Baldwin says now. "There is no other ghetto out of which one cannot escape."

Even outside the ghetto (from nine to five), his neighbors were still in it, the mark of their caste irrevocably branded upon their skin. It was easier, and far less painful, to give up at once than to persist against seemingly insurmountable odds. Either way the end result was apt to be the same: unconditional surrender.

And so Baldwin watched the boys drop out of school and troop downtown to the menial jobs that were the only kind available to them. His father, from motives at least half economic, urged

Jimmy to follow the same course. But he jibbed at that, not even sure why.

As a child, he had tried to insulate himself against rebuff by spinning a cocoon of reverie about the future, about the time when he would be grown-up and successful. The dream had been recurrent:

Clad in a gray suit, he would drive his big Buick uptown—uptown, from somewhere in the shining, white citadel—to the block in Harlem where his family lived. And they would all be there waiting for him, proud of him now, his father as well as his mother, proud of their son, James Arthur Baldwin, so wealthy and so famous. Then they would all pile into his car and he would drive them to his country house. And they would dine there together or in a restaurant, all of them close and loving.

Much of this, but not all, was to come true (although Baldwin, whose distrust of mechanical devices extends to cars, has never learned to drive). But, at fourteen, immersed in his dream, he saw no practical and legitimate way of translating it into reality.

He couldn't make it by boxing (like his first hero, Joe Louis) or singing (even though he had been a soloist in church when he was very little). But he was mutely resolved not to settle for less than the counsel he had proffered himself through Pete the tramp: "You do the work that you're best fitted for, as well as you can do it, and you'll be successful at it."

Today Baldwin says he is glad he never went to college: "Because, so far as I can tell, what colleges *mainly* do is teach you how not to think," he comments. "They certainly teach you how not to *live*, y'know. They make—as far as I can tell, basing it on what I've seen of college graduates—they give you a system which is supposed to conquer life. I think life tells *you*; you don't tell *life*."

But, as a boy, he had secretly wished he could go to college. "Oh, I did at one time in my life," he says, shrugging. "It's very long ago. But I *did*, yeah." That may partially explain why he held out against his father's counsel.

As the heat rose in waves from Harlem's sidewalks and gutters, and the acrid tenements simmered under the sun and only the kids frolicking in the fire hydrants' spray were reasonably comfortable, his acquaintances grappled downtown with Mr. Charlie for the dollars that staved off starvation but not defeat.

With their meager salaries, some bought bus tickets to the Harlems of other cities, or wine or the exorbitant oblivion of heroin. Many retreated into the Army as soon as they were old enough. Others congregated after dark in the rank, musty hallways and passed around a bottle, merry enough at first, then subsiding into tears as they cursed fitfully at the man they had not yet learned to call "whitey." Watching, Baldwin was afraid for them and himself.

The corruption he witnessed seemed to him to have seeped into his soul. The division between morality and immorality, hitherto so broad and incontrovertible, diminished and then disappeared. His pulse pumped with fear. He thinks now that a portion of his terror came from the recognition that he desperately wanted to be *somebody's* little boy."

Appalled by the revolution of his senses, he fled. He sought deliverance, and found reprieve, in the church. There, encapsulated against the world, he considered himself impregnable. He was, he observes now with a scorn verging on contempt, hiding from himself, hiding from life. But all he felt then was relief.

The agent of his conversion was a fellow student at junior high school, two years his senior, Arthur Moore, slight, quick, lighthearted, then devoutly religious. With his parents, Moore worshipped at Mount Calvary of the Pentecostal Faith Church, known more simply in Harlem—and outside it—as Mother Horn's Church.

Now a postal clerk with a pretty wife and an elfin daughter who is Baldwin's godchild, Moore says: "I was probably his closest friend at Douglass. Once in a while, at recess, he would play ball or ring-a-levio, but he wasn't really athletic. Mostly I'd be playing handball and he'd pass by on his way to the library or on some other urgent errand. Sometimes he'd wait for me. We both liked to read. We used to go to the used-book stores at 125th Street and buy a book for a nickel—or six for a quarter, when we had the money."

As they sauntered home from school, Jimmy would talk about his favorite English teacher, Maude R. Robinson, a plump, sweet woman with Boston in her accent and posture (her name draws from him now a blank stare and, struggling to place her, he asks, "Was she a Negro?" But Moore says: "She and Jimmy had rapport. She's the one he'd have liked to have known he really did become a writer, but she died years ago"). To Moore, young Baldwin would also enumerate his difficulties with his father ("Jimmy never said anything particularly good about him").

It was during this period that Baldwin began to seek out as substitute parents a series of older women, some of them more paternal than maternal. Curiously evocative in personality of David Baldwin, they often shared many of his surface traits: his granite strength, his commanding presence, his overbearing assertiveness, occasionally even his strictness and severity, a constellation usually identified in our society with the aggressive male.

But, unlike his stepfather, each of these confidantes evinced a positive and sympathetic interest in Jimmy Baldwin. They were replicas of David Baldwin, but replicas without fangs, more giving, less punishing. In these relationships (which continue in kind today), the youth may have found the mythical father-mother, that hangover from early childhood, who accepted him without consuming him.

"It was natural for him to kind of attach himself to people who showed affection for him," Moore says indulgently. Mother Horn belonged in that category for a while. She was a tall, dynamic woman, the leader of a large flock, in her own way as opinionated and domineering as David Baldwin. But he was glacial in the pulpit and hardly less so out of it; and "Mother Horn was warm, ingratiating—and encompassing," says Moore. "She had a lot of power within her. Her church was a huge loft of a place on the second floor and it was a mecca for tourists. My father was a trustee. Mr. Baldwin never went there. I was a member at thirteen, and I got Jimmy to join."

Baldwin was later to describe his initial meeting with his friend's pastor, "an extremely proud and handsome woman" of forty-five or fifty, who smiled at him and inquired before he could be introduced, "Whose little boy are you?" This time, Baldwin reports, his heart had replied at once, "Why, yours."

"He liked Mother Horn very much," Moore says. "She lived over the church and Jimmy would visit her there. He liked the church almost immediately. It was a solace for people like him, who needed hope. You could emote a great deal. He says there's still no music for him like that music, no drama like the drama of the saints rejoicing. You could spend all day Sunday there. I think he was happiest when he was going to church."

One night toward the end of that summer, when Mother Horn had finished her sermon, Jimmy Baldwin underwent a religious crisis. In "Down at the Cross," he wrote: "One moment I was on my feet, singing and clapping and, at the same time, working out in my head the plot of a play I was working on then; the next moment, with no transition, no sensation of falling, I was on my back, with the light beating down into my face and all the vertical saints above me."

He was "saved"—saved spiritually, but also saved from the menace of Lenox Avenue, from the demands of his own flesh and most of all from David Baldwin, who sooner or later might have suspected the sexual imagery distracting the adolescent by day and besieging him at night, and then consigned him to perdition.

Once Jimmy Baldwin became a member of their tabernacle, George and Jeannette Moore more or less adopted him. Art's father referred to Jimmy fondly as "my adopted son" and Art's mother says:

"Baldy—my whole family called him that, and we still do—was like my own boy. He was very serious, not like Art, who is kind of carefree, not inclined to worry about anything. Baldy was at my house all the time. He was freer and more relaxed with us. I'd take him on little trips. Once I invited him to go to Albany with me. He ran home to get permission and came running back with his things. We had a fine weekend visiting my sister. I took him to the museum, and he loved the prehistoric animals."

"I loved Mrs. Moore," Baldwin says now. "I still do."

At home, Baldy was constantly ducking lines of wet diapers and David Baldwin's whiplash criticism. "Mr. Baldwin was very tall, very grim," says Mrs. Moore, "and he never smiled." Mrs. Baldwin was too pressed to give her firstborn individual attention. "She was the light of his life," Art Moore claims. But Mrs. Moore muses: "With so many kids and so little money, Mrs. Baldwin had very little time for Baldy. She was nice but very subdued. I think he's closer to her now than he was."

The Moores, a small and closely knit unit, were an avidly attentive audience. For them Baldwin recited both his short stories and his woes. "I'd try to make him realize his father wasn't mean," Mrs. Moore says. "That he was just a disappointed man who hadn't reached his goal. But there wasn't much of a bond between the two. I think he kind of compared Art's closeness to his father with the way Mr. Baldwin treated him. Still, I don't think Baldy suffered as much as he thinks . . ."

Now and then Art would stop off at the Baldwins' dank and dreary flat, where he was always treated with "reasonable" courtesy: "But Mr. Baldwin—that's how his wife addressed him, too, I remember—was on the stark side. He'd move around in bathrobe and slippers, like a dark cloud. I remember one instance when he ordered Jimmy to do something and Jimmy said he had to study. His father looked at him and said, 'Cease studying.' Like that. 'Cease studying.' "

When the Moores later parted with Mother Horn and affiliated themselves with the Fireside Pentecostal Assembly, a small church at 136th Street and Fifth Avenue, it was natural for Jimmy Baldwin to follow them. But it must have been a wrench for him to tear himself away from Mother Horn, whom he was to memorialize years later in the character of Sister Margaret, the indomitable evangelist of THE AMEN CORNER.

The Moores' new minister was Theophilus A. Sobers. "Not very old himself," says Art Moore. "Very pleasant, very reasonable—and very different from Jimmy's father." Sobers, the founder of Fireside Pentecostal, still its pastor, was mild and friendly, with a cello-rich baritone.

It was there at this storefront house of prayer, where beating tambourines and pounding feet and clapping hands and lifted voices attested to the glory of God, the sound swelling higher and higher, drowning out misery or sanctifying it, that Jimmy Baldwin decided he must be more than just "another worshipper."

"I was discussing it with him one day," Mrs. Baldwin recalls, her tone soft and wondering. "He told me, 'Mama, there's nothing I want to do more than be a preacher.' I was really surprised. I was shocked. It wasn't a common thing to preach so young. And he was so shy. But I knew he was sincere."

Baldwin disputes this. He attributes to his fourteen-year-old self "a deep adolescent cunning" that led him to the pulpit. But it is unlikely that the metamorphosis of this painfully withdrawn youth into a shouting, hellfire-and-brimstone, Holy Roller sermonist was as contrived as he now supposes.

For fourteen years he had been an outsider, even within his family—most of all, within his family. But as young Brother Baldwin he was at last an insider, close to the center of operation, close to the core of the mystery. "Being in the pulpit was like being in the theater," he wrote later. "I was behind the scenes and knew how the illusion was worked."

The cries of "Hallelujah!" and "Amen!" and "Praise His name!" were balm for his bruised and battered psyche. For three hysteria-tinged years he preached the Word, reveling in a most unholy fashion over his superiority to his stepfather as a ministerial drawing card.

"Jimmy was even more devout than I was," Moore says. "He went to church more and more. We'd often go together, several nights a week, arriving about eight and coming home at eleven or twelve. The Pentecostal faith believes you must be in the world, but not of the world. You mustn't smoke or dance or go to the movies. Jimmy and I didn't swear, didn't smoke, didn't go to the movies, didn't dance.

"To be a young preacher, first you have to get your calling. You hear a voice from heaven telling you to be a minister. Then you study a lot, asking God to give you assistance. You can preach before you're ordained. The format is to get the text from the Bible and then you elaborate on it, as God gives you utterance, with passion and fervor and conviction."

Brother Baldwin, abundantly furnished with all three, spoke once a week on Young Ministers' Night (along with two or three others a bit older than himself), sometimes on Saturday afternoon, once in a great while even on Sunday. "He was good," Moore says, hitting the adjective hard. "He was inspired. He was a very hot speaker." (Jimmy Baldwin concurs. Assessing his adolescent performance, he says candidly, "I was a great preacher." And, of course, he still is.)

David Baldwin, omnipotent at home, provided the barest minimum of professional competition. On the rostrum, he had a chilling grandeur. But his disdain equalled his arrogance, and he refused to disguise either. He was outraged by all-night parties (whose shrill gaiety entranced his children as they lay sleepless in bed), caustic about the energy squandered on shattering the Commandments.

His asperity endeared him neither to his neighbors nor to his parishioners. Constantly dwindling in popularity, he went from small to ever smaller congregation. His engagements were so sparse that the Moores think of him as "a minister without a church."

There was little opportunity now for him to bark at Jimmy,

"Cease studying." The boy's commitments to religion and family left him less time for homework, although he needed more. On September 12, 1938, five weeks after his fourteenth birthday, he was admitted to De Witt Clinton High School, a low, sprawling edifice in the scholastic-Gothic tradition, set down in a park-like landscape that even today retains a deceptively pastoral air.

This was the only school he attended outside Harlem, and thus his first brush with integrated—or partially integrated—education. Actually there were few Negroes among the all-male student body since Clinton at that time offered only academic courses, and it was customary (then as now) for the majority of New York's Negro youngsters to be shunted off into vocational schools.

The transition from the congestion of Harlem to the comparatively wide open spaces of the Northern tip of the Bronx must have been jolting for Baldwin. More—much more—than a lengthy subway ride was involved. He was now surrounded by white boys ("boys with red hair, boys with blond hair," says Randy Douglas, "and I wasn't accustomed to that"), some of them Christian, many of them Jewish, all of them theoretically his peers.

But his stepfather preached with vein-swelling virulence that this was the enemy. Jimmy Baldwin, so long deprived of intellectual companionship, thirsting for it, had now to choose between loyalty to David Baldwin's concepts and the covenants that normally sustain a schoolboy through the throes of adolescence.

The contingent that had gone from Douglass to Clinton was initially at a disadvantage in the senior high school. "We felt the difference when we met youngsters from an enriched background," recalls Lionel McMurren, who trailed Baldwin to Clinton after a year. "We were bright, but we had to study what the other kids just absorbed from their environment."

For Randolph Douglas, the academic shift was less disturbing than the jarring sense of relocation: "It was a pleasure to ride the subway into what seemed to me to be a far, far away land. It was really an adventure because I felt I was escaping—something, I didn't know what. I was being released into a new atmosphere. The green around Clinton—I remember that. It seemed beautiful. And the sadness when it grew dark and I had to return to Harlem. I remember the let-down when I realized I was back again, back to that place I loved and yet resented . . ."

Jimmy Baldwin experienced a similar letdown. "I wasn't a bad student," he says. "And I got along very well with my playmates and all that jazz. Nevertheless, when the school day was over, I went back into a condition which they could not imagine, and I knew, no matter what anybody said, that the future I faced was not the future they faced."

But he went back to David Baldwin, "a condition" the other Negro students did not have to contend with and which most of them (if not all of them), might have had just as much difficulty imagining as Jimmy Baldwin's white "playmates."

Randy Douglas, returning to Harlem so reluctantly at nightfall, was nevertheless returning "to people I loved, who loved me." Baldwin returned to a man ravaged by mental disease who had demolished himself and appeared bent upon extending the destruction to his stepson. That set Baldwin well apart from the Negroes as well as the whites.

During his first year at Clinton, he was a very bad student indeed. His I. Q. of 122 established his above-average intelligence (the chances are that he would have rated even higher if such tests were not devised, as is now generally conceded, by the middle class for the middle class), but his grades toppled from an overall 81 for his three years at junior high to a doleful 60 his first term at Clinton (he failed two subjects, Spanish with 55, plane geometry with 20; even in English, he dropped from 90 to 65). In his second semester, he managed to pull himself up to a lusterless 66.

He still saw himself with his father's eyes. "I assumed," he was to write later, "that no one had ever been born who was only five-feet-six-inches tall, or been born poor, or been born ugly, or masturbated, or done all those things which were my property when I was fifteen."

Racked by guilt because he was not as unblemished in thought and deed as he felt a preacher should be, Jimmy Baldwin fell far short of his potential during his first year at Clinton. His grades there were never distinguished. Flunking a total of four courses, including physical training and physiography (called earth science today), kept him from graduating with his class; he received his diploma six months later, on January 29, 1942.

But that is not the whole story. On his New York State Regents examinations, he scored handsomely in English (93) and medieval European history (93), earned an eminently respectable 83 in American history (he now derides the history taught in the United States as a compendium of the wishful thinking indulged in by the Western world). Moreover each of the three entries on his General Organization Character Card, recorded in 1941 when he was nominally an upper senior, amounts to an accolade.

On February 19th, Marcella C. Whalen wrote: "Showed outstanding character in unselfish work as editor of The Magpie. A talented, modest boy of fine character. Will go far!"

On May 21st, Gertrude G. Lavery noted: "James Baldwin was outstanding for his modest, unassuming attitude in a class where he was an intellectual giant."

On May 28th, Wilmer T. Stone commented: "James Baldwin has contributed brilliant articles to The Magpie and has also put in many hours of work in reading, suggesting improvements in, and passing judgment on the work of others."

Significantly all three instructors taught Baldwin English and two of them, Mrs. Whalen and Stone, alternated as faculty adviser to The Magpie, Clinton's literary-art publication. Baldwin, eventually the magazine's editor-in-chief, was a constant contributor. Poems, short stories and plays flowed from his pen, some of them bearing a remarkable resemblance in theme and style to his mature work.

Miss Lavery, who classified Baldwin at sixteen as "an intellectual giant," has a ready explanation for the inconsistency of his marks: "He just didn't apply himself. He liked English, so he did well in it—it was easy for him. But he didn't bother about the other subjects, such as physiography and math and physical training.

"I was fond of him. I liked his general sweetness. He was boyish and smiling and smart and cooperative. There was none of the bitterness he has now. He used to pal around with a slight Jewish boy, I remember. The period in which I taught Baldwin followed lunch and he'd always come in gaily, sometimes pausing at my desk to chat very amusingly.

"I'm chagrined now when I think of it because it must have been just at that time—he was a lower senior—that he was suffering so much. He was in such agony and he covered it so well. I never suspected. I realize it now only from reading his books . . ."

That agony was never a deterrent to his writing. It was while

Baldwin was at Clinton that he overheard at home late one night some harsh words between his parents. From that fragment of domestic conversation, he relearned what he had earlier suppressed: that David Baldwin was not his father. The shock heightened the adolescent's acute sense of dislocation. For several weeks his spirits sagged. Yet nothing impaired his prolific output. Instead of blocking his productivity, his turmoil fed it. "One thing about him," says Art Moore; "he always had faith in himself as a writer." What was more important, he always wrote.

Mrs. Whalen, still The Magpie's adviser, confirms that. An expansive, gray-haired, portly woman, robustly pretty in a heather tweed suit, a charm bracelet dangling from her wrist, rhinestones twinkling in the pink frames of her glasses, she at once labels herself Baldwin's "discoverer." (When this is relayed to him, Baldwin's eyebrows arch. "We *hated* each other," he says. But Mrs. Whalen genially contradicts his summation. "I liked him," she insists.)

On the door to her cramped office is a poster urging, "Draw and Write for Magpie," which boasts that "among the editors who became well-known people are George Sokolsky, Sid Skolsky, Paddy Chayefsky, Paul Gallico, Counte [sic] Cullen, Jerome Weidman, Richard Avedon and James Baldwin, to name a few." Baldwin's place at the tail end of this list would suggest he is not Mrs. Whalen's favorite author.

"He was such a quiet boy," she says. "Except that I feel his work even then reflected the bitterness of his attitude. I remember him very, very well. The eyes haven't changed in the least. He was very shy but he put a poem, I think it was, in the basket we kept in the library for Magpie contributors. I sent for him and he became a regular contributor."

Defying his father's edict, Baldwin crossed the enemy lines and established alliances with two white boys, Richard Avedon and Emile Capouya, both of them Jewish. All three were closely identified with Magpie, Avedon and Baldwin serving in turn as its ranking editor, Capouya winding up as second-in-command. For the first time in his despairing life, Jimmy Baldwin had companions of his own age with his own absorption in literature and his own conviction that they would abide there forever. It granted him access in some degree to the "human warmth" he had been hunting since childhood.

With his new friends, he could trade confidences, pool enthusiasms, reel off critiques, test his reactions, unlock a few—a very few—of his fears and doubts. "Baldwin and Avedon were inseparable," Mrs. Whalen reports. "The two of them were perfectionists, Avedon more so than Baldwin. Their work never had to be edited." But to her Baldwin revealed none of the blitheness that captivated Miss Lavery. "He was secretive and guarded," Mrs. Whalen says.

Her view meshes with that of Frank Corsaro, a year behind Baldwin at Clinton, now a director with the Actors Studio Theatre. "He was the only Negro boy on the magazine and he tended to hide behind his needs," Corsaro says. "I found him curiously removed from the people around him. He used to be arrested by the theater and I was involved with the dramatic productions. It's very funny—he was the saddest looking little soul, with none of the fire I see in him now. He would hover about, shy, almost droopy, very remote, always on the edge of things."

The Harlemites who had been with Baldwin at Douglass had little contact with him in high school. He had never been one of them. Now he drifted farther away. Almost twenty years later, he was to suggest to a Clinton News reporter that he had been penalized by his fellow Negroes: "I was rather atypical. I wrote for The Magpie and had white friends, and was not trusted by the other Negro boys for it." But it is conceivable that he shunned his few Negro classmates, as he might have shunned himself if that had been physically possible.

The color line, no longer a nebulous concept in his mind, had come sharply into focus. Once it had had "no weight" for him, but now he began to stagger under its impact.

"When I was brought up, I was taught in American history books that Africa had no history and that neither had I," he has said. "I was a savage about whom the least said the better, who had been saved by Europe and who had been brought to America. Of course, I believed it. I didn't have much choice. These were the only books there were. Everyone else seemed to agree. If you went out of Harlem, the whole world agreed. What you saw was much bigger, whiter, cleaner, safer. The garbage was collected, the children were happy. You would go back home and it would seem, of course, that this was an act of God. You *belonged* where *white* people *put* you."

He then made his "worst discovery: it was not only that society treated me like a *nigger* and thought of me as one, but that *I myself* believed it—that I *believed* what white people said of me."

His links with Avedon and Capouya intensified his problem. He treasured their friendship even though they were white, perhaps more because they were white. But he could never entirely forget that they were exempt by birth from his own handicaps and that they belonged to the race that had subjugated his.

That conflict, which was to reach crucial proportions some years later, still impinges on Baldwin's thinking, often twisting his emotions into corkscrew convolutions. But in many respects he was neither secretive nor guarded with Avedon and Capouya.

Clinton's tower, a romantic anachronism which has since been designated as a fire hazard and ruled out of bounds, was Magpie's headquarters in those days. It provided cloistered asylum for members of the Publication Squad, who escaped there as often as they could, sometimes cutting gym to lose themselves in the intoxication of planning the next issue.

"The first home I found outside of my own home was that tower," says Avedon, now an illustrious photographer who collaborated with Baldwin in 1964 on a picture book of America, NOTHING PERSONAL (which is, of course, strictly personal). "I remember Jimmy as a friend and as someone I could talk to—and I had very few friends. He was one of the few students I cared about. We were interested in the same things—the same writers, the same movies."

Avedon, far from enjoying the felicity Baldwin attributes to the offspring of his paler countrymen, was almost as wretched in his school years as Baldwin himself.

"Clinton was a nightmare for me, as elementary school had been," Avedon says. "You know a high school that size is a pretty lonely place for a potential artist. But the tower wasn't lonely at all. We had the most wonderful time there. We stayed as long as we could and left only when they shut the doors."

Wilmer Stone, long since retired, was revered by The Magpie clique. "He was a great teacher," Baldwin says simply. Avedon argues that the sum total of the knowledge he acquired at Clinton was contained in a flash exchange with Stone: "He read a poem of mine and then asked what magazines my family read. I said, THE LADIES' HOME JOURNAL, THE READER'S DIGEST and HARPER'S BAZAAR. And Stone said, 'Oh, that explains it.' That sentence, that lesson, was all I learned at high school. I've never forgotten it."

Exposed to Stone and Dostoevsky and the skepticism of unbelievers, young Brother Baldwin faltered in his determination to gain heaven—which might prove, after all, to be just another ghetto.

He still saw Art Moore, who would periodically ascend to the tower and wait there for Baldwin. But for the most part he concealed his pulpit duties from both students and faculty. His religious ardor had cooled. He was beginning to suspect that "Faith, Hope and Charity" had less connection with ecclesiastical ceremony and custom than "Blindness, Loneliness and Terror."

As his writing brought him more and more satisfaction, his sermons tapered off. His father said one day, "You'd rather write than preach, wouldn't you?" The boy was startled by the rare intimacy of the question. "Yes," he said. The conversation ended there.

But with Capouya ("my best friend in high school"), now a writer, editor and teacher, Baldwin used to discuss his activities at the Fireside Pentecostal Assembly. "Jimmy told me he was a preacher," Capouya says. "He once took me to a Holy Roller church in Harlem similar to his own, where he was not known. I think he wanted someone to know what his own atmosphere was like. I understood from Jimmy that the saved in his congregation regarded all whites as *ipso facto* Satan.

"Jimmy was race conscious, but he had no chip on his shoulder. He understood what every Negro boy with wits about him understands: that he was going to have a difficult time.

"He was subject to very strict home discipline. His was an old-fashioned, patriarchal family that told him, 'You get in at such-and-such a time or you'll get strapped.' He had to let them know where he was every minute. He had had religious scruples about movies and was just beginning to go to them.

"Some of his associates his parents didn't approve of; in general, since they regarded themselves as the elect, they felt any relationships Jimmy had outside the church would be contrary to the good of his soul.

"He talked to me about his stepfather. He had a curious respect for the man and, at the same time, a terrible resentment. And what was so odd in so young a boy was that he had pity for him. Jimmy recognized the economic and psychological and moral and spiritual trap his father was in. He spoke of him as someone you couldn't like but had to respect.

"Jimmy was one of the most naturally sweet boys I ever knew. He had a simple generosity, an intellectual generosity. He was never one to argue with another man's idea because he didn't think of it first. He was cordial and curious. From the very beginning, he was a literary type, with a lyric talent that was very touching. I can't recall a time when he didn't want to be the poet and prophet he turned out to be."

Although Baldwin's prose grew steadily in power, the quality of his work was uneven. A sonnet, entitled "To Her," began, "How did we reach this Fairyland/Of our love?" Its author, confronted with a copy almost twenty-five years later, read the eight lines in a glance and recoiled, muttering, "Jesus Christ!" But there was also a splendid character study, "Aunt Tina," penetrating by any standard, which would certainly not embarrass Baldwin today.

His pieces in The Magpie constitute a precise graph of the adolescent's preoccupation with the sacred and his increasingly pessimistic view that profane principles were guiding the church. In the spring edition of 1941, three stories appeared under Baldwin's byline, each with a strongly religious—or anti-religious—theme.

"The Woman at the Well," foreshadowing the mood and the bite and the savage grief of BLUES FOR MISTER CHARLIE, had as its central figure a saintly pastor who was really an idealized composite of Jimmy Baldwin and his stepfather.

"Mississippi Legend" was essentially an assault on an obdurate, egotistical deacon who refuses to heed the vision of God granted Mattie Jones (a woman "so blame holy that she wouldn't even straighten her hair, or light her stove on Sunday"). Deacon Jones declares: "Ise de Deacon. Look like ef de Lawd had somethin' to tell de church, He'd tell me."

But "Incident in London" is neither more nor less than a nine-paragraph epitaph to the dissolution of Jimmy Baldwin's faith:

The small chapel stood on the white, still street, and seemed, in

81

the darkness, to be a thing eternal, a bulwark and a refuge from strife and from fear. And the man hurried toward it.

The man was no longer young, and he stooped a little as he hurried. His hands were large and rough, and he carried shrapnel in one leg. His face was scarred with the scars of many battles, and his eyes were bleak and hard.

And the chapel beckoned in the dim, frosty moonlight, and he hurried towards it.

Long before, when the man was young, and before he had gone off to the many wars that were always being fought, he had believed implicitly in the faith he had been taught. He had believed in God, in peace, in righteousness, and the dignity and decency of man. But after he had fought, and had seen how strife degraded and destroyed humanity, his faith had lost its glory and had disappeared.

But now, still another war had come, and his family and his loved ones had perished, and he was alone and lost without them, and being lost, knew not what to turn to.

And the chapel beckoned in the cold moonlight, and he hurried towards it . . .

And as he hurried, the stars winked and trembled in the heavens, and as he entered, they, for an instant, hid themselves, and the man knelt before the rough, heavy crucifix and closed his eyes.

And suddenly the skies blazed fire, and the stars were blotted out, and a roar of fury filled the universe. And slowly the chapel crumbled to the white, still earth.

And the street was as it had been before, save that the chapel had been destroyed, and the snow was no longer pure, but filthy, and the man was dead.

Not long after he had written that, Jimmy Baldwin delivered his farewell sermon. "I remember my last sermon," he says. "I remember it because I knew it was my last. It was a sermon to me. 'Set thy house in order.'"

The Reverend Mr. Sobers today refuses to discuss Baldwin. "He's angry with me," Baldwin says, himself angry, "because he was the minister when I left the church. We had a row the last day I saw him. I was to meet a friend at two P.M. We had tickets to a matinee of H. M. S. PINAFORE. I was sitting in the front of the church and I kept hoping he'd finish the service before I had to leave. But he didn't.

"So I tiptoed out. His little boy came after me and said, 'Daddy wants you back inside.' I said, 'Tell him I have an appointment.' Then 'Daddy' came out after me himself. And *ordered* me back inside. If he hadn't ordered me, I might have *gone*. But when he made it an order, I said, 'I've already told you I have a date.'"

It was an open break. But the minister was no more unhappy about it than Jimmy Baldwin. "It was agonizing for me to face the fact that I didn't believe any more," he says now. "I didn't believe the lies I was telling . . ."

He felt dishonest and betrayed: he had not been cleansed by the blood of the Lamb; he had not been purified. He was still black. And wasn't God white?

"My own apprehension of my *own* *life* is that—it's up to *me* to do it, to *live* it, to discover it, y'know. With whatever tools I can make out—out of *me*. I don't want to be fitted into this society. I intend to survive it, if I *can*—but, in any case, do whatever I do on *my* terms, including going *under,* on *my* terms . . ."

Seven

David Baldwin's health was deteriorating. The Baldwins, who had never risen economically, could not fall very far. Their decline, not swift, not steep, was barely perceptible. But all hope seeped away. The days, crammed with the minutiae of monotony, were yet as blank as an empty horizon.

Of the four Baldwin brothers, only the eldest could stick it out through high school. Young David, seven years Jimmy's junior, quit at fifteen. "You'd have to know something about being poor to understand why," he says. "Like watching your mother work all day and meeting her at the subway late at night to walk her home. That does something to you. So does being on relief. You have no privacy, no life.

"George and Jimmy used to shine shoes. At six or seven, I'd work in the meat store for one dollar a week. We all had chores to do. And we all used to sell chop-wood. You'd go into an old house and tear the wood off, take it down to the curb, get a tomato bushel basket and chop the wood up. People were still using woodburning stoves, so you'd sell the wood for ten cents a basket. Or, if you were hard up, five cents a basket. Or you'd go over to the coal yard and pick up coke.

"George and Wilmer and myself would work on a horse-and-wagon, selling vegetables. That was after Jimmy stopped preaching. He was trying to become a writer. Then the rest of us went into the Army. So we got off relief."

But that was later. Back in 1942, David was only ten, and the Magpie's former editor-in-chief, just out of Clinton, was now a porter or a handyman or an elevator operator by day. At night, he was beginning to sweat out the first draft of his first novel, GO TELL IT ON THE MOUNTAIN. Then called "Crying Holy," it was not to be completed for a decade.

"That book cost him a great deal," David says. "What happens to you, you can't say it didn't happen. The only way to survive is to start understanding. Jimmy had to understand a lot before he could write GO TELL IT ON THE MOUNTAIN. Everything that happened to him, in and out of the family. Ten years," says David. "It's a life."

As he wrestled with himself, trying to understand but not yet able to understand, Jimmy Baldwin was ground down by his father's baffling behavior and his mother's interminable struggle and his own fumbling efforts to improve their situation. He felt caged in. "Like an animal," he says. He was imprisoned by his own helplessness, but he thought his condition rooted entirely in the black ghetto. He was sure he would strangle if he didn't break out.

He had depended on school to peel away the multiple layers of his sorrow and remove him from the subfusc gloom of Harlem. PS 24 and Douglass and De Witt Clinton had failed him in that mission. So had Christ. Now, witnessing the collapse of his stepfather, for so many years the keystone of his life, a symbol of indestructibility, of terror and superhuman might, Jimmy Baldwin was obsessed by flight. He could not bear to see that proud, black man crumbling into ruin.

Always as remote as a mystic communing on a mountain top, David Baldwin now seemed more dazed than awesome. One night, on his way back from work, he stepped off the subway and sat down on a bench in the station at 135th Street and Lexington Avenue, lost in some never-never land of his own, until his stepson, coming in search of him, coaxed him to his feet and, half-supporting him, led him home.

The youth could not bring himself to ask what was wrong. In any case, it is doubtful whether David Baldwin could have told him. Jimmy Baldwin must have suspected then, even though he could not admit it to himself, that his father's illness had reached an advanced stage. The boy's world, desolate as a dead planet, yet the only world he knew, was caving in. From the havoc of demolition, he ran away. He thought only of escaping from Harlem, but he was also trying to preserve his godlike image of his father—and his hate against the desecration of pity.

"I was born in Harlem," Baldwin often says now, "I was raised in Harlem and, indeed, as long as I live I'll never be able to leave Harlem." In a sense, this is true. Harlem is an extension of his family; he carries it with him wherever he goes. But the facts are that he left Harlem in 1942, when he was not quite eighteen, and has never really returned.

When Emile Capouya graduated that June and landed a job in Belle Mead, New Jersey, not far from Princeton, Baldwin gladly joined him there. Capouya's friend, Tom Martin, a poet in his early twenties, had pioneered the way. A big, handsome, gregarious Irishman, Martin had married and settled in Rocky Hill, a short distance from Belle Mead, where he was working on the construction of the Army's Quartermaster Depot.

The convivial Martin, encountering few problems there, eventually rose to foreman. But Rocky Hill was tiny and he dearly loved company. At his invitation, Capouya, who had turned down a partial scholarship to Harvard (he was later to study philosophy at Columbia and comparative literature at Oxford), boarded with the Martins in the pleasant, frame house they had rented, hitchhiking to Belle Mead and back.

"All the employes there were civilians and the wages were munificent for those days," Capouya says. "The depot had to have a railroad connection and I was laying track. The base pay was eighty dollars a week. But we often worked seven days, so we really earned a lot more than that. I was in touch with Jimmy, and he came out and rented a room from the Martins, too."

Mrs. Martin, a pretty, vivacious girl, took to Baldwin at once. "Jimmy was very engaging and she liked him very much," Capouya says. She did the cooking and the four young people ate together. The evenings were short, almost nonexistent; exhausted by their exertions in Belle Mead, the men retired soon after dinner. Capouya recalls with a grin, "You had to talk fast to be heard."

For Capouya, with his middle-class background, manual labor was "a stimulating, new experience." But it was scarcely a novelty to the youth from Harlem. "Jimmy wasn't romantic about the job," Capouya remarks. "He knew better."

A lanky six-footer, Capouya managed to get through the work day without generating undue friction. Martin could spar his way, with words or fists or bravura, out of any difficulty. But Jimmy Baldwin, small, unprepossessing, touchy and provocative, could only flare up in anger as he floundered from one crisis to another.

On the other side of the Hudson, he had regarded himself as an expert on discrimination, familiar with every nuance and every inflection in the perverse catechism of bigotry. But in Jersey he learned he was just a novice. Expecting emancipation, he was thrust on the rack.

"People—you know, the way people treated one—*me*, because of the fact that I was colored, was a great *revelation*—to me, y'know," Baldwin says now, pain giving its own accent to the act of remembering. "And although, much later, you put up all kinds of defenses and you forget—you *make* yourself forget—how you felt, apart from everything *else*, it breaks the *heart*, you know.

"I've really never written about that period and I—*hardly* ever. I've written about the end of it, but not the time itself. It was—it was, as I say, a great revelation that people could—could *be* so—so *monstrous*. It makes you angry. But, before it makes you angry, y'know, it demoralizes you. It—it *hurts*. To be *treated* that way. And I realized I was going to be treated that way all my life, in one way or another."

But what he apparently did not realize, and still does not realize, is that his martyrdom in New Jersey was essentially a continuation of his martyrdom at home. He actually had been "treated that way," exactly that way, all his life. Oppression had been his native state. Only the color of the oppressor and the setting had altered.

While the vengeful minister who had taught the boy everything he knew about hate sat in Harlem at a living-room window, incommunicado, doomed by psychosis to the equivalent of solitary confinement, self-inflicted but none the less real, Jimmy Baldwin was discovering that he was still in bondage. He had burst forth from Harlem. He had crossed one wide river. But his chains had not dropped off.

Somewhere he must have nursed the hope that, liberated from the ghetto, he would be infused with the security of belonging. Instead the seventeen-year-old, unwary and unprepared, was plunged into the torrents of racism.

The Martins' home was Baldwin's sole sanctuary, as once the hill in Central Park had been, and then the tabernacle and, later still, the Magpie office in Clinton's tower. "Jimmy was pleased to be with friends in Rocky Hill," Capouya says. But, when Baldwin walked across the threshold, he was at war.

At Belle Mead, he was initially a railroad hand. Too slight for that job (although heavier then than he is now), he was transferred to the cinder gang and then to the warehouse, where he loaded and unloaded boxcars. But, whatever he did, the skinny kid from Harlem was encircled by enmity. The more he battled, the more he stiffened the opposition. The hostilities were not to abate from that June to the next.

"I was working with a lot of Southerners," Baldwin, who had never met a white Southerner before he went to New Jersey, says now. "And I caught *hell*. They just thought I was—I guess, in their terms, I *was*—very cocky and very sure of myself. Or I *seemed* to be very sure of myself. I *wasn't* . . ." His voice fades out. Then, just audible, he says again, "I wasn't . . ."

Baldwin has devoted considerable space in his essays and in his talks to Negro role-playing: to the bland and subservient character the American Negro pretends to be in the presence of whites.

But he himself has never lent himself to this kind of mock adaptation. Far from submerging his real identity, Baldwin has accentuated it.

More porcupine than chameleon, he can bristle with a belligerence that is apt to invoke more of it in a society where the dominant order relies for much of its superior status upon the Negro's seeming acquiescence. It was in Jersey that Baldwin trained himself for what has proved to be a prolonged endurance contest.

"It wasn't until I was out of Harlem and on my own in a very different world that—I could see how the problem of color applied to me directly," he says now. "To *me*. I didn't know what they saw when they looked at me—but they did their best to kill me."

He might be temporarily enlisted as a wartime laborer, but he knew he was not a serf. High school had not readied him for degradation. Acknowledged there as a writer and an intellectual, he was lurchingly confident, even at seventeen and eighteen, that he would develop into a novelist and playwright. He could not accept the servile role for which the Southerners had typed him. Responding by reflex to his pigmentation, they completely ignored the human being under it. Jimmy Baldwin, entombed in his brown skin, was virtually buried alive.

The wounds he incurred then have never healed. But he would not beg for a truce. He would not "yassuh" and "nosuh" his fellow workers or his bosses or the townspeople. He would not pose as a nigger. He flaunted his refusal. His tactics may have been short on wisdom, but they were long on valor.

Under Baldwin's feline nervousness and brittle delicacy is a store of genuine toughness. He drew—and overdrew—on that reserve in Jersey. "It seemed to me," he says, "not *possible* for me to think of myself as a nigger, you know, and let myself be treated that way."

Incensed by the animosity directed at him, he was ostentatiously bellicose—and almost maddened by fright. Shaken by the terrible scenes in which he stubbornly participated (and which he often initiated), he was afraid at last to go anywhere. But he went everywhere. Children tittered at him, as though he were crazed. Indeed he thought he might be.

Three times he lined up with Princeton undergraduates at a

cafeteria counter, waiting much too long to pick up his hamburger and coffee, before he was politely informed by the management that it should have dawned upon him by then that Negroes were not served there.

But there was nothing even pseudo-polite about the vocal clashes precipitated by his subsequent appearances. His obstinate one-man stand-ins accomplished little since he never again ate there, but they did permit him to siphon off for the first time in his overdisciplined life some of the rage he had been hoarding for eighteen years.

Baldwin says he neither drank nor smoked in Jersey. He had only an occasional beer. He slashed from his budget every item that was not a basic necessity. Every week he sent most of his salary to his mother, an act of repentance that drained his father's pride.

Jimmy Baldwin went home only once that year. David Baldwin would not talk to him. It would seem that the old minister talked very little to anyone; his heavy silence was broken only by a stray phrase from an old song or a murmured hallelujah. But in his stepfather's attitude the youth inferred accusation: he had forsaken his family, and his generous subsidy was nothing more than Judas silver.

Tutored by David Baldwin, the youth had learned how to fight. In Belle Mead he fought back openly, even excessively, with a boldness that had until then been rigorously prohibited. Exposed to the brutality of white strangers, he could at last discharge the resentment and the fury that had traveled with him, waiting to be tapped. And they were tapped, regularly and often.

In every figure cloaked with authority, he must have envisioned David Baldwin. Even today Jimmy Baldwin is tiger-ready to spring at the commanding voice, the dictatorial manner. "I'll not listen to anybody like that," he exclaims with sudden, unwarranted heat. "I can't be told what to do. By *any*body. In any tone whatever. *I can-not* be told what to do. If you want me to do something, the best way to do it is to tell me not to do it. You know, I *can-not bear* it."

There had of course been only one authoritarian "like that" who had incessantly told Baldwin what to do and how to do it and when. But in Jersey any aberrant impulse to strike back at his stepfather had to be repressed more than ever. For as the young defense worker rushed into combat, David Baldwin was rapidly sinking into the acute phase of paranoia.

He had been out of communication with the world around him for so protracted a period that the change didn't impress his family as significant. His friends had long ago abdicated, driven away by his barbed tongue. Only when he refused to eat, insisting that his wife and children were trying to poison him, were the Baldwins compelled to recognize how far gone he really was.

By then it was too late for psychiatry to aid him. Perhaps it always was. He was formally committed to Central Islip Hospital, a state mental institution in Long Island. As he neared death in July of 1943, Emma Baldwin was awaiting the birth of her ninth child.

A month earlier, when the baby's arrival and David Baldwin's departure seemed imminent, Jimmy Baldwin had sped home. By then his stay in New Jersey, which had evolved from release into banishment, had ended in melodrama.

Engaged in overt warfare, he had twice been fired, then re-hired through Martin's intercession. But even Martin, with all his Gaelic persuasiveness, could not sweet-talk Baldwin back on the payroll a third time. Emile Capouya had already resigned and returned to New York, but a relative of the Martins' took Baldwin to Trenton for a last-night fling that was intended to wash the sour taste of dismissal from his mouth.

As it turned out, the evening was more of a disaster than a celebration. It was like a reprise of the indignities to which Baldwin had been subjected in all the preceding months. In diners and bowling alleys, in restaurants and bars, his eyeball-to-eyeball confrontations with the naked manifestations of white supremacy had roused in him a homicidal resentment: "a kind of blind fever, a pounding in the skull and fire in the bowels," he has written.

He has compared it to "some dread, chronic disease" that, once contracted, can always recur: "There is not a Negro alive," he wrote in 1955, "who does not have this rage in his blood—one has the choice, merely, of living with it consciously or surrendering to it. As for me, this fever has recurred in me, and does, and will until the day I die."

It is Baldwin's thesis that he orginally contracted these symptoms during his year in New Jersey. But his reaction to his collisions with Jim Crow was so explosive, so consuming, so totally devoid of self-protectiveness, that it suggests the violence had been locked up within him all the time: only the detonation occurred in New Jersey.

Baldwin whipped himself into a maniacal frenzy that night in Trenton. In retrospect, he detects an element of deliberateness in his conduct. From a counterman in a diner, he ordered a hamburger and a cup of coffee. "I do not know why," he wrote later, "after a year of such rebuffs, I so completely failed to anticipate his answer, which was, of course, 'We don't serve Negroes here.'" It is obvious that Baldwin preferred the luxury of letting go.

Back in the street, he felt "a physical sensation, a *click* at the nape of my neck as though some interior string connecting my head to my body had been cut." What had been cut—and very nearly severed—was the rigid restraint that had always prevented him from counterattacking his father.

The emotion that sprang up flooded Jimmy Baldwin. He was almost swept under. His friend called out to him but Baldwin went down the block, prowling trouble. He caught up with it in "an enormous, glittering, and fashionable restaurant" where, he now admits, he knew "not even the intercession of the Virgin" would gain him service. He pushed through the doors and sat down in an empty seat. The waitress moved toward him.

In the instant that she did, she was transformed into a blood-red bull's-eye for his accumulated ferocity. He hated her and her pale face and her frightened eyes. And when she repeated the counterman's words rather apologetically, her timidity enraged him even more. He wanted to kill her, just as he had long ago wanted to kill those two laughing policemen who had frisked him in a Harlem lot.

"I wanted her to come close enough for me to get her neck between my hands," Baldwin has written. But she took only a short step toward him and then stopped. He picked up a mug of water on the table and flung it straight at her head. She dodged. The missile splintered the mirror behind her.

The crash of glass against glass restored Baldwin to sanity. He leaped toward the door, A man gripped the back of his neck and punched at his face, but Baldwin kicked him off and bolted into the street. His companion, who had followed him there, urged, "Run!" Baldwin obeyed. His friend remained behind to detour the pursuers and then the police.

Back in Rocky Hill, in his bedroom in Martin's house, Baldwin could not throw off the horror of that climactic moment when he had been willing and even eager to commit murder. His fever had subsided. He saw one thing clearly: ". . . That my life, my *real* life, was in danger, and not from anything other people might do but from the hatred I carried in my own heart."

A dozen years passed before he set down on paper the events of that night. They may have loomed larger with the passage of time. But Jimmy Baldwin is convinced that only the sound of cracking glass deflected him from homicide at eighteen.

He has never again resorted to physical violence. He rechanneled the tide of his passion: it now rips through his speeches and his plays and his books. "It doesn't matter any longer what you do to me," he says. "You can put me in jail. You can *kill* me. By the time I was seventeen, you'd done everything that you could do to me."

That soliloquy is a monument to his vendetta against New Jersey. When he recrossed the river and went back to Harlem, he was a battle-scarred veteran of almost nineteen. It was the middle of June and his stepfather, riddled with tuberculosis, weakened by self-starvation, was slowly expiring on a hospital bed.

The Harlem to which Jimmy Baldwin returned was not the Harlem he had left: it was worse. War had sharpened the tensions within the ghetto and a race riot was fomenting early in that long, hot summer of 1943. Baldwin noticed a new stillness in the streets. The maelstrom of motion to which he was accustomed had frozen into immobility, like a trick shot in a newsreel.

Policemen could be seen pacing uneasily, always by twos, a routine precaution in danger zones, their faces too florid or too pallid under their jaunty caps. Standing together in tight clusters, the muted residents watched obliquely. Baldwin observed within these groups strange alignments that violated the ordinarily stringent demarcations based on political, moral and religious affiliations.

Injustice had unified Harlem. The prejudice operating against Negroes even in the nation's Armed Forces and defense plants had touched almost every family in the ghetto, igniting long-smoldering grievances.

The ominous mood of the streets was an appropriate backdrop for the events hurtling upon the Baldwins. Their father's critical condition had only deepened the pall he had always cast upon his family. His wife, in the eighth month of her pregnancy, could visualize nothing ahead but catastrophe. She reminded her unresponsive offspring that it was the invalid who had held them together.

If Harlem had changed, so had Jimmy Baldwin. Jersey had stripped him of the compliance that had made him "very easy to raise." His dissidence, no longer counterfeiting docility, startled and dismayed his mother. The innately conservative Mrs. Baldwin reproached him for neglecting his filial obligations. She wanted him to visit David Baldwin in the hospital, a duty the youth had deliberately shunned.

With a flick of the anger he now didn't attempt to conceal, he replied fiercely that he hated his father and refused to play the hypocrite. Mother and son bickered for several weeks, increasing his dread of looking upon a fatally stricken David Baldwin.

The Army was to grant Jimmy Baldwin a deferment ("for undue hardship," he says). But his old comrade, Art Moore, almost twenty-one, had been drafted six months earlier. Avedon and Capouya had both elected to join the Merchant Marine. The vacuum in Baldwin's life was filled by the many quick (and one or two enduring) associations he had established in Greenwich Village.

At sixteen, intent upon exploring the area outside Harlem, Baldwin had been attracted by the traditions of creative nonconformity swirling around Washington Square. He had experienced there a freedom that repeatedly lured him back. "I thought it was a great place," he says now. "You know, like all American kids do. I started hanging out down there. When I ran away from home and to New Jersey, I didn't come in to New York very often, but when I came in, I went to the Village."

It was there, in the bohemian stronghold he now disparages, that Baldwin went for solace during that interminable July. Dramatizing his renunciation of parents and church, he was beginning to smoke and drink ("giving himself airs," his father's older sister commented tartly). Among his new acquaintances, he tried to forget his mother's remonstrances.

But he finally acceded to her wishes. On July 28th, with the aunt who seems to have been the model for his portrait of "Aunt Tina," he rode out to Long Island to pay his first—and last—visit to his hospitalized father. The old woman, bound to her brother by a devotion that had revealed itself only in the intensity of their reciprocal recriminations, was no less apprehensive than the youth.

On the seemingly endless train trip, she nagged at her nephew about his smoking, periodically lapsing into a meditation so profound that she appeared unconscious of his existence. During these intermissions, he puffed at his cigarette and studied her furtively. Once beautiful and lively and loving, adored by her brother's children, she was now haggard and fretful. Age had crumpled her spirit as well as her face. He was overcome by revulsion and the pity that he didn't want to feel for his father.

By the end of the pilgrimage, both were unnerved. But there remained before them the sight of the dying man. He was almost unrecognizable. Wasted by disease, he had shrunk into "a little black monkey." His breath rasped in his throat. A tube attached to a needle in his arm fed him intravenously.

His sister wept and his stepson was inundated with the sorrow he had been warding off for a year. He wanted to reach out, to touch his father and speak to him. But David Baldwin, the David Baldwin both visitors had known, was gone. By morning he was dead.

Jimmy Baldwin's long, futile endeavor to achieve a sense of his own worth by gaining his father's approval should at last have been over. But, mutinous, unappeased, he could not share in the relief of his younger brothers and sisters.

"I didn't feel it *then*," Baldwin says now. "I felt betrayed—that he died before I could prove myself to him. Which, I guess, sums up what I really felt about my father. I really *loved* him. Somewhere. And I wanted to prove to him that—that . . . I wanted us to be *friends*."

Bereft of the father he had never had, Baldwin could not stay at home that day. The compulsion to put distance between himself and the site of his depredations, which now keeps him wandering on four continents, made him desert his distraught mother and the bewildered children. Leaving them to the ministrations of neighbors, he rushed downtown.

A few hours later, before his return, his mother gave birth to her last child. Jimmy Baldwin named David Baldwin's posthumous daughter Paula Maria.

In the essay he wrote twelve years later, Baldwin recorded

August 2nd, his nineteenth birthday, as the day of his father's funeral. But he inadvertently telescoped the past. The service for David Baldwin had actually been held twenty-four hours earlier, on August 1st.

"Wait," Jimmy Baldwin says now. "Let me think." He shuts his eyes. When he opens them, he nods. "Yes," he says. "That's right. That's what must have happened. The funeral must have been on August first."

On that day, in Harlem Hospital, he heard his despairing mother sob, "I'm a widow forty-one years old with eight small children I never wanted." Her lament obsessed him. For a year his family's financial bulwark, Baldwin did some simple arithmetic, and was appalled by the result.

"I figured out," he explains, "that by the time the youngest kid would be able to take care of herself, I'd be thirty-six. And it would be harder to begin a career then. I'd seen a lot of brilliant, unhappy, *miserable* and *evil* people trapped in Harlem in various basements, being janitors. And they really *were* brilliant. That's why they became so monstrous. And I could see it happen to me. It *would* happen to me—if I stayed." His decision made, he postponed the announcement.

During the afternoon, gulping scotch in a girl's flat in Greenwich Village, he was gnawed by anxiety because he had nothing dark to wear at the obsequies that evening.

Baldwin was not quite sober when he sat in the chapel, attired in his somberest clothes and a black shirt his friend had managed to locate for him ("I remember her ironing that shirt"), chewing gum to disguise the smell of alcohol on his breath, listening to his aunt moan aloud as the preacher eulogized the considerate, gentle, kindly man David Baldwin had never been.

Seated near Jimmy was his half brother, Sam, faithful to the bitter vow of a decade earlier. "He left home saying his father would never see him alive again," Baldwin says now. "And he never *did* come back. He never *wrote* his father. Daddy used to make me write letters to him when I got to be a preacher, but Sam never answered them. He answered *me*—we were very good friends when we were little—but he never answered his father. He came home when his father died—to *bury* him."

Assailed by nausea, reeling from the heat, Jimmy Baldwin was beset by fragmented memories. He remembered, wondering how he could ever have forgotten, scraping his knee as a tot and his father's solicitude. He remembered his church solos when he was very small, and David Baldwin's radiant pride. He remembered his only real conversation with his father: "You'd rather write than preach, wouldn't you?"

The casket was opened. A deacon led the family, one by one, up the aisle for a final glimpse of the deceased. When it was Jimmy's turn, he advanced reluctantly toward the bier. The gray, powdered face inside resembled David Baldwin no more than the subject of the sermon had.

In the narrow box lay the body of the man who was not his father but yet had made Jimmy Baldwin so much that he was: a child, achingly aware that he was black and little and ugly, who pressed pennies against the lids of his bulging eyes "to make them go back"; a boy, the eldest and the brightest, a buffer between his parents, who diapered the younger kids, spanked them, corralled them, always knew where they were; an adolescent forced by the pressures of his role to be ("ironically") just what David Baldwin had wanted his own children to become; a youth still up in arms against a foe retired by death. It seemed implausible to Jimmy Baldwin that the product of the mortician's art contained by the coffin, diminished, quiescent, could ever have been capable of procreation and tyranny.

At just about that time, in the lobby of a Harlem hotel, Patrolman James Collins was trying to arrest a colored woman, Margie Polite, for creating a disturbance. When she resisted, Private Robert Bandy, a Negro military policeman who happened to be off duty that Sunday, came to her aid. He grabbed Collins' nightstick and knocked him down. Margie Polite disappeared. Bandy might have done the same, but Collins dropped him with a bullet. The wound, in the fleshy part of the shoulder, was slight. But a rumor sped through the stifling streets that a Negro soldier had been slain by a drunken, white cop. The story fell on ears already inflamed by reports of Negroes mistreated and abused in the Army.

Later that night, when Baldwin must have been downtown going through the motions of ushering in his birthday, Harlem's stillness was finally shattered by riot. Stores were smashed and looted, others set afire. Five Negroes were shot to death. Hundreds more were injured and jailed.

David Baldwin's cortège the next day drove through streets littered with wreckage. Gazing at the destruction, seeing in it a hint of the apocalypse which his father had threatened and he himself had scorned, Jimmy Baldwin hated the streets, hated the Negroes and the whites who had together made them that way.

At nineteen, in his mother's absence, he was really his father's chief mourner. He still is. Bequeathed an ambivalence, Baldwin is torn between the love and the hate ("they are equally terrifying—I think they really *are*") he felt in childhood for the psychologically maimed minister whose wretchedness was strewn on all around him.

In "Notes of a Native Son," published in 1955 and surely among the most memorable of all American essays, Baldwin wrote his father's epitaph: "I do not remember, in all those years, that one of his children was ever glad to see him come home."

Yet after so remorseless a judgment Baldwin continues to pursue his stepfather's specter in life and in art. The spoils of such a chase can only be grief. Over and over again, Baldwin has re-enacted his relationship with his father, first creating David Baldwin's image, then charging against it, savagely, blindly.

It was this compulsion that wrecked his friendship with Richard Wright, the author of BLACK BOY and NATIVE SON. Baldwin repaid the kindness of his boyhood idol by castigating him in print and then, in a lengthy postmortem apologia, nailed down the factor underlying their clash: "He became my ally and my witness, and alas! my father."

The trauma that is David Baldwin's legacy still inflicts pain. Several years ago, in Stockholm, Jimmy Baldwin was stabbed by envy when Ingmar Bergman, the Swedish film director, casually remarked that after an interlude of conflict he and his father were close friends. In Chicago, after dining with Elijah Muhammad, the head of the Black Muslim movement in the United States, Baldwin wrote: "He made me think of my father and me as we might have been if we had been friends."

To be friends with David Baldwin, to attain his love, to punish him for withholding it, Jimmy Baldwin habitually resurrects his stepfather. The only description of Emma Baldwin provided by her eldest son outside the pages of his first book is the fleeting reference to her in "Aunt Tina," where she is observed "making a vain effort to be dictatorial." But David Baldwin haunts his stepson's work, an apparition part god or part devil, sometimes both.

In his fictional autobiography, GO TELL IT ON THE MOUNTAIN, Baldwin tells the story of John Grimes, a Harlem boy who turns preacher at fourteen, huge-eyed, undersized, bright, poetic—and born out of wedlock, a circumstance his mother's husband, himself a clergyman, never forgives. In this volume, Baldwin creates two fathers, the one he knew and the one he wanted.

For the clergyman, John Grimes cherishes a hatred that cannot be quenched even by death: "The grave was not enough for punishment, for justice, for revenge." Then there is John's natural father ("completely imaginary," Baldwin explains), Richard, young, sullen, bitter, tense, incandescent in his quest for beauty and knowledge, who commits suicide after the humiliation of a false arrest.

So urgently does Baldwin still long for a scene of affection and warmth between father and son that he fitted it into his earliest play, THE AMEN CORNER. In BLUES FOR MISTER CHARLIE, by a reverse twist, it is the son (another Richard, both in name and character) who dies, shot by a white man; the minister-father, respectable, upright, cowardly, but transfigured by the murder into an ardent civil rights crusader—cries out: "Would God—would *God*—would God I had died for thee—my son, my son!"

In the short story, "This Morning, This Evening, So Soon," dazzling in its insights, Baldwin conscripts a veritable platoon of David Baldwins, each reflecting the other in dizzying array. The narrator, an American Negro who triumphs in Europe as an actor-singer, names the son he adores for the father he despised. In a movie, the American is cast as Chico, a mulatto who hates both his parents—and, consequently, everyone else. When Chico must appeal for a job to a Frenchman who reminds him of the father who betrayed and disowned him, the scene lights up the nightmare of the star's own past. He is overwhelmed by fear that his son may some day feel for him the contempt he had for his own father.

David Baldwin, it would seem, populates his stepson's universe. In his periodic tirades against his father, sloughing off any semblance of moderation, Jimmy Baldwin uses the identical vocabulary of vituperation he wields against sheriffs in the South, bigots in New Jersey, white liberals in the North and—once—the men in a Swiss mountain village:

"He was righteous in the pulpit and a monster in the house. Maybe he saved all kinds of souls, but he lost all his children, every single one of them. And it wasn't so much a matter of punishment with him—he was trying to *kill* me. I've hated a few people, but actually I've hated only *one* person. And that was my father."

It was shortly after the funeral of his father that Jimmy Baldwin mustered up the strength (the courage? the egotism?) for a very long shot:

"The long shot was simply that I would turn into a writer before my mother died and before the children were all put in jail—or became junkies or whores. I *had* to leave Harlem. I had to leave because I understood very *well*, in some part of myself, that I would never be able to fit in *anywhere* unless I *jumped*. I knew I had to jump *then*."

He did jump. He jumped to Greenwich Village. He jumped to five years he has since characterized as "desperate." Once he had moved in, the Village's bloom rubbed off. Fast. In Harlem, he had been too busy looking after his brothers and sisters to familiarize himself with temptation. In Jersey, Jim Crow had wholly absorbed his attention. But in the Village all the sins catalogued by his father were thrust before him.

Whatever defenses he had so painfully evolved in the past were suddenly, abysmally ineffectual. He was too young, too small, too poor, too black—in short, he says, too "visible."

"I got into trouble with cops," he recalls. "I got into trouble with landladies. I get into trouble with *everybody*. The cops wanted to know why I wasn't uptown. The Village wasn't then like it is *now*. There were only half a dozen Negroes scattered *throughout* the Village. And I was the *youngest*. And people—you know, people that you thought were friends would—you know, you'd go to somebody's party—and get beaten *up*. That's *right*.

"And I went with a lot of white girls in those days, without realizing that—there was no *love* in it, y'know. It was just kind of a—I was a *stud*. I didn't know that *either*. Until I found out all these things—the *hard way*. I made a lot of discoveries in those years—*all* of them *horrible*."

"The whole effort of *being* a writer is—is really very—is really *frightening*. In any circumstances. Even under the best of circumstances. But it seemed, you know—it seemed, on the face of it —*grotesque* and *ludicrous*—that I should try to be it—to do it. Because I had, so far as anyone could tell, no equipment at *all*. In the world's sense, anyway. No *education*."

Eight

It was during the desperate years that Jimmy Baldwin became a writer. His qualifications may have seemed dubious, his consecration never.

In Greenwich Village, which he now classifies as "more treacherous" than New Jersey, he received his first fellowship, convalesced from his first literary setback, sold his first essays, honed his prodigious talent and rage.

"When I hit Publishers' Row," Baldwin says, his eyes glaring like stoplights, "I was about nineteen. I had just come out of Harlem, you know. And you couldn't have been greener than I was. And why *not* take a gamble on me, y'know, since I was the first one out since Richard Wright?

"And nobody cared whether I could write or *not*. You know? I was such a cute little black boy. And it was *interesting* that I wanted to try. You know? They wanted to be nice to me. Like a dancing dog, y'know? I've been in the profession for twenty years. And the people who ever really bet on me—I would use one hand. And have most of it left over!"

Baldwin's adjustment in the Village was complicated, as it had been in Jersey, by the upheavals and disruptions of World War II: "There were people from Texas, from Georgia—people from all over this dreary country. They'd go to the Village—in uniform and *out* of uniform, you know, and bounce *chairs* off your head."

There are cynics in the Village who contend that Baldwin was less victimized than subsidized by whites and that most of the thorns in his path budded from his own eccentricities and penchants. He shrugs at this, half amused. Then, abruptly, he is irate.

"I've won a few fellowships," he concedes. "Probably because there was no one around to *give* them to. And they pick their Negroes. No, I think white people—you know, white liberals or people who *say* that I've been subsidized by whites—are deluded.

"The principal thing they are saying is that I made it because of *them,* you know. And they think that because I am now a star that it proves something about them. It doesn't prove anything about them at *all*. It proves that I managed to *survive*—and that's *all* it proves."

Certainly Baldwin worked for his rewards. He worked right around the clock on a regimen that came close to destroying his health and his reason. During the day he held down a series of full-time jobs in defense plants, in restaurants, once on the newspaper PM (where Max Lerner remembers him as "a bright, vivid copyboy"). At night, almost all night, he wrote, sleeping three hours or four, establishing the topsy-turvy schedule he adheres to today.

"Crying Holy" was progressing handsomely. Gratified, Baldwin read portions of it aloud to friends, basked in their praise, changed the book's name and, somewhat prematurely, on his employer's machine, typed out what he called "a reasonable facsimile" of the title page:

IN MY FATHER'S HOUSE
A Novel
by
James Baldwin

For a year, he worked in shipyards, then in a factory making rifles. "You know, I made a lot of money during the war," he says. "I wasn't drafted because my father died. I was supporting the children. I was 3D or something." But there came a day when he heard the alarm clock ring in the morning and couldn't get up.

"Because I'd only *gone* to bed about an hour *before*. You know, I really—by the time I was twenty, I had—I *really* had a kind of nervous breakdown. That's when I started working in restaurants —because I couldn't—keep up the pace."

Even when tips were most lucrative, he earned far less than he had in industry. His allocations to his family fell off; they were to remain at best small and sporadic until fame yielded him royalties worthy of that designation.

Baldwin has a propensity for imbuing the past with the bleakness of Gethsemane. "Those were terrible years, I must say—they *really* were," he says now. "They really were terrible. Terrible because of—you know, you can't be a writer unless somebody *admits* it. You can't make any *money* at it. You know?"

It was actually not too long before somebody admitted it, although it was to be very long before Baldwin made any money at it: enough money to live on, instead of not quite enough to get by on.

He was twenty ("broke, naturally, shabby, hungry and scared"), with some sixty pages of "In My Father's House" completed, when a friend ("a very nice girl named Esther") arranged a meeting between him and Richard Wright. On a winter day, Baldwin and Esther took the subway to Wright's apartment in Brooklyn and there the two writers, one acclaimed, one still unknown, were introduced.

"Hey, boy!" Wright said in his light, sweet tenor, and brought out a bottle of bourbon. Baldwin's stomach was empty. Awed by his host, ranking himself as an intruder on Olympus, he drank the liquor and talked about his book—talked, he was sure, too much and too brashly. But Wright was understanding as well as receptive.

"There was very little he could tell me, y'know," Baldwin says. "Except that being a writer was very difficult. Which I'd already begun to suspect. And—he hadn't *read* anything of mine—because there was nothing to read."

Baldwin remedied that a few days later. With more than his usual quota of trepidation, he mailed the first section of his novel to Brooklyn. Wright read it, liked what he read and maneuvered for Baldwin a Eugene F. Saxton Memorial Trust Award. "And that was *almost* the extent of our relationship then," Baldwin says.

"You know, it was very funny. I can see now—kids who are coming to *me*—I'm still—I'm not *used* to it yet. Maybe I never *will* get used to it, you know. I don't—I *know* I must be different [now] in many ways, but I don't *feel* any different, you know. But they're scared shitless of me—as I was scared shitless of *him*.

"And there was nothing *he* could do about it—and nothing I can do about it, y'know. That's just the way it is. And a lot of things I *should* have done (I think now), I didn't do—because he was really a very nice man and I was very fond of him. But I was just too *shy*, y'know.

"I never would have *dreamed* of calling him up, or—you know, asking for his *advice* or *anything*. Y'know? (I was just a *kid*. I wanted to stay out of his way.) But I think he wouldn't have minded if I *had*. It might have been better for us if I had. Anyway, I *didn't*."

But the Saxton was his; and it was tangible. Baldwin has never spurned the financial benefits of his art. Indeed, he regards them as insufficient, pointing out dourly that white colleagues of comparable stature earn immeasurably more. But his is not a banker's mentality. The monetary value of his work is for him primarily a gauge of his reputation. The Saxton conferred upon him something he prized more than cash: the status of a writer. He sent a portion of the grant to his mother. Then, elated, incredulous, he set out to prove that he deserved the bonanza and Wright's trust.

Baldwin worked and reworked his novel. He worked too hard on it. He listened to the advice of too many people. And he ruined the book. He couldn't finish it—or, rather, he finished it too many times. Then he had to stop. "I got paralyzed," he says, even now a trifle defensive.

"There were *two things*, really. It was not *entirely* my fault. It was also the fault of—of the publishing *industry*. They thought of me as being another Richard Wright. And I didn't know I *wasn't* another Richard Wright. The whole idea never entered my—you know, I never thought of myself as anybody at *all*. I just thought of myself as trying to get to be a *writer*.

"But I had to *balk* at the direction in which they were *driving* me, you know—without having worked out any direction of my *own*. I still knew I couldn't go *that* way. But I *tried*. And, you know, that's what—it was that collision that wrecked the novel.

"And I was very ashamed of myself, you know. For not being able to bring it off. And, y'know, I was ashamed—I thought that I'd done something *terrible* to Richard—because he—he *counted* on me—as I *thought*, y'know, to *do* it. And I'd failed. It was very sad, y'know. It's a little funny to think about it now, but it was, you know—it was *awful* then."

Awful, but invaluable: the collapse of the novel forced Baldwin to reassess his career and start again on a less ambitious level. He began to learn his craft slowly, meticulously, as a journeyman: "Which is, you know, not *poetic*. It's just a matter of writing a sentence. And it's also a matter of writing every day, y'know."

He wrote a sentence. He learned to write it sinuously, sweetly, knifed through with emotion. His prose sang—and bled. He wrote as fervently, as fanatically, as once he had prayed. Writing, for Baldwin, is a distillation of prayer. It may be that writing is his only religion.

He holds fast to it whatever happens to him. He held fast to it through the many years of famine and the few of plenty. His tenacity is enduring. Pushing himself too hard and too long and too fast, pushed by others whose motives are not always selfless, burningly aware of his dolor, memorializing every moment of anguish, inclined to be amnesiac about his remissions from pain, Baldwin has consistently managed to squeeze out of his scrawny body and staccato personality the formidable energy required to stoke the process of creativity.

His apprenticeship was grueling. But it made of him, long before that was acknowledged, a professional with something to say and his own way of saying it. "I'm not a writer," he says, "I'm a re-writer." While writing and rewriting in the Village, he waited on tables at the old Calypso for eighteen months.

Connie, who ran the restaurant, was a Negro woman with bubbling humor and a tender heart. She was fond of Baldwin, as Mother Horn had been, and threatened to adopt him. There was also a very pretty Negro girl, Kay, to whom Baldwin warmed at once. He congratulated himself upon stumbling upon "a marvelous job."

When Corporal Arthur Moore came home on furlough, he took a snapshot of Jimmy with Connie, big, smiling, amply upholstered. To Moore, Baldwin seemed "reasonably happy in the Village—he felt he belonged there." That was reflected in his rambling reports to his former schoolmate while Moore was in the Army, from 1942 to 1945.

The letters, disarmingly signed "the Ace Boon Doon," contained philosophical outpourings on "the business" of the artist, excerpts from pieces he was writing, an assurance that his first published work would be dedicated to Moore (in ornate—and misspelled—German), a poem composed at three in the morning, a description of his first apartment—cheap (twenty five dollars a month), large (six windows, two toilets and a roof garden), convenient (close to a bar, a liquor store, bookstores and a pawnshop).

"Jimmy's letters were tomes, four or five pages each, written on both sides of the paper," Moore says. "They had drawings in them by an artist friend showing 'Le Baldwin at Rest,' 'Le Baldwin at Work.'" There were days when Baldwin was almost as low as he now remembers (once he confessed he wanted to beat his breast and howl at the moon) and then his communications were mired in depression.

Physical exhaustion could account for some of Baldwin's despondency: moderation has never been his vice. His shifts at the Calypso, which usually extended a couple of hours beyond midnight, the official closing time, were enervating After the last patron had departed and the tables had been cleared, Connie would call it a night. Baldwin couldn't. Too wound up to rest, he would have a few drinks with friends, gradually—and strenuously—decompressing. He was acquiring a taste for scotch as well as a phenomenal capacity.

But the overripe kitchen odors he inhaled on the job left him faintly (and, it may be, permanently) queasy, with little inclination for food. He still "can't stand" hamburgers, shudders at the recollection of lunch counters and cafeterias, would rather not eat at all than eat alone, all of which he views as the residue of the occupational hazards to which he was exposed as combination busboy-dishwasher-waiter.

It was usually three or four in the morning before Baldwin was alone in his room. Until dawn streaked the horizon, until seven, eight or even later, he would write (in long hand on unruled sheets, typing out a passage after he had finished it). By then there was likely to be someone at the door, advising, "You can't write all the time, Jimmy—relax!" Baldwin heard that admonition so often that it seemed to him to swell into a stentorian chorus.

Seldom did he retire before ten, often not before noon. Somewhere around four P.M., he would rise, pull himself together (then a fairly short routine, since he "never had hangovers and things like *that*" in those days) and, yawning, lope back to the Calypso "to set it *up*."

He was on the verge of "a crack-up." But perhaps the most remarkable aspect of this cycle is that he survived it. His abhorrence of New York, which he berates as "tight" and "unbearable to live in," crystalized then.

"I've *always* hated it," Baldwin says now of the city of his birth. "It began with the racial thing, y'know. Much, much later, I realized it was not just race. It was *everything*, y'know. The way people *treat* each other there. The fact that people don't dare to be friendly with each other at all! Except at the most hostile level. It's the *only* way they can talk to each other. The result is what New York *is*. Chaos."

In the Village, much of the chaos was internal. Baldwin was worried about his separation from his family, his religion, his race. He was uncomfortable with what he called "hep-cats" and impatient with intellectuals who prattled of socialism and literature but hated Jews.

Reassessing God, man, and sex with youthful ardor, he fluctuated between euphoria and melancholia. One moment, he knew himself a writer destined for greatness; the next, dissatisfied with his life, he wondered if he were a traitor to his people. But he managed to retain enough vitality to take note that spring had arrived "safely and in good spirits."

At twenty-two, he sold a piece to THE NATION ("a book review—

a book review on Maxim Gorki, as a matter of fact"), then another. Next he did some reviews for THE NEW LEADER ("about the Negro problem, concerning which the color of my skin made me automatically an expert").

These early samples impressed COMMENTARY, the publication of the American Jewish Committee. Baldwin was asked to do an article on Harlem. It was his introduction to the late Robert Warshow, whose memory evokes in Baldwin today an unreserved enthusiasm:

"He was the *greatest* editor I ever *had*. He was marvelous. He really worked very hard with me on that piece. He worked with me for six months and he taught me a lot. He was a very nice man and a *very* good editor for *me*. I think—in fact, this could be taken as a generality—a good editor is someone who knows what the writer is trying to do, and helps him to do it. He doesn't think the writer is trying to do what he *isn't*.

"I guess he senses the writer's intention. And helps him to get closer to it, y'know. And he also has to be very ruthless. He can't be nice to you. He has to, y'know, tell you when it's shit. When you're showing off. Or when you're avoiding something. Which means that Robert *did*—y'know, on that first piece, all the things that I was avoiding was what he kept pressing me for.

"And, y'know, I was very grateful to him. I still am. Because he taught me—I really *learned* in that six months. We sweated that piece out—because I was really afraid of it. Naturally. And there was much more *in* it than I was willing to deal with. He saw that—and *forced* me to. To deal with it—especially the whole question of anti-Semitism. Which was a very delicate and dangerous area, y'know. Which I'd really never consciously explored. And he forced me to do that. Which was a great liberation for me."

Ever since he was a student at Clinton, Baldwin has felt more profoundly involved with Jews than with any other segment of America's non-Negro population. He has a special affection for Jews that wells up "out of the depth of my sympathy, my love and imagination." All of this was a deterrent when he had to analyze Negro anti-Semitism. But Warshow persisted.

"He made me feel like a *writer*, y'know," Baldwin says. "He said that—there was not much he could do to *help* me, except keep turning it back to me—because I was much too good a writer to—for him to help me in any other *way*.

"But he knew that I could *do* it—if I *would*. And that was the first time I realized that writing was not simply the act of writing —that it was something *else*, something much *harder*. Which is to tell the truth."

The truth as Baldwin saw it, pressed from him by Warshow, appeared in the February issue of COMMENTARY in 1948. Entitled "The Harlem Ghetto," it was a very different appraisal from the one its author had produced for Bill Porter back in junior high school. Sardonic but controlled, Baldwin described the Harlem he knew, its housing, its leaders, its newspapers, its churches and its relation to the Jew.

"I remember meeting no Negro in the years of my growing up," Baldwin wrote, "in my family or out of it, who would really ever trust a Jew, and few who did not, indeed, exhibit for them the blackest contempt."

In Baldwin's opinion, Harlem's anti-Semitism was derived partly from the nation's, partly from its own humiliation ("whittled down to a manageable size and then transferred"), partly from its disappointment in Jewish tradesmen, rent collectors, real estate agents and employers for failing to secede from "the American business tradition" of exploiting Negroes.

"Just as society must have a scapegoat," Baldwin concluded, "so hatred must have a symbol. Georgia has the Negro and Harlem has the Jew." The piece kicked up a mild controversy. Negroes were abashed, Jews aghast. The sentiment was that while Baldwin's proposition was hardly new, he had overstated the case.

But, after "The Harlem Ghetto," his market slowly expanded. The "little magazines," the avant-garde of America's intellectual elite, provided him with an occasional outlet. Unfortunately they could extend to their contributors less pay than prestige. Baldwin's income lagged far behind his debts.

"We published some of Jimmy's early essays," says Philip Rahv of PARTISAN REVIEW. "He worked hard when he began. He was poor, terribly poor, of course—fifty dollars was a lot of money to him. He was very plain, very bright. He did stories and poems."

The critic, who was later to perform a notable service for Baldwin, recalls that he never had to edit the young writer, never had to shift his paragraphs around or amputate them: "He was talented and interesting and I liked him. He was," says Rahv, "a pro."

Broadening his scope again, Baldwin had tackled another novel, "Ignorant Armies" (now reposing in a duffle bag in his mother's apartment), seeded by the bizarre Wayne Lonergan case.

Lonergan, a debonair Canadian of twenty-four, ruggedly good-looking, twice rejected by the United States Armed Forces for homosexuality, was married to a pretty socialite, the former Patricia Burton, twenty-two, heiress to an eight-million-dollar brewery fortune. Prominent, popular, with a baby son, the couple lived in a lavish triplex on Manhattan's East Side. There, on October 24, 1943, Patricia Lonergan's nude body was found in the bedroom, where she had been bludgeoned and then strangled.

Lonergan, who had enlisted in the Royal Canadian Air Force, was on leave in New York that day. He was later arrested in Toronto and charged with the slaying. In his confession, which he later repudiated, he admitted quarreling with his wife about extramarital dates, beating her on the head with a brass candlestick and then choking her to death. On April 1, 1944, he was convicted and sentenced to prison for a term of thirty-five years to life.

The trial, covered by the New York press like an extravaganza, "fascinated" Baldwin. "'Ignorant Armies' was probably a very bad book," he says. "I was dealing with—it was a very halting attempt to deal with some element in myself, which I had not, at that point in my life, really come to grips with at *all*. The whole *sexual* element. The whole—how can I put this? Because now I have the vocabulary, but then I didn't . . .

"Well, the whole—what I was grappling with *really*, without knowing it, was the—all the implications in this society of being *bisexual*. Though I could not have put it that way *myself* then. It was just—you know, just—I was really, you know, *untouched*. Another reason the Village years were so difficult . . ."

The concept of the Negro male cherished by white men and women threw him off-balance. "Let's try to imagine," Baldwin says now, "what it would be like to be a Negro adolescent with those people to whom you are a phallic symbol . . ." For him, it was a "terrifying" burden.

There were conventionally romantic episodes that apparently did little to allay his fears or quell his doubts. "I've been

—I've *been* nearly married—*three* times," Baldwin says impulsively, not without appreciation for the impact of his line.

"The first time was a white girl"—her successors were both Negro—"and I thought that was *it* for a while. And that would never have worked. Because we were both too young. And the pressures were too—at that point I was—my God, how old was I? I must have been—I had to be twenty. *Yes, I had* to be twenty.

"Later on, a couple of years later, I was living—in 1946, I was twenty-two; at that time I started living with a Negro girl. I was with her until 1948. And *even* bought the *wedding* ring, as a matter of fact. And then—but when *that* broke, and it wasn't *her fault*—when it broke, it was *not* my fault *either*: it was partly—it was partly—what I call the whole question of being a *writer*, you know. Which is a *concrete, economic* question. And I couldn't support *myself* then. And—she was *working*. I was working. But I wanted *children*, you know. If I get *married*, that's what I *want*.

"And I didn't want to—I couldn't take—I couldn't take that chance, y'know. I could *see*—because I'd seen it happen to *friends* of mine, and I could see *how* it would happen that, you know—the energy (at that point, I was working all night and working all day) would have to be turned *fatally* in some other *direction*: that I'd never be able—that I would never become a *writer*. Which I had to become before I could become anything *else*. D'you know?

"And I'm *older* now than I was then. So that, you know, the—what I *thought* of then, what I was beginning to *suspect* then—as being an insuperable obstacle to my—to *marriage* (that is, the whole bisexual question), no longer strikes me that *way*. I know much more about myself and the world—and *life*—than I did *then*."

His confusion stretched from sex to race, encompassing both. His identity, never sharply focused, never very clear to him, blurred dangerously. He was trying to be white—"trying not to act like a nigger," an ambiguous phrase he then interpreted very literally as the negation of the classic assortment of stereotypes: "Acting like a nigger meant eating with your hands or scratching yourself or cursing or fighting or getting drunk or having nappy hair—all those things."

He assiduously slicked down his hair, modulated his voice, perfected his already good table manners—and learned, of course that "it didn't help at all." The "iron corset" of constraint he wore was invisible, as his skin was not. And it was his skin, not his nappy hair, not his voice, not his very personal amalgam of human frailty and strength, that predetermined the attitude of white strangers. They didn't really see Jimmy Baldwin any more than New Jersey had. His color made him simultaneously conspicuous and anonymous.

Excluded from Eden, he reasoned that self-reform was useless: "It didn't make me white. And it didn't make me a man, either. And it meant I couldn't talk to white people, because I was talking in a certain kind of way, and I couldn't talk to black people either, because I was too busy not being one of them. And I hated white people from the bottom of my heart. And I hated black people for being so common."

Yet, even at this juncture, he did not allow his work to stagnate. With photographer Theodore Pelatowski, Baldwin did a documentary on Harlem's store-front churches that was never published. But it won for him his second fellowship, this time from the Rosenwald Foundation.

He wrote his first short story, "The Previous Condition," which was his own present condition, encircled by the thinnest shell of fiction. "I wrote it in white heat," Baldwin says. "People accuse me of writing in white heat now, but I wrote that story about four *times*. I wrote—I finally *finished* it, from beginning to end, in one night—which is the way it's published [in COMMENTARY, in October, 1948]. It's something you can do when you're very young . . ."

He wrote the story in the first person, casting himself as Peter, a young actor. To Peter, the author attributed his own grievances, his own experiences with the police, his own contempt for the Negro, his own furious ambivalence toward the whites who wanted to help him but didn't know how.

The venom that had infiltrated Baldwin's bloodstream races through Peter's veins. "I felt that I was drowning; that hatred had corrupted me like cancer in the bone," Peter says. And to the "Jewboy" who befriends him, Peter, from the abyss of Baldwin's sorrow, cries out:

"I know you think I'm making it dramatic, that I'm paranoiac and just inventing trouble! Maybe I think so sometimes, how can

I tell? . . . I know everybody's in trouble and nothing is easy, but how can I explain to you what it feels like to be black when I don't understand it and don't want to and spend all my time trying to forget it? I don't want to hate anybody—but now maybe, I can't love anybody either . . .' "

By the fall of 1948, Baldwin's morale was so fragile and his confusion so apparent that a girl warned, "Get out—you'll die if you stay here." He passionately concurred with this prognosis. Two years earlier, his friend (and cohort in a brief venture into socialism), Eugene Worth, had committed suicide at twenty-four by jumping off the George Washington Bridge. Baldwin saw in Worth's fate a portent of his own.

"I could not be certain," he wrote later, "whether I was really rich or really poor, really black or really white, really male or really female, really talented or a fraud, really strong or merely stubborn. . ."

With his intuitive sense of timing ("I know when to leave the party, baby"), Baldwin recognized his exit cue. Recklessly he booked passage for Paris, planning to cover the price of his fare with the final installment of his Rosenwald grant. But the ship sailed three days before his check arrived.

Slipping the precious piece of paper in his pocket, he wandered about, feverishly indecisive, numbed by the conflicting advice lavished upon him, all of it oracular. At the end of four days, terrified he would fritter away the $660, he bought a one-way plane ticket to France. Then, and only then, did he break the news to his family. His mother said nothing. Baldwin knew she was frightened, but so was he.

"What happened is this," he says now. "That I was born in Harlem, which is not New York. And, at a tender age, I left Harlem, which seemed, you know, like a *prison*, to come downtown—which *is* New York. And *uptown*, you know, I've been beaten up half to death—and got almost slaughtered *downtown*, y'know.

"So that by the time I was twenty-four—since I was not *stupid*, I realized that there was no point in my staying in the country at all. If I'd been born in Mississippi, I might have *come* to New York. But, being born in New York, there's no place that you can go. You have to go *out*. *Out* of the country. And I went out of the country and I never intended to come back here. Ever. *Ever*."

And, so intending, Jimmy Baldwin climbed aboard the plane on November 11, 1948, scared yet jubilant. Flying across the Atlantic, he promised himself nothing worse could happen on another continent than was bound to have happened to him in the United States. "Even if I go there and drop *dead,*" he told himself darkly. "Catch syphilis and go *mad.*"

"I've always been afraid. But I was lucky, y'know. Because if you're frightened *enough*, there's just nothing to be frightened *of*. So you just have—to keep *moving*, because—if you *don't*, if your fear is *great* enough, you'll just simply— you know, you'll *perish*—in it. In that case, you just *might* as well commit *suicide*. Overtly—and *swiftly*, instead of doing it—instead of dragging it *out* . . ."

Nine

Fog shrouded Paris. As the plane circled and recircled the field, Baldwin's fear rapidly outstripped his jubilation. It was a rather forlorn American who finally set foot on foreign soil with forty dollars in United States currency and a French vocabulary consisting of little more than "bonjour."

"There I was," Baldwin says now, "and Paris was awful. It was winter. It was gray. And it was ugly."

But he was cheered by a waiting friend who took him straight to a café in St. Germain des Pres, Les Deux Magots, the nepenthe of several generations of Americans, then an existentialist hangout where Jean-Paul Sartre often held court. There Baldwin spied a more familiar figure chatting with the editors of ZERO magazine: Richard Wright.

"Hey, boy!" Wright called out. He looked surprised and pleased. Baldwin's spirits levitated. But Wright merely ushered his young compatriot to a hotel and then bowed out.

"I knew forty dollars wasn't going to last very *long*," Baldwin says. "But I had no idea it would go so *fast*. I didn't know what I would do when it was *gone*. And, when it was gone, I—I had no way of getting any *more* money."

His welcome evaporated as swiftly as his resources. When he couldn't pay his bill, he was locked out of his room. He moved to another hotel. Borrowing funds from a Negro architect he met in the bar, Baldwin recovered his baggage. But the reunion was brief. He sold his clothes, then his typewriter. "What else could I do?" he asks.

Right after Thanksgiving, he "went to pieces," a process begun at home but hastened by his exposure to the chill of Paris (indoors as well as out), the inadequacy of his apparel and the knowledge that, 3,000 miles from friend and foe, he was now—"*really*"—on his own.

"I'd gone to pieces a bit *before* I left New York, y'know," Baldwin says. "But I really *did* go to pieces when I got to Paris. Thank God I went to pieces there! It was very lucky—because I fell ill in a hotel that was run by a Corsican woman who *liked* me. And so she nursed me. And I ran up a *ferocious* bill.

"I caught—you know, Paris was, for Americans, extremely badly heated. And I was always on the *streets*. And I—I really didn't have any *clothes*. So I—something went wrong with my bronchial tubes or something. Anyway, I was very *sick*."

He neither went mad nor died, of course. But he did learn that he could be at least as hungry, as cold and as scared in Paris as in his own country. Countless men of arts and letters have made the same discovery, but Baldwin claims on behalf of his privations a special intensity and depth. Any suggestion that other writers of lighter hue have had experiences comparable to his tarnishes his mood.

116

"Well," he says, at first almost sullen, "they didn't work as *hard*. They didn't have to go for broke. I *had* to go for *broke*. If I hadn't made it [in Paris], I wasn't going to make it at *all*."

Then, fuming, he declares: "I also knew *this*, I must say—if I didn't make it, my family would perish. There was only *one* thing I could do. I did not have three or four choices. And I had no one to fall back on, y'know. I could not write home for money. Yes, they *sent* me money. But—like—in some *terrible* emergency. But I *could not* write home for money."

His brother David swoops to second this. "When Jimmy wrote for money," he says, his words tumbling over one another, as though he were defending Baldwin against a charge of treason, "it was because he was down up to—like dying. Just before the last difficulty went over his head, he says, 'Well, *send* me something.' But the whites say, 'Mama, I need two hundred dollars.' And they get five hundred dollars if they ask for two!"

Whether or not they were unique, Jimmy Baldwin's vicissitudes were extreme. During the years he lived there, Paris, much as Baldwin learned to love it, was never the New Jerusalem. From the outset, it was dismayingly large, inconvenient and indifferent. The Parisians gave no indication of rejoicing in his presence.

His earnings, small and whimsical, aroused in a series of concierges grave—and justifiable—doubts about his ability to pay the rent. Sizing up his old adversary, the police, from the sidelines, Baldwin concluded that the gendarmes were more picturesquely attired than their American counterpart, but no less vindictive.

If some of his contemporaries were shrill in their insistence that bad food, bare lodgings and no income constituted the Great Adventure, Baldwin harbored no such illusions. He wondered gloomily "which would end soonest, the Great Adventure or me."

He was even imprisoned for eight days in a ludicrous mix-up over a "stolen" bedsheet that an acquaintance had filched from a hotel. Before the case was dismissed in a courtroom suffused with merriment, Baldwin, duly fingerprinted, mugged, handcuffed and confined to a frigid cubicle that reduced him to tears, had ample opportunity to investigate the intricacies of French bureaucracy and the shortcomings of the French penal system.

What kept Baldwin abroad almost a decade was an unaccustomed and exhilarating sense of individuality. In the United

States, he had felt himself an alien—and an enemy alien at that. But divided from the land of his birth by an ocean, liberated from the collective anonymity that transforms American Negroes into faceless and nameless men, Baldwin slowly began to reconcile himself to what he was.

"I got over—and a lot beyond—the terms of—all the terms in which Americans identified me—in my own mind," he says now. "And I realized I'd never be controlled by them *again*. I didn't have to worry about acting like a nigger. I didn't have to prove *anything* to *anybody*.

"I didn't have to walk around, you know, with one half of my brain trying to—to *please* Mr. Charlie and the other half trying to *kill* him. Fuck Mr. Charlie! It's his problem. It's not my problem. I felt that I was left alone in Paris—to become whatever I *wanted* to become. That it was up to me, y'know.

"I discovered—I began to—I could *write*, I could *think*, I could *feel*, I could *walk*, I could *eat*, I could *breathe*. There were no penalties attached to—these simple human endeavors. Y'know? Even when I was starving, it was *me* starving. It was not a *black man* starving.

"The trouble I got into in Paris was *me*. And there was no wall between—between my trouble and myself, as there always had been here. This was *me*. And, if I fucked it up, it was me. It wasn't—you know, it wasn't some weird abstraction called 'The American Negro.' That's what it *did* for me."

But it didn't happen overnight. Outside the ghetto, he was still its victim—physically and emotionally sapped by the ordeal instigated by his stepfather and extended by his nation. The process of sloughing off the carefully cultivated defenses that concealed Jimmy Baldwin from himself was gradual, and only partial; he could not shed what he once described as "the profound, almost ineradicable self-hatred" with which the United States endows its Negro citizens.

Perhaps it was inevitable then that he should initially seek to forget his race. It was after all inextricably bound up in his mind and in his blood with all that he had suffered at home. During the eight and a half years he remained in France, Baldwin infrequently associated with Negroes. His past humiliations were linked in his memory not only with his white oppressors but also with his colored kin. He had been a fugitive from both when he fled his country.

If in France he exchanged his racial tag for a national one (even in jail, his fellow prisoners and the guards regarded him primarily as an American, not as a Negro), that was unquestionably the lesser evil. On a conscious level at least, Baldwin no longer had to defy the color clichés. Relieved of the complexities of the black man's burden, he could listen to the records of Bessie Smith, taste watermelon, stop worrying about the texture of his hair.

Nevertheless, then as now, his intimates, always few in number, were usually white. "When Jimmy was in his twenties in Paris," one of Baldwin's friends explains, lowering his voice several decibels, "he thought seriously of never being a Negro again—certainly never a Negro in America."

Reality did not, of course, conform with this fantasy. Even life in sanctuary, and that is what France represented to Baldwin, was not devoid of dilemma. In cutting himself loose from the United States, he had hoped to obliterate the psychology of the outcast But geography could not perform so radical an operation.

Baldwin had run away from his native land to escape not only the Negro condition but the condition of being Negro. It was not long however before he sought to reverse his opinion of himself by repairing his opinion of his race. One seemed to hinge on the other. He longed for revelations of African superiority that would convince him his inferior image of himself and his people was a subversion of history. But unfortunately the reflex judgments he had damned in his countrymen had become his own.

Confronted with Europe's abundant testimony to Western culture, he searched there for a reflection of himself (or of what he assumed to be his African heritage), then despairingly concluded he was an interloper. He subjected himself to merciless self-examination, and later wrote:

"What was most difficult was the fact that I was forced to admit something I had always hidden from myself, which the American Negro has had to hide from himself as the price of his public progress; that I hated and feared white people. This did not mean that I loved black people; on the contrary, I despised them, possibly because they failed to produce Rembrandt. In effect, I hated and feared the world."

Baldwin contends that he has since purged himself of this hate and this fear. But the fury bubbling up in his prose and erupting in his speeches invites skepticism. In any event, it was in Europe that Jimmy Baldwin began to recognize both his nationality and his race. It was in Europe that he became an American.

While planning his exit from New York, Baldwin had imagined that he might find people treating each other "in a more human way" outside the United States. But once he was in France he never made the mistake of confusing the golden legend of Paris with its impenetrable natives. Yet their very impersonality, their immunity to curiosity or interest in strangers, proved therapeutic. The claustrophobia that had overwhelmed him in Harlem and Greenwich Village receded. Parisians left him alone to find out who he was. Paris granted him the freedom to uncover his identity or conceal it.

"Something *struck* me in Paris," Baldwin says. "I didn't realize what a *Puritan* I was—until I got to Paris. I *know* now I am a Puritan. But then I *didn't*. It was—it was really kind of—*humiliating* to *discover* it. Because I never thought of myself that way at *all*. Until I found myself dealing with people—you know, whose morality was entirely different from my *father's*, which was the morality with which I—carried *around* with me, really.

"And I watched *myself*, you know. Just like any other little American, I was doing my best to avoid all the things which I thought of—that I'd been *brought* up to believe—were amoral. But I couldn't—I couldn't on the other hand avoid realizing— because I was dealing with the streets of Paris—with Arabs and Africans and French whores and pimps and *street* boys, you know—that there was something very beautiful, no matter how *horrible*.

"You know, I saw some—I saw some *tremendous things*. And some of those people were—*very* nice to me and—in a way, I owe them my *life*. D'you know? These were people that everyone else *despises* and *spits* on. And it was—it *humbled* me, in a way. It did something—very strange for me. It opened me *up*—to whole *areas* of life."

Baldwin writes as he lives: hard. Whatever leeway he gained by reappraising his stepfather's morality and his own did not eliminate the inhibitions that have led him to compare his creativity to the hazards of "forever treading the thin, wavering line between adjustment and surrender." His labor pains are intense and prolonged.

There are always, as he confided several years ago in a letter to an editor at Dial Press, "the unforeseeable and demoralizing snags" that occur "when the writer, in working, disturbs one of his sleeping lions, the rage of which he's by no means prepared to face; or, to put it more simply, when the truth concerning one of his characters—or all of them—becomes crucially and unflatteringly involved with the truth about himself. Then the typewriter stammers day after day, the wastebasket overflows, his sentences become impenetrable and uncontrollable for the very good reason that the real impulse behind them is to keep something in the darkness instead of bringing it to the light. All that can be done at such moments is to hang on to the typewriter and sweat . . ."

Baldwin hung on. And he sweated. He had been abroad only six months when he wrote "Everybody's Protest Novel." Out of bitter knowledge, he set down in this piece his view that "the oppressed and the oppressor are bound together within the same society; they accept the same criteria, they share the same beliefs; they both alike depend on the same reality."

Tracing the history of social protest fiction from Mrs. Stowe's UNCLE TOM'S CABIN to Wright's NATIVE SON, Baldwin scathingly denounced both for robbing the black man of his humanity and thus perpetuating the very myth they were intended to destroy.

The day this article was published in Paris (ironically, in ZERO magazine), Wright accused his former protégé of betraying him. Baldwin, proud of the essay, even hoping ("sad and incomprehensible as it now sounds") to be patted on the head for his originality, was stunned. The differences between the two Americans were never patched up, although Baldwin used to dream that some day they would be. That dream, like an earlier one, was blasted by death and Baldwin, hymning Wright's elegy, wrote, "The man I fought so hard and who meant so much to me is gone."

Baldwin says today of "Everybody's Protest Novel" that it described his state of mind. "And it still is im-*por*-tant," he asserts. "It's written from a particular point of view. And I was trying to save my life as a writer. And it was a protest against all the stereotypes—you know, all the white—liberal and illiberal—stereotypes which come out, in action, to be *exactly* the same thing. In terms of you, as a Negro, facing your life and dealing with all the stereotypes—every one of which you've got to *break through* and make somebody look at *you*. That's what I was trying—still what I'm trying—to do."

To "break through and make somebody look at you" has been the American Negro's epic effort. W. E. B. Du Bois and Ralph Ellison and Chester Himes have attested to that. Baldwin's agony over the stereotypes was his own, but it was also that of every American Negro.

The Paris in which Baldwin staged his lifesaving struggles was hardly the tourists' Paris. He was plagued by hunger as well as sleeping lions. Chronically skidding on the edge of starvation, he wore hand-me-downs that were usually several sizes too large for him, the pants belted around his chest.

But there was, he says, not the same kind of penalty attached to this level of poverty as there would have been at home: "If you walk into a bar in Paris looking the way I looked in those days, if you have the money for a drink, you can *buy* the drink."

Since the temperature of his hotel room approximated winter on the Siberian steppes, Baldwin quickly learned to accommodate himself by lingering in the cafés, thawing himself with innumerable cups of coffee and numerable glasses of liquor. At twenty-five, scrounging sandwiches and beer in a bar, Baldwin met there one day a lean, quiet, dimpled youth with a seductive voice and a determination to paint. His name was Lucien Happersberger and, at seventeen, he had just run away from his family in Lausanne.

"It was in one of those horrible—*dives*—where I had *credit* in those days," Baldwin says. "Actually, the place was *awful*. But it was run by a very nice woman—from Brittany, I think. Lucien was *skinnier* then. We *all* were! And—I don't know—we formed a kind of an alliance because—well, partly because, I suppose, I had the habits of an older brother, really."

Their friendship has weathered Happersberger's first marriage (the elder of his sons, Luc James, is Baldwin's godchild) and perhaps his second. Until 1964, when he moved to Manhattan, Happersberger shuttled between his first wife in Switzerland and Baldwin in New York or Paris, intermittently serving the writer as manager-buffer-companion. "That's my best friend," Baldwin then said of him fondly.

Distance has veiled with nostalgia the youthful adventures of the two men. Baldwin remembers a rainy Thursday in Paris when they hadn't eaten for a couple of days. "We lived in this terrible place on rue Jacob, way up on the top floor," he says, smiling.

"Lucien and I went downstairs because we thought we could eat around the corner at this woman's restaurant. On credit. And it was *closed*." The smile is now a grin. "And we had no cigarettes. And no money. *Noth*-ing! And it really was *like that*."

"What did you do?"

Laughter cascades from Baldwin. "Why, we went back upstairs. It was *raining*." He rocks back and forth, helplessly, joyously, his eyes squeezed shut, laughing so hard that a tear courses down his cheek.

But Baldwin shied away from the Parisian quarters where his American confrères clustered. He was sure he would be patronized by colleagues possessed of more influence or affluence than he, and his equilibrium was still too precarious for convulsive encounters.

"*They* didn't put me on the defensive—*I* did," he says. "It wasn't their fault; it was my fault. You must remember that I was still a dark horse. Very improbable, from their point of view. Not at all respectable, from their point of view. You know, I might just as easily have perished as have made it. And more *likely* to perish."

But not all Americans were barred from his company. At the home of some mutual acquaintances, he was introduced to Mary Painter, a Swarthmore-educated economist from the midwest, a thin, laconic girl, indifferent to the purity of her features. "It was at a brunch for Americans," Baldwin says. "And we didn't fit *in* with these people. So we—you know, we talked to each *other*. And we got to be friends." They still are. Fiercely loyal, unswervingly generous, Miss Painter flew from Paris to New York not long ago to hold Baldwin's hand at the Broadway première of BLUES FOR MISTER CHARLIE.

Tom Michaelis, an American patent attorney of German origin, befriended Baldwin in Paris, furnishing him with a job as an office boy and championing him through The Affair of the Stolen Bedsheet. Today Michaelis functions as Baldwin's behind-the-scenes legal adviser.

Beauford Delaney of Tennessee, a middle-aged painter Baldwin had known back in Greenwich Village, eventually turned up in France. A chunky mystic who has been described as "a guru—

a venerable and compassionate teacher," the artist had inspired Henry Miller to write an essay called "The Amazing and Invariable Beauford DeLaney." Still a Paris resident, Delaney is the only Negro in Baldwin's sparsely populated inner circle—always excepting, of course, his brother David. Delaney's portrait of Baldwin, bold and vivid, done in pastels almost twenty years ago, usually hangs in the author's Manhattan apartment, like a prophetic statement of what its subject has since become.

Baldwin has commemorated three of these relationships by dedicating GIOVANNI'S ROOM to Happersberger, ANOTHER COUNTRY to Miss Painter and GOING TO MEET THE MAN to Delaney.

Then there were occasional American benefactors, like Ed McGee of Alabama, whose kindness Baldwin recalls with pleasure: "Ed was a writer, around my age, maybe a couple of years older. What was nice about Ed, to put it briefly, was that he understood that I was starving and understood that I was proud. He would say, for example: 'I heard of a wonderful French restaurant down the road and I speak no French. I understand you speak a little. I wish you'd come and help me out.' He wrote a great book, which was never published, so far as I know. I don't know where Ed is now, but I'll never forget him."

Later in that hazardous period, Baldwin established warm ties with novelists James Jones, Philip Roth, William Styron ("I adore them") and, on a charged, on-again-off-again basis that is at once closer and more threatening, Norman Mailer. But the incestuous atmosphere of literary parties made Baldwin uneasy. And still does.

While he was growing thinner and shabbier on the streets of Paris (and sometimes in its gutters) and recognizing his leftover puritanism and relishing his freedom and selling an occasional article and revising (again) his novel, an editor back in New York approached one of his writers.

"There is a young man in Paris by the name of Jim Baldwin," Elliot E. Cohen of COMMENTARY said to Dr. Kenneth B. Clark, the psychologist. "If we can keep him alive, he will emerge as one of the greatest writers America has produced."

"What's his name again?" Clark asked.

"James Baldwin," Cohen said. "Don't forget it."

In the autumn of 1951, after investing almost ten years in the making of GO TELL IT ON THE MOUNTAIN, Baldwin scrapped it, presumably for the last time. Then, suddenly, so suddenly that he later said he had felt as though he had been "hit by a hammer," all the pieces he had been manipulating and remanipulating fell neatly, felicitously, into place.

In three months he had whipped the book into final form, completing it high up in the Swiss Alps, in the chalet belonging to Happersberger's parents, in Loeche-les-Bains. Only three hours from Lausanne but virtually inaccessible in the winter, the village had six hundred inhabitants, no library, no theater, no bank, no moving-picture house: in short, few distractions.

It was there, on February 26, 1952, that Baldwin typed out the closing line of the novel ("'I'm ready,' John said, 'I'm coming. I'm on my way.'") and was swept by "a *tremendous* sense of elation." (Only later would he experience the hollowness of fruition.) Giddy with joy, he went down to the foot of the mountains with his friend and mailed the manuscript to Helen Straus of the William Morris Agency in New York. That night, Happersberger scrupulously recorded the event in his journal.

Miss Straus had been introduced to Baldwin in his Greenwich Village phase by another client. "He said Jimmy had talent and asked if I would help him," she says. "And so I became his agent. Jimmy was very sweet, very ingratiating and very helpless."

Baldwin was back in Paris when Miss Straus notified him that Knopf might publish his book. Four years had elapsed since he had exiled himself from his country. Intent upon pushing the sale, he decided to visit New York. But he had another—unspoken—motive: he wanted to test the interaction between the United States and himself.

"I was curious about—what it was like, by that time," Baldwin says now, "and what *I* was like by that time."

He had just enough money to pay his hotel bill or ship fare. While he was mulling over this choice, Marlon Brando arrived in town. The actor and the writer had met in New York at the New School for Social Research when, twenty and stagestruck, both were gravitating toward the theater (Baldwin, who feels he could have been "a great actor" and occasionally toys with the notion that he yet will be, contends that preaching and acting evolve from "the same bones, the same nerves").

Bailed out of Paris by Brando ("he's a beautiful cat—he really is a beautiful cat"), Baldwin arrived home stone broke. He tipped his steward with a ten-dollar loan from his brother David, who was at the pier. Armed with borrowed cash and a borrowed suit, Baldwin reconnoitered New York.

"It was a nightmare," he says in a funereal whisper. "I'd been away just long enough to have lost all my old habits—all my old friends, all my old connections, you know. So I came back into a kind of limbo."

He stayed with his mother in Harlem. It was as familiar to him as his own body, yet he felt like a phantom, more ectoplasm than protoplasm. He floated through his former haunts, weightless, discarnate, unable to bridge the four-year hiatus.

He was best man at David's wedding. "That was part of it," Baldwin notes: his brothers and sisters had grown up in his absence. They had been kids when he left. Now, abruptly, seemingly without transition, they were adults. He needed time to adjust to their new status. He moved downtown to Greenwich Village, but the shift did not dissipate his panic.

Dropping in at the San Remo on MacDougal Street, a popular rendezvous when he had been working at the Calypso, he was gripped by shyness. His old companions still hung out there but now they pretended they hadn't seen him. "Because I was a—I was, you know, a world traveler," Baldwin says contemptuously. "And, you know, a writer—and all that shit. And I'd *made* it. They didn't know that the suit I was wearing was my *brother's*. I was suddenly, you know, the cat from *uptown*.

"And it created very real tensions. Once I realized that, I couldn't talk to them *either*. Y'know, I couldn't go over to them. And it—it was like *that*. It was as though one had to apologize for—for having attempted to survive. D'you know?

"When I said 'Montmartre' to those cats, they thought—they'd never been to Montmartre; they didn't know that I was talking about the *gutters*—what Montmartre was really *like*. And, of course, what happened to *me*, I began to *despise* them. For being grown men and women and being so—innocent and so envious. Envious, after all, of *what?* Y'know? And there was a great *rupture*. Do you know? And there was no place—in those days—for me in the entire *city*, it seemed to *me*. It was—really, I think, the *worst* three months of my *life*.

"It's very hard to describe this because something was happening which I was not aware of. I'd been away—and I had, on the very bottom of my mind, a kind of—a kind of secret card up my sleeve, y'know. I thought to myself (but very, very privately—and scarcely to myself), 'Maybe one day I will grow up enough to be able to come back to America—and it won't bother me.'

"I'd become, in those four years in Paris, much more myself than I'd ever been before—in twenty-four years here [in New York]. And it was just precisely *that*, which I did not *realize* then, which made me absolutely out of *kilter* completely—and not because I was colored. I think that was the thing which, probably at bottom, threw me *most*. Because I didn't think of myself any more the way I'd thought of myself, you know, all those years before. So I had no frame of reference, I had nothing to *hang* it on. Do you know? At *all*.

"It was—it was just *me*. In this terrifying city, alone. I didn't know *why* I was here, what I was doing here, how I could stand it. But it was—it was—there was no objective *reason*—for it. D'you know? I was—after all, I was *young*, I was *alive*, I'd finished my first novel—and it was going to be published.

"So, objectively, you know, I had all kinds of reasons to be proud and happy. When, in fact, I wasn't. I was simply—I was *scared*. I didn't know what to—how I was going to handle the rest of my life. And I guess I went back to Paris to figure that *out*. Really."

He went back to Paris as soon as he received Knopf's check from Miss Straus. But the city of light had somehow dimmed. Paris had been his haven, his prop. And now Jimmy Baldwin felt he required neither. "I really *had*, as it turned out, y'know, liberated myself of a great *many* things," Baldwin says wryly. "And I *missed* them. I missed all the crutches."

He was almost as lonely in Paris as he had been in New York, and even more dismayed. He sought an antidote in work. He made a false start on what was to emerge years later as ANOTHER COUNTRY, had an acute attack of second-novel jitters and told himself he should not attempt another book of fiction right away.

Reverting to the ambition he had proclaimed fifteen years earlier in The Douglass Pilot, he plunged into his first play. He wanted to learn how to make people reveal themselves when

127

there is no way to describe them "except for them to describe *themselves.*"

He wrote about a store-front church, insular and defensive, and "what those brothers and sisters were like when they weren't wearing their long white robes." He wrote half of THE AMEN CORNER, which revolves around a too-pious, too-dedicated woman evangelist who uses religion to exorcise love, trying to find within the tabernacle a fortress where she can barricade herself and her adolescent son against life's incursions.

But Baldwin could not exorcise his own dejection. He says the play was even harder for him than the novel had been, impossible as that may seem, because he was "more scared." For economy's sake, he was living in Gallardon, a village near Chartres, pooling his scanty resources with a Frenchman who painted, a Norwegian girl who sculptured and a German-African woman who wanted to write.

On a morning in May, it was Baldwin's turn to try his luck at reviving the communal exchequer. He set out by bus, but a strike obliged him to proceed on foot from the gates of Paris. The day was wet and dismal, the kind of day on which all Paris is submerged in gray and the entire population appears to be in mourning. Trudging into the American Express office, Baldwin prayed he would find there a check from New York that represented salvation.

His mission proved a grotesque failure. No money awaited him although ten spanking-fresh copies of GO TELL IT ON THE MOUNTAIN did. Magnificently burdened with these testimonials to his success, Baldwin sloshed through the streets in rain-logged sandals to the bar he and Happersberger had frequented in Saint Germain des Pres.

Stacking his books on a table, he sat down behind them, dripping water into miniature puddles, cadging beer and waiting hopefully all day (alas, in vain) for someone to lend him enough money to get back to the country. It was hardly the most auspicious augury for a fledgling author. "I was," he observes grimly, "absolutely broke and *starving.*"

Jimmy Baldwin's time sense doesn't correspond to any known calendar or clock. Highly subjective and internal, it operates entirely on his own theory of relativity, whose laws are considerably more erratic than Einstein's. Baldwin may be several hours late for an appointment or fail to appear at all. Once he arrived with most unnatural punctiliousness at the exact hour and day set for a business conference—but a week behind schedule.

Not unexpectedly, then, his memory of the past is inclined to be impressionistic. Events are often compressed or expanded by the significance and the emotional tinge with which he imbues them. Referring on several occasions to the same phase of his life, he may date it in different years, even in different seasons. But, if the sequence is variable, the nuance is constant.

"I was living near Chartres," Baldwin says now, his brow furrowed as he conscientiously tries to reconstruct the continuity of an earlier decade. "And it was at some point *after* that that I went *back* to the mountains *again*. And that's where I finished 'Stranger in the Village'—in the mountains, where I'd gone to work on my play."

But his return to the Swiss Alps was also a retreat. The wind of critical acclaim blowing across the Atlantic ("Brilliant!" said the reviewers; "Exciting!" Honest!") had not dispelled his melancholy. Loeche-les-Bains was a glacial sanatorium where he could teach himself to carry on without "all the crutches" that had so long supported him.

This was his third or fourth sojourn at the Happersberger chalet. But, to the villagers who had never seen another Negro, he remained an oddity. They kept him under ceaseless surveillance, often amiable, occasionally malicious, always speculative. They fingered his hair. They touched his hand to see if the color rubbed off. They regarded him as a source of wonder, never of humanity.

"The question of who I was," Baldwin later reported in analyzing his years on the Continent, "was not solved because I had removed myself from the social forces which menaced me—anyway, these forces had become interior, and I had dragged them across the ocean with me."

He had dragged them across the mountains, too. In the naïve villagers, primitives preserved in ice, Baldwin fancied he saw the makers of the modern world: "Out of their hymns and dances come Beethoven and Bach. Go back a few centuries and they are in their full glory—but I am in Africa, watching the conquerors arrive." He was disdainful of their ignorance and envious of their security.

Even their simplicity seemed to him suspect. There were women who smirked at him, others who looked away. But in the eyes of some of the men Baldwin thought he detected "that peculiar, intent, paranoiac malevolence" he associated with the expression "one sometimes surprises in the eyes of American white men when, out walking with their Sunday girl, they see a Negro male approach."

All of this roused in him again "the rage of the disesteemed"—and a new maturity. In Loeche-les-Bains, Jimmy Baldwin finally came of age:

"No road whatever will lead Americans to the simplicity of this European village where white men still have the luxury of looking on me as a stranger," he concluded in the superb essay that so perceptively defines the nature of America's conflict and his own. "I am not, really, a stranger any longer for any American alive. One of the things that distinguishes Americans from other people is that no other people has ever been so deeply involved in the lives of black men, or vice versa."

Jimmy Baldwin was to "dawdle" in Europe four more years. But, once he had written those lines, the days of his expatriation had to be numbered.

"There's a point where you feel your nerves beginning to snap, you know. And you begin—and the terrible thing is that you begin to take it out on people around you. Obviously because the pressure is too great. And you can't—you can't deal with all the people you've got to deal with. In my own case, it always also means that—this is hindsight; it's what I've discovered—it also means I'm working on something and I haven't got it clear yet. My attention is really fatally distracted from what I should—from the objective I'm pregnant with. And it's at that point that you split . . ."

Ten

Still prodded by uneasiness, by that inexplicable sense of menace that flares up within him periodically like a recurrent bout of malaria, Baldwin deserted Paris for the south of France, settling down in a hamlet not much larger than Loeche-les-Bains, on the outskirts of Cannes.

The travel-poster attractions of that region are lost on Baldwin. He prefers the muted light of dusk to brilliant sunshine. Gambling bores him. He swims ineptly and doesn't drive ("My friends insist that if I buy a car, it'll be like buying a *tomb*"). But, "pregnant" with a book he had never intended to write, he sequestered himself from the fatal distractions of the outer world for a period of intensive work.

In Les Quatre Chemins, Baldwin wrenched out of himself ("out of the same depths that love comes or murder or disaster") almost all of GIOVANNI'S ROOM, his favorite among his books, as a mother's most troublesome child is often her favorite.

From time to time, Baldwin broods over the notion that he is fated to live his novels before he can write them. The compulsion to shape life into art, to impose form and order on private chaos, is not uncommon. But, more than most fiction, his weaves together clearly discernible strands of his experience. No face, no incident, no passion is wasted; sooner or later, everything is salvaged and shuttled into the fabric of a novel, a play, a short story, an essay. It is the only economy Baldwin practices.

Yet GIOVANNI'S ROOM concerns itself entirely with the white world. Not a single Negro enters its radically segregated pages. The leading character, David, a tall, blond, handsome American, oscillates between Hella, his tense, glittering fiancée, and Giovanni, the beautiful, black-haired Italian barman he meets in Paris.

Although most of the book was completed within a two-year span, between 1953 and 1955, its genesis can be traced back to the Wayne Lonergan case. "I could say 'Ignorant Armies' might be considered a first draft of GIOVANNI'S ROOM," Baldwin muses. "Anyway, one *character*—who turned out to be *David*—is carried over *intact*, almost entirely, you know, to the other."

Giovanni too is a reincarnation. His previous existence had been that of a peripheral figure in the novel Baldwin abandoned before turning to THE AMEN CORNER. But Giovanni and his morbid situation had proved too obtrusive. Baldwin found he had to deal with that "conundrum" before he was free to return to ANOTHER COUNTRY.

Baldwin conceives of GIOVANNI'S ROOM as a fable illustrating a basic tenet of his philosophy: that experience which destroys innocence also leads one back to it. It is his conviction (a conviction that has led him to remain enthusiastically receptive to life's sometimes flattering, often demonic attentions) that the man who struggles to preserve his innocence is doomed to sink into corruption.

"It is still, I think, the masculine necessity to look outward on life as it is," Baldwin commented in a questionnaire he filled out for his publisher in 1956, "to face himself as he is: neither is ever as we would like it to be. But before anything can really be dealt with, it must be faced. David's dilemma is the dilemma . . . of many men of his generation; by which I do not so much mean sexual ambivalence as a crucial lack of sexual authority."

Baldwin, who can take seclusion only in limited doses, left Les Quatre Chemins before he had entirely resolved David's dilemma. Although he insists he enjoys both solitude and silence, Baldwin risks neither except under the lash of urgency. Even when he is on deadline, working through the nights to complete a manuscript long overdue, he wards off loneliness by filling the emptiness around him with recorded music, the volume turned up high until the walls resound with the voices of Ray Charles and Mahalia Jackson.

One summer in southern France, forsaking isolation to visit a farm near Bordeaux, Baldwin discovered he could master a horse. For a confirmed nonathlete whose only spectator sport consists of sipping a drink on a terrace and watching people, it was a day of high drama.

"This friend of mine," Baldwin recalls gleefully, "had a stallion, a young stallion, whom he called Black Boy." A smile fans out from the corners of his mouth until every feature is engaged. "It was named for *me*. That's one of the nice things about *living* in France, I must say. Somebody could get a horse—a beautiful, *beautiful* horse, and call it Black Boy, you know—out of *love* for you.

"My friend was very proud of this horse. And, you know, it was my *horse*. And my friend helped me up on the horse—and the horse *promptly* ran away with me. Scared me *half* to death. But it *excited* me, too. And the horse was trying to *throw* me, but *didn't*. I *never* got thrown." Baldwin, beaming, leans over and raps wood. "And I rode a few years. It's the only thing I've ever done that way I liked."

But he was now marking time in France, no matter how beguiling the diversions. In the summer of 1954, like a deep-sea diver trying to prevent the bends, Baldwin gingerly edged himself back into the United States for nine experimental months. "It went better," he says. "It wasn't, you know—it wasn't *heaven.*"

To this day, Baldwin is uncertain why he slid back into his own country at that particular time. "I'm not sure I *know*," he says. "It was a complex of reasons. It was—I guess I was making up my mind, in some interior, strange, *private* way, about what I would do with the rest of my life. And I think I was *suspecting*—though I don't think I could have put it that way then—that—that I couldn't really—hope to spend the rest of my life in France. That it would—that the *attempt* would *kill* me."

What is remarkable is that Baldwin refers not even once in this recitation to the precedent-shattering event of May 17, 1954, when the United States Supreme Court outlawed segregation in the nation's classrooms. Nor does he indicate that the unanimous verdict reversing the doctrine of "separate but equal" school facilities, which was to sire the Negro revolution, contributed in any measure to his discontent with Europe.

"I wasn't in the *least* prepared to come back *here*," he says, gathering momentum and intensity with every syllable. "But, on the other hand, I—I was out of kilter in Paris *too*—because I couldn't get along with the bulk of the American colony, especially the American *Negro* colony who, so far as I could see, spent most of their time, y'know, sitting in bars and cafes, talking about how awful *America* was.

"And I didn't cross the *ocean* to do *that*, you know. And I wasn't prepared either to be used by the *French*—or any *other* European—as a stick to beat the United States over the *head* with. Y'know, it seemed—I was perfectly willing to say anything about the United States *to* the United States, d'you know?

"But I didn't feel that I had the *right* to allow myself to be used so *gratuitously*. For, after all, it was *my* country. And France was really no *better*—you know, *no* country is. And for the French to—complain, y'know—to be indignant about the way America's treated Negroes—seemed to me absolutely *hypocritical*—since I knew the way they treated their *own* black people.

"I couldn't—I couldn't *bear* it. And I couldn't, on the other hand, bear the Negroes who—who *allowed* this to be *done* to them. And neither could I bear the bulk of the American *exiles*, who were so romantic about *both* countries, their own *and* France. D'you know? And it seemed to me that, if I were going to live *that* kind of life, I might as well go back to *Harlem*. D'you know? But the whole prospect of coming back to America, I must say, gave me pause for a *very* long time."

What he calls his "second return" to the United States was a notably productive period. Between the summer of 1954 and the spring of 1955, progressing with rare smoothness and speed, Baldwin wrapped up his novel, his play and his first book of essays, NOTES OF A NATIVE SON (dedicated to the baby sister he had named, Paula Maria), whose bitter grace was triumphantly received.

Baldwin's early essays are rather like a running autobiography —communiqués from the front reporting the various advances in his own development as a human being, a Negro and an American. While no less ardent, no less committed than he is today, Baldwin was then primarily concerned with clarifying his own thinking. He gave the impression of wanting to set the record straight for himself, and only after that for his readers.

It was essentially a form of self-analysis, although Baldwin may wince at that term. But he himself says as much another way: "What I am trying to accomplish in my writing is what—I think —everyone tries to accomplish in whatever way is possible to him: to begin to understand and accept the world and my own place in it."

That effort permeates his review of André Gide's MADELEINE, printed in THE NEW LEADER at the close of 1954. To his appraisal of the French author, Baldwin brought his own sensibilities, his own ambiguities and his own distress.

Contributing to his dislike of Gide, Baldwin wrote, was the Frenchman's Protestantism and homosexuality. Basically no less moralistic than his subject, Baldwin expressed the opinion that Gide's homosexuality was "his own affair which he ought to have hidden from us."

"That was meant," Baldwin says now, "as a commentary on *myself*. I was accusing myself, perhaps not directly enough, of a certain fear and a certain hypocrisy. I do *think* that his *Protes-*

tantism, you know, accounts for a certain *coldness* in him—in his *work.* But I wasn't trying—it really wasn't meant as a judgment on *Gide.* It was meant as a judgment on *me.*

"I thought he was too defensive about his homosexuality. And it seemed to me pointless to be defensive about anything which is—in the *first* place, the *vocabulary* isn't the *same,* y'know. No one knows enough *about—anybody*—no one knows enough about *himself*—or *herself,* y'know?—to—accept those categories as—as *given.*

"Life is not *that way!* I know *that* much about it. Life is much more—much more difficult than *that.* And people are capable of all kinds of things, y'know. And what people look for—in spite of what, you know, people in this terrifying time and place *say*—I don't think people go around looking for sexual *fulfillment.* They go around looking for *love.*

"I don't think they can have anything resembling sexual fulfillment unless they—unless they *do* love. Otherwise, you can do—*otherwise,* you can do it with your *hand.* What I'm *finally* getting at is that no one—*no* one can really dictate who he or she is going to fall in love with. You know, you really—you can *try,* but you *can't.*

"You don't *tell* life. I think that if you accept what happens to you, you—you can keep *moving.* From one place to another. And you—you can *discover* things. But I think if you make up your mind about it—that 'I will do *this* and I *won't* do *that,*' I'll go *here* and I won't go *there*'—I think you—I think one makes a great *error.*

"I think one needs to learn how to—it's a very *delicate* matter because, you know, it can also be an excuse for the most *excessive libertinism.* But I'm not *suggesting* that. I'm suggesting that one try to listen to one's own *heart.* And—and roll with those *punches,* y'know . . ."

Reverting then to his discussion of Gide, Baldwin reiterates, "I was objecting to his defensiveness." Reminded that his review suggested Gide had been excessively "explicit" about his sexual problems, Baldwin exclaims: "No, that's the other comment on *myself.* It seemed to me, if I remember myself correctly . . ."

He jumps up. "I have the essay here." He slides a book from a shelf. "But again I was talking about *myself.* It was—it was . . ." He is flipping through the pages to locate the passage he wants. "And my point, finally, was that because he was so defensive *about* it, that he couldn't, you know—that he could not establish a relationship with his *wife* and he couldn't establish a relationship with any other man *either.*

"And he spent all of his time in North Africa with, you know—with little North African boys who—for whom he didn't take any responsibility. My point was that if you're this self-conscious, this *guilty* about yourself, this is the *inevitable* result. That you have no relationship with *anybody.*"

He has found what he was hunting for: "Yah," he says. "This paragraph." And he points to the end of it, to a sentence on Gide which says: "If he were going to talk about homosexuality at all, he ought, in a word, to have sounded a little less *disturbed.*" Baldwin nods, satisfied.

But the man who reads this passage aloud is more comfortable with himself, and conceivably more tolerant of himself, than the man who wrote it. In that earlier period, Jimmy Baldwin was only beginning ("*just* beginning") to be a little more secure, emotionally, professionally and economically.

In the spring of 1955, Howard University produced THE AMEN CORNER. Baldwin went down to Washington about a week before the opening. He was very casual about it. Then he saw his first rehearsal—"and almost died." His dialogue was too verbose for the stage, he decided. He felt bombarded by his own literature ("an unbearable experience"). Rallying, he cut the length of the speeches, although probably not as ruthlessly as he supposed. But, when the final curtain descended, he was proud of the play.

The pleasure he absorbed from the performance was more than counterbalanced by the depression into which he was hurled upon the completion of GIOVANNI'S ROOM. The homosexual theme had initially frightened Baldwin; now it made the publishers draw back. But they issued paternalistic warnings to Baldwin that they were rejecting the book for his own good, really, since publication would surely "wreck" his career.

"They said I would—I was a *Negro* writer and I would reach a very special audience," Baldwin says now. "And I would be *dead* if I alienated that audience. That, in effect, nobody would accept that book—coming from *me.*" His eyes smolder. "My agent told me to *burn* it."

Helen Straus denies that she ever offered him such advice. "I never told him to burn it, thank God," she says. "I just thought he could do better." It is her recollection that she eventually succeeded in selling the book, first to Dial Press in the United States, then to Michael Joseph in England.

But Baldwin angrily disputes her version. "*I* went to England—Mary Painter is a witness to that," he says. "And when I went to England, the book was *not* sold. I borrowed some money from Mary to *get* to England. Mary *took* me to England. And we hung around England for a *week. I* sold it to Michael Joseph. *I* did!

"What happened was that I wrote Helen from England—from London, saying that Michael Joseph—Michael Joseph was *wonderful*. He said, 'I'm not sure my lawyers will *let* me publish it, but I'll give you $400 against this or anything *else* you ever write.' Which was an *enormous* advance for a relatively unknown writer —in *London*. And for *that book*. I almost *cried*.

"But then Helen got busy and sold it to Dial Press in New York—which was easy for her to do, because Philip Rahv had been telling George Joel, who was the president of Dial, that he should pick me *up*."

Rahv, then a consultant for Dial, told Joel that James Baldwin was "the most brilliant Negro writer in America." Rahv did not regard GIOVANNI'S ROOM as a great novel, but he did deem it worthy of publication. The late George Joel is not favored with posthumous laurels from Rahv.

"Joel was not the most perceptive editor," he says in his slow, heavy voice. "When I brought him the manuscript of Orwell's ANIMAL FARM, he said to me, 'We don't publish kid stories.' So don't get the idea he *understood* Baldwin. But I believed in Jimmy as a writer. I was glad to help him because he was talented and made sense. And Joel's calculation was that Baldwin had potentialities."

The contract Baldwin signed with Dial in 1955 incenses him now. "This was George Joel's opportunity to pick me up for *nothing*, y'know," he says. "I signed a contract for GIOVANNI'S ROOM *and* for ANOTHER COUNTRY—which hadn't been *begun*—for *two* thousand dollars." (Eight years later, when Dial, under the direction of Richard Baron, signed up Norman Mailer with an advance of $125,000, Baldwin stormed: "Don't talk to me about it! That's *my* money!")

Whether or not Baldwin's account is accurate in every respect, the history of GIOVANNI'S ROOM permanently soured its author on the American publishing industry. He still aches to extract from its members full compensation—not all of it financial—for what he was forced to undergo then.

"One thing that Jimmy's got that's good is that he's stubborn," his brother David observes. "When they said, 'GIOVANNI'S ROOM will destroy your career,' he said, 'I'm sorry—that'll have to happen.' If he'd allowed them to frighten him that way, he'd never have been able to write again."

Back in Paris, Baldwin was not yet finished with the book. James Silberman, then Dial's editor, had suggested by mail several revisions that coincided with Baldwin's own ideas. This impressed the writer as a good omen (and, indeed, his relationship with Silberman was to remain a happy one).

The last section of GIOVANNI'S ROOM was typed in red—not for emphasis, but simply because the blue half of the ribbon had worn out and Baldwin, always rather helpless in such matters, had been unable to buy a new one for his American machine. "If you could send me a good, sturdy, old-fashioned American ribbon," he once wrote from Paris to Dial, "there's scarcely any telling how much brighter the future of American literature becomes . . ."

It was not until April 8, 1956, that Baldwin dispatched the final draft to Helen Straus in New York. Having been delivered at long last of David and Giovanni, their creator could now resume work on the book they had interrupted. By the following month, he was again "carrying a very precious egg," as he put it.

Like many writers, Baldwin borrows the vocabulary of obstetrics in speaking of his books. But his allusions tend to be persistent and extensive. He frequently estimates time in nine-month stretches. His descriptions of his periods of incubation and productivity teem with phrases like "I am pregnant" and "the newborn child" and "fatal miscarriage." A few years ago, conducting a guided tour around his psyche for a national magazine, he referred in the course of the taped interview to "all those strangers called Jimmy Baldwin." Identifying first "the older brother" and "the self-pitying little boy," he said candidly: "Lots of people. Some of them are unmentionable. There's a man. There's a woman, too. There are lots of people here." It would seem that all of them are inclined to think of themselves as perennially involved with the process of gestation.

A five-year struggle with the mammoth manuscript of ANOTHER

COUNTRY lay ahead. But Baldwin was rapidly gaining in self-possession. The literati no longer intimidated him as they once had. In Paris' American colony, or in that wing occupied by the writing contingent, he was looked upon as one of its own: charming, talented, amusing, easily moved to laughter.

"Fun to *be* with," says a woman novelist. "There was a beautiful, tall, blonde, Scandinavian girl I used to see with Jimmy," reminisces another member of the coterie, his eyes quickening with this backward glimpse into Baldwin's youth and his own.

In the next decade, Baldwin was to circulate among the famous more and more frequently ("exclusively," corrects an acid commentator), although he still draws many of his cronies from obscure strata. But the public Baldwin was beginning to emerge, small, sleek, seasoned, leery of traps, equally familiar with the boulevards and the alleys of Europe's capitals.

In the summer of 1956 Baldwin and Norman Mailer met at the Paris home of Jean Malaquais, who was then translating Mailer's THE DEER PARK into French. The two young Americans took to each other at once. Both short, rash and impulsive, spectacularly articulate and egocentric, streaked with a wild and vivid originality, capable of brandishing their weaknesses with desperate bravado, they circled each other warily ("the toughest kid on the block was meeting the toughest kid on the block").

They stayed up late that night, drinking and shouting and posing and mutually showing off, as Baldwin wrote later. During the next few weeks, Mailer and his second wife, Adele, saw a great deal of Baldwin. Then on the downcurve of an affair, he envied Mailer his success, his love and his swaggering exuberance. But there was a connection between them, a warmth and a vitality. Their friendship has since been marked, however, by an exasperation no less genuine than the affection: for Baldwin, a fairly typical cycle.

Mailer, given to flexing his muscles physically and verbally, tends to be overly authoritarian, the trait that infuriates Baldwin: "I'll not *listen* to anybody like that." They respect and value each other—nervously. Baldwin worries on occasion about their flashes of mutual antagonism; Mailer plans "one day" to do a book on Baldwin. And both have explored some phases of their uneven friendship in print.

"I like Jimmy a lot," Mailer says. "I think he likes me. He's very good company, a marvelous conversationalist, a very lively presence. He's able to contain such opposites in himself. Jimmy is very delicate and at the same time very strong. That's a rare mixture.

"He's certainly not a powerful man physically, yet he has what amounts to a power in himself. The thing about Jimmy is that he has a nice combination—a toughness that is good because he's so sensitive that you wonder how he stays alive. He gives off an enormous awareness of complexity and ambiguity, of moments and moods.

"He's always in motion, in the sense that you see him one moment and the next you don't—because he's always going some place else. I never saw Jimmy for more than a couple of hours at a time, except when he came up to see me in Provincetown for a couple of days when he was doing a piece on me (I thought it was a well-intentioned piece of work; no one is ever satisfied with a piece on himself, but I thought Jimmy did it as a friend).

"I think all good writers live in a kind of dread—and it takes different forms. Some drink, some travel. A good writer feels he is dealing with secrets about the nature of things. It inspires almost a biological fear. The thing about Jimmy is he must live in a very intense fear—we all do, but he's not a big man and he is saying very dangerous things that haven't been said before. There's danger of retribution."

In 1962, Baldwin and Mailer had a falling-out under well-publicized conditions. Both were in Chicago to cover the Patterson-Liston fight, Mailer for ESQUIRE, Baldwin for NUGGET, a magazine with less status than his friend's sponsor, a situation that may have made him excessively prickly ("Norman and I are alike in this, that we both tend to suspect others of putting us down, and we strike before we're struck").

Baldwin chose a cocktail party to advance an argument of long standing. Baring his teeth at Mailer, he snarled that he'd rather spend his time with a white racist than a white liberal, since with the racist he knew at least exactly where he stood.

This was a very low blow, as Baldwin well knew, since Mailer's disdain for liberals rivals his own. Mailer retaliated by calling Baldwin an impossible sort of Negro who didn't know the difference between a liberal and a radical.

"I got sore," Mailer confesses. "I almost slugged him. Because, to me, 'liberal' means someone who is not engaged, not serious and always ready to cash in a good cause for a compromise. The one weakness in Jimmy's vision is that he doesn't believe that there are whites who constructed their own moral universe by identifying with the rights of the Negro.

"What I'm getting at is that I don't think Jimmy thinks there's one white man alive who has a genuine rather than a complicated love for the Negro. And I'm not certain he knows that the Negro revolution—or, rather, the American revolution—in all sorts of different ways has a profound meaning for these whites. It's as moving to them, perhaps, as it is to many Negroes."

Both Baldwin and Mailer fancy themselves as political sages. Mailer, who once aspired to New York's mayoralty, remarks gravely that Baldwin "might even be an important political figure on the scene."

And Baldwin observes just as gravely: "In a way, and Norman will hate my saying this, one could almost say that I'm more *ambitious* than that. In any case, my attention is somewhere else. It seems to me that what's real is—is *behind* what's real. You know?

"I don't think that the symbols and the things that we deal with—*touch* and *taste* daily, I don't think that's *reality*. I think the reality is contained *in* those things. But one has to keep watching those *things*. Among those things is *politics*.

"Norman and I fight too much. I don't even know what we're fighting about, you know. It's just—I have great respect for Norman, for Norman's talent. It's just that he and I temperamentally can't hit it off. I don't know why. Maybe we're too much alike. I was very sad about it for a while. But now I'm resigned about it."

So much for the rollicking evening that started at Malaquais' home. Not long after, Baldwin, bogged down in his third novel, prepared to lock himself away with "the monster" on the island of Ischia, just a stone's throw from Capri (he is fond of island havens, particularly in their off seasons).

Irradiated by that "almost biological fear" of which Mailer speaks, Baldwin wrote his editor, "I wonder if anybody knows just how scared a writer can get?" Nevertheless, he was already projecting his fourth novel and had even selected its working title, "Lead Me to the Rock."

At the last minute, Baldwin substituted Corsica for Ischia. There, in a house overlooking the sea, miles away from the town of Calvi, he dug himself in for the winter with a dog and his typewriter for company.

He spent Christmas in Paris, but for most of the time ("it was—it was about nine months, I think") he remained in Corsica, his isolation was virtually unbroken. He took a daily walk to the post office, but complained that he was beginning to talk to himself.

It was on Corsica that Jimmy Baldwin, for the first time in his years of exile, began to feel homesick for America. His mood may have been due in part to the gratifying reviews accorded GIO-VANNI'S ROOM back in the United States, in part to "the violence and loneliness and horror and sort of writhing beauty of New York" that he hoped to recreate in ANOTHER COUNTRY.

But there was something more, something new to him: he was propelled homeward by a realization that "whatever's happening in your country is happening in you." In July of 1957, still reluctant to be betrayed into light and air again after almost nine years in Europe's womb, Baldwin returned to the United States. He told himself he had forgotten so many details about New York that he needed a refresher course to make the setting of his book authentic. But that was rationalization.

"I knew," he now says flatly, "I was coming back for good."

"That accident of birth, you know, is really what controls you in all other things. The only other element in it which is really *impenetrable* and always next is *who you are*. Because everything depends on how you meet this. And the terrible drama in this, you know, is—according to me—that you never know who *you* are. And you begin to discover who you are only in terms of how you meet it. So that, you know, the course you follow is on the one hand charted by things beyond your control, d'you know—I mean *outside* you; and it's charted by something *else* beyond your control—which is *you*."

Eleven

Jimmy Baldwin came home to an America in revolution. It was still little more than a beat pulsing faintly in the distance, but he heard it. It was the sound of the Negro revolution he had been waiting for, praying for and writing for, but it was a revolution that had begun to march in his absence.

The sound had reached him across the ocean. It had grown louder on the day someone had asked him about Little Rock. The thought occurred to him then that it would be "more honorable" to go to Little Rock than to try to explain it in Europe, particularly while enjoying the privileges of an American passport.

But now that he was back in the United States, he was still far behind the lines. The battlefront was to the South and the West. New York itself was unchanged; Baldwin's antipathy had not diminished during the years he had been away.

It was hard for him to adjust to a system he was "determined not to adjust to." For a couple of months he languished in a hotel room, snarled in the thickets of introspection. Immobilized by fear, he sat around, moping, drinking too much, uncertain what to do next.

"I thought—the thing to do, you know, if you're really terribly occupied with—with *yourself*," he says now, "the thing to do is to, at any price whatever, is get in touch with something which is *more* than you, y'know. Throw yourself into a situation where you won't have time to weep. So I went South. Because I was *afraid* to go South."

Baldwin was—and is—"scared to death" in the deep South. His terror springs from his unfamiliarity with the intricate code of behavior observed by both races there, a "weird kind of etiquette" that cannot be cultivated "surface-wise." Deliberately exposing himself to Southern segregation patterns for the first time, Baldwin penetrated the frontiers of what Northern Negroes often call "the old country." It is his recollection that he went there initially on an assignment from LOOK.

"But much more than to write about it—though I finally did—was to see it," he says. "To expose myself to it. And I was *right*. It *did* do something for me. It—oh, it *released* me from—from—some danger that every artist has, I think."

On that initial journey, so long dreaded, so long fantasied, the forerunner of a score of others, each equally terrifying, Baldwin concluded that the artist's role is to bear witness to what life is and what life does.

"I began—I *understood*—and I think I *really* understood, and probably for the first time, that—that *what* you are *doing*, as a writer, or any kind of artist, was not designed to—you know, to—to make you *special* or to—even to *isolate* you," he says, speaking very slowly, with long pauses. "It was designed—what your *role* was, it seemed to *me*, was to speak for people who cannot *speak*. That you are simply a kind of conduit. D'you know? You're at the mercy of something. Which has nothing to do with *you*, nothing to do with your *career*, nothing to do with your ambitions, nothing to do with your—*loneliness*, nothing to do with your *despair*."

His voice, quickening with intensity, just brushes the air, light, rapid, the rhythm of the italics crisply accented.

"It had to do *simply* with the division of labor in the world—and this was *your* job. This is what *you* were *here* to *do*, y'know—to translate somehow, if you *could*, by whatever means you could find, the way *I* see *it*. In any case, you know, I found myself in the deep South, looking at the eyes of a black boy or girl of *ten*. Y'know? To make it *real*. To force it on the world's attention."

He speaks now with a missionary's fervor. For in the fall of 1957 he had undergone another conversion, very different from the first and even more compelling. Jimmy Baldwin, who had absorbed from America's climate the polluted and polluting concepts of Negro inferiority, assaulted almost from birth by the mortifications of the Negro's America, acquired in the South what he had desperately hoped to acquire in Europe: a fierce and healing racial pride. It was as though the preacher he once was, surviving intact within the unbeliever, had regained his faith through a new religion and by that act again been "saved."

Baldwin was thirty-three when he first visited that section of the United States previously known to him only in nightmares. But his roots were in the South. His parents had been raised there. His stepfather's mother, born in slavery, had lived with the Baldwins in Harlem until her death; Jimmy, then seven, had been her favorite grandchild.

It was painful for him, remembering this, to witness the virulent varieties of discrimination—all of them bearing official or unofficial governmental sanction—practiced below the Mason-Dixon line. Yet he was exalted by the spirit of his people. His joy in them was the real culmination of his European exile.

"I met some—I met the most beautiful people I ever met in my life—down there," he says. "I mean Negro grocerymen, for example, whose stores had been bombed, who had to go through all *kinds* of—*hassles* and *danger* to get some beans to put on the shelves to sell. Because nobody [white] would *sell* to them. Y'know? Whose wives and children were insulted, menaced and in *danger*. Who nevertheless went *on*. It was just *incredible*."

Exhilarated and stirred by the day-to-day heroism of Negro civil rights crusaders, Baldwin made a long swing through the South. Instead of remaining three days in Charlotte, North Carolina, he stayed fifteen. He flung away his schedule, bouncing along by instinct, relying on his eyes, ears and empathy.

He interviewed Negro children who were defying the violence and the obscenities of white mobs to enter desegregated schools. And Baldwin, himself buffeted by insults and frayed by ridicule in his classroom days, marveled that these young Negroes could face every morning the dire realization "that it was all to be gone through again."

In their gallantry and that of their parents, he felt himself regenerated. Without planning to, he shifted from spectator to participant. The transformation was so natural that he was never conscious of having submitted his role to deliberation and decision.

"What I *did* was to write the essays I wrote about the South when I came back—and publish them," Baldwin says. "And I suppose the depth of my own involvement began then, because I—was forced to *understand*—that people *talked* to me as though I were a messenger. To get—to get the message *out*. You know? And the kids trusted me. Which had a great *effect* on me. And of course I was not then, you know, as *famous* as I am *now*. And all that—jazz."

His reports on his voyage of self-discovery eventually appeared in HARPER'S MAGAZINE and in his old stand-by, THE PARTISAN REVIEW, which paid him its standard rate of a cent-and-a-half a word ("It was an excellent piece," says Rahv; "we were glad to take it").

Meanwhile GIOVANNI'S ROOM had caught on with the reading public. "Everywhere you turned, there was somebody that had the book under his *arm*," Baldwin says. "I'll never forget *that*, my God." Back in New York after his baptismal journey, he learned that a play based on the novel was optioned for Broadway and a writer assigned to the dramatization.

Beleaguered by would-be Giovannis, Baldwin tried to dodge them all. He was determined not to do the adaptation himself. When a composer telephoned him to boast, "I have a Giovanni for you," Baldwin cursed him out roundly. "I really do have a Giovanni for you," the composer persisted. "I'm going to give a party. I won't even say you're coming. You can just look at him." Baldwin sighed and consented.

His apathy evaporated when he saw the young actor, Engin Cezzar of Turkey. "He looked like he could *do* it, and I took him to the producer," Baldwin says. "And everything was all *right*. Until I saw the script. It was—semi-poetic, sentimental—oh, just *awful.*

"I went to Engin's house after I'd spent two days wrestling with it, with my conscience—in despair." Cezzar read the script and grimaced. "Why don't you write it?" he demanded. "And we sat down on the kitchen floor," Baldwin says, "and worked out a sort of tentative structure for it. Which worked. I did write it."

It was never produced, however: "But I learned a lot out of the dramatization; we did it at the Actors Studio Workshop. Engin played the lead. He was very good. It would have been done on Broadway if we'd ever found a star to play *David*. But—we couldn't. And subsequently I got involved with many other things. And I was never really fascinated with the idea of dramatizing GIOVANNI'S ROOM. I'd like to do it as a *movie* one day. It would really make a marvelous movie."

Cezzar has since returned to Istanbul ("he and his wife are the young Lunt and Fontanne of Turkey"), thereby providing Baldwin with one more city to add to his roving itinerary. In recent years, whenever closer hideaways fail to immunize him against his own social susceptibility, he jets to Istanbul for a stay with the Cezzars or, in their absence, with one of their equally hospitable relatives.

But his contact with the Studio had whetted Baldwin's hunger for the theater. Late in 1958, Baldwin apprenticed himself to Elia Kazan as a kind of playwright-in-training. Clutching a clipboard as his symbol of office, he trailed the director through Archibald MacLeish's J. B. and Tennessee Williams' SWEET BIRD OF YOUTH.

"Jimmy went through the two plays with me, taking notes for me at run-throughs and rehearsals," Kazan explains, reclining on a couch between telephone calls, his arms crossed under his head. "I think he had the time of his life. He met professional actors for the first time and he was very much taken with Geraldine Page, Rip Torn—all of them. I think he responded to it like a great adventure."

The adventure was not without friction. Alfred de Liagre, Jr., the producer of J. B., was offended by what he regarded as Baldwin's arrogance: "He was paid something like twenty-five or fifty dollars a week by a foundation or some theater society," de Liagre says, "and he was allowed to sit in the rear of the house. Occasionally I'd ask him to make himself useful—he was not particularly willing to offer his services."

During the tryout in Washington, D.C., MacLeish made a number of revisions. Since a stenographer was not immediately available to incorporate the changes into the script, de Liagre turned to Baldwin. "I asked him to help out with the typing," the producer says. "Which he did. But he made a few comments about MacLeish and the quality of the play which I thought were unnecessary. Completely gratuitous. I didn't," he concludes with distaste, "see much of Baldwin after that."

But Gadge Kazan, whose own difficulties with Baldwin still lay several years ahead, maintains that he harbors for his erstwhile aide an undiluted affection: "Jimmy is warm, companionable, sympathetic, loving. His heart just bursts out. It's marvelous to talk with him—he has complete candor; you feel you can say anything to him and he can say anything to you. I really love him. He's one of the nicest men in the world."

Between rehearsals, Kazan and Baldwin discussed the Emmett Till case. Till, a Negro youth, had been killed in Mississippi in 1955. A white man, tried for the murder and acquitted, blandly confessed the details of the slaying to William Bradford Huie, whose article was released in a national magazine with a fanfare of publicity.

"I thought the Emmett Till case would make a great movie," says Kazan. "But Jimmy said no, he wanted to do it as a play."

Although grateful for this "germ" of an idea, Baldwin is less than effusive in describing the period of his association with Kazan. "I *like* Gadge *very* much," Baldwin observes. "Working with him is very *exciting*. But I had decided, when I was working with Kazan, that I was *not* going to *work* in the theatre.

"I was not about to get involved in all these—you know, I had enough *problems*. Who needed—*who needed* to get involved with *Broadway*, for Crissake? All those—I'm not talking about the *actors* now; I'm talking about—about the *economics* of it, about the—the illiteracy of—you know, so many of the people in *charge*.

"I saw *everything* while I was working with Gadge. I got more and more and more and *more depressed*. Leaving J. B. and SWEET BIRD out of it entirely, why would anybody want to produce a show called TALL STORY, for example? Why—would *anybody* in his *right* mind who *reads* that *wretched* script, y'know . . . ? Or AFTER THE FALL . . . ?

"Y'know, they get all these people involved *in it*. All this energy, y'know, for weeks and weeks and *weeks*, and all this nervous *strain*. People on the edge of—*death*, practically. And *hysteria*. Wow! And the older I become, I wonder: 'What have you got on the *stage*—after all that *effort* and all that *money*? A *crock*, y'know. A *pure crock*. Worth about a *dime*. Well, *no!*"

It was in part this disappointment that sent him scudding back to Paris, low in spirits and funds, but with a richly detailed knowledge of theatrical ventures that would lend substance to the bisexual actor-hero of ANOTHER COUNTRY, Eric. There was, however, small comfort in that during the summer of 1959.

Baldwin can generally be relied upon to unburden himself to his confederates by mail, abjuring them (sometimes only figuratively), "Pray for me." In this way they can track his moods half a globe away. But now his communications dwindled. Sitting on a cafe terrace, he dashed off an appeal to his publisher for $500. And got it. For months after that, Dial heard nothing from him. Brooding over a liaison that had proved exorbitant, he went underground.

But by November he had recovered enough to withstand again the glare of the world and was rallying his American friends to an elaborate Thanksgiving feast. The flat he then occupied was about a block away from Beauford Delaney's in Petit Clamart, a Paris suburb: his rooms were directly above a country restaurant-bar, run by a tiny, amiable couple he had dubbed Pierrot and Pierrette.

"Jimmy took over the whole restaurant for Thanksgiving," says Robert Cordier, a Belgian-born writer and director who was one of the beneficiaries of Baldwin's bounty on this occasion. "Pierrot and Pierrette prepared the food while Jimmy supervised. The table was carefully arranged with autumn decorations. It was really a banquet for twenty people. Jimmy's a gourmet, a connoisseur of wine and cognac. That was a great night!"

On November 25th, the Wednesday before Thanksgiving, Gérard Philipe, the film star, had died at thirty-six. Baldwin, just a year younger, had been jolted. Not quite six weeks later, on January 4, 1960, Albert Camus, the Nobel Prize-winning novelist, was killed in an automobile crash. Baldwin was chatting with Cordier at the Café Flore, across the street from Les Deux Magots, when he heard the news.

"The waiter came over and said, 'It's terrible—Monsieur Camus has died in an accident,'" Cordier relates. "Jimmy stood up and cried out, 'Bobby!' And he ran outside. I ran after him. He looked sick and he was shaking all over. He said to me, 'I'm going to be the third to go!'"

Death—his own death—looms constantly over Baldwin, both a curse and a promise. In almost every one of his books, a boy dies, by murder or suicide: Elizabeth's lover in GO TELL IT ON THE MOUNTAIN, Giovanni in GIOVANNI'S ROOM, Rufus in ANOTHER COUNTRY, Richard in BLUES FOR MISTER CHARLIE. "I guess it's obvious," Baldwin commented not long ago, his smile apologetic, "that I'm afraid the dead boy will be me." It is as though, damned to perdition in his childhood by his stepfather, Jimmy Baldwin remains there still, holding fast to the chains of his guilt, forever atoning for nameless and unremembered sins.

Perhaps it is to alleviate this affliction and ward off worse that Baldwin so frantically surrounds himself with people. "The people who are in one's life or merely continually in one's presence reveal a great deal about one's needs and terrors," he has written. He is rarely without an entourage.

From Clamart, he would travel by bus and Metro to Paris. There his path generally took him from the American Express office, where he would stop off for mail, to a cocktail date. En route, like a sprightly, goblet-eyed Pied Piper, he invariably gathered up any acquaintances he chanced to meet. By dinner time he was likely to be the center of a merry, mobile troupe that lost some of its partisans and gained others as Baldwin completed his late hour circuit of the cafés and bars. When he headed home at last, he was infrequently alone.

Still alarmed by the Philipe-Camus sequence, Baldwin fled his appointment in Samarra, zigzagging back to New York. Early in 1960, he was commissioned by ESQUIRE to visit Harlem. The landscape of his childhood had never inspired his affection. Now Harlem winced under the yoke of his displeasure.

As a youth, Baldwin had never derived his kicks from the antisocial activities—truancy, stealing, gang war, knife-play—regarded as a test of masculinity in the adolescent subculture of the streets. He had been too rigidly policed by David Baldwin and his own fears to dabble in delinquency. Dropped for a term from De Witt Clinton's highly esteemed Publication Squad after a single experiment with hookey (his mother was summoned to the principal's office when he was found wandering through the corridors of another high school), he had been thoroughly chastened by his punishment.

Moreover, much as he now disparages it, Baldwin had learned very early to attain gratification from such socially approved outlets as writing and preaching. The truth is that he really had little need and less opportunity to resort to illicit diversions, a circumstance that led some of his classmates (and hence, of course, himself) to question his manhood.

It may be that Jimmy Baldwin was hell-bent on avenging himself for the constraint of his childhood when he went back to the neighborhood where he had been reared. Once known as the Hollow, it had been rechristened Junkie's Hollow in rueful tribute to the pastime that grants one segment of Harlem an illusion of life, liberty and the pursuit of happiness.

Where the tenement in which he grew up once stood, Baldwin found one of the high-rise housing projects he regards as anathema in Harlem ("A ghetto can be improved in one way only: out of existence"). However it was Riverton, a private residential complex then occupied by Harlem's elite, and still eminently respectable, that bore the brunt of his ire.

Assailing in a fashion still incomprehensible to them the educators, business executives, lawyers, social agency administrators, doctors and high-caste civil servants dwelling there, Baldwin described the building as "a slum" and then proceeded to flay its inhabitants with the startling claim that "they had scarcely moved in, naturally, before they began smashing windows, defacing walls, urinating in the elevators, and fornicating in the playgrounds."

This broadside was viewed by Rivertonites (and, indeed, by a substantial proportion of upper-strata Negroes everywhere) as heresy. They protested that he had confused their project with another one just across the street. Far from retracting, Baldwin issued a denial that was later included in reprints of the essay as a less than tactful footnote. In effect it was a declaration that the kid from Harlem's lower class had no intention of paying fealty to middle-class traditions.

Repercussions from this dispute may still be heard at Harlem soirées. In the homes of some of Baldwin's keenest admirers, even in homes where he has been an honored guest, there is apt to be at least one renegade whose resentment has not abated since that June day in 1960 when ESQUIRE hit the newsstands with the issue containing "Fifth Avenue Uptown: A Letter from Harlem."

Baldwin is a thorn in the side of prosperous Negroes. They almost uniformly repudiate his leadership, sneering at him as "White America's Negro spokesman." Every now and then one of them barks at him, "You don't speak for me, Jimmy Baldwin!" He pretends indifference, but he is supersensitive to any criticism from his own race.

The unenthusiastic reception a few Negro publications gave his first book still rankles. "The Negro press has been unfriendly, I think, because I come from the streets," Baldwin remarked years later, losing sight of the fact that he not only doesn't come from the streets but was rarely permitted to tour them. "I wasn't part of the Negro middle class."

For that matter, he still isn't. Even in success, he remains apart, his anarchy too ingrained—and perhaps too precious—for rehabilitation. He shuns the standards and protocol of that group of Negroes who, having forged far ahead in their chosen fields, can now be distinguished from their Caucasian prototypes only on the basis of complexion—and often not even then.

The imbroglio over Riverton left both camps embittered. "Those Negro leaders and white liberals who wanted me to return to America in 1957," Baldwin informed a reporter in his noblest, wounded-warrior accents, "now want to pay my fare back to Europe."

Yet he could rise above such infighting and vanquish his bouts of self-pity. Undergraduates, both black and white, were beginning to look to him for guidance. At Kalamazoo College in Michigan, Baldwin delivered an address that was a model of lucidity. It was also an American sequel to the essay he had written in Switzerland, "Stranger in the Village." Speaking without a text, as he usually does, Baldwin told the students:

"No one in the world—in the entire world—knows more—knows Americans better or, odd as this may sound, loves them more than the American Negro. This is because he has had to watch you, outwit you, deal with you, and bear you, and sometimes even bleed and die with you, ever since we got here—and this is a wedding. Whether I like it or not, or whether you like it or not, we are bound together forever. We are part of each other. What is happening to every Negro in the country at any time is also happening to you. There is no way around this. I am suggesting that these walls—these artificial walls—which have been up so long to protect us from something we fear, must come down . . ."

At the Florida Agricultural and Mechanical University, a Negro institution perched on the highest of Tallahassee's seven hills, the "separate but equal" version of all-white Florida State University, Baldwin had bull sessions with activists and their more reluctant fellows, exchanged views with some of their elders, watched a joint CORE chapter from both universities plan a protest prayer meeting—and contemplated the vast gap between the students' youth and his own.

"They remind me of all the Negro boys and girls I have ever known and they remind me of myself," he wrote in MADEMOI-SELLE magazine; "but, really, I was never like these students. It took many years of vomiting up all the filth I'd been taught about myself, and half believed, before I was able to walk on the earth as though I had a right to be here."

Baldwin's popularity was increasing on the campus. Yet he could still, with a fair degree of accuracy, entitle his second compilation of essays NOBODY KNOWS MY NAME. It was this "private logbook," with its wrenching report on the Southern condition, that riveted the attention of the nation. The volume became a 1961 best-seller—and the self-styled "dark horse" was transmogrified into a literary lion.

"It was at this point that I began to be officially involved with the civil rights movement," Baldwin says now. "And the students in the South began to—in some way, they *grabbed* me. This was the point where I meant something in their lives. And they began to *depend* on me more. And in effect began to *demand* of me more.

"And—it turned out that money could be raised on my name, y'know. And they needed money—to get—to pay all those terrible, terrifying court costs. And fines and bails, y'know. To get people out of *jail*—and off chain gangs. And so I began donating my time to *do* that."

For almost three years, Baldwin rode the civil rights hurricane. At any hour of any day during that incalculably wearing period, he could be deflected from the central and avowed purpose of his life, writing, by an urgent request for his presence at integration rallies, protest marches, fund drives.

"What is *interesting* about it, for me, is not so much the surface of it—the obvious drama, you know, the obvious revolution, but what one learns about people, black *and* white," Baldwin says. "Because there's no real difference *between* them. In terms of their real motives, their real terrors—and how, speaking as a novelist, you discover *really*, you know, the terrible operation, the terrible conjunction between the person and his time and his place."

But that conjunction, in his own case as fortuitous as it was terrible, elevated Baldwin to a unique position in the country. Without the freedom movement, he might have gone on articulating the Negro's interior rage and frustration as he had been doing since 1946, achieving only limited recognition for his intensely personal essays, with their flashing insights and stinging eloquence.

What thrust him into the foreground of the American scene was the swift procession of sit-ins, sleep-ins, boycotts and demonstrations staged by Negroes for Negroes. The United States was precipitated into a moral crisis that forced its citizens to take sides almost as decisively as they had been required to do during the Civil War.

For many Americans Baldwin became the egghead symbol of his race, just as Martin Luther King emerged as its spiritual touchstone. Yet the author's appeal as a polemicist, unlike Bayard Rustin's diamond-hard reasoning, was not primarily to the intellect. Always more emotional than cerebral, Baldwin was a hot, blue flame licking at the nation's collective guilt.

His passion, vast, vibrant, untrammeled, translated the mass agony of the nation's Negroes into an individual experience: his experience. White Americans had to participate in what he suffered. The Negro was no longer a comfortingly remote figure, sweating in the fields or even performing in a nightclub; now he was Jimmy Baldwin, with his accusing eyes, his disquieting words and his reassuring dimensions. Reading Baldwin, listening to him, Americans were transformed from jurors to defendants.

Some of his countrymen, not just as a mark of contrition but out of an earnest desire for justice, espoused the Negro cause by identifying themselves with James Baldwin. By them, by Negro students and by a scattering of their white contemporaries, by other Negroes who did not—perhaps could not—read him yet recognized in his fury their own, Baldwin was acknowledged as a prophet in his own country.

Even the segregationist forces—the white conservatives and ultra-conservatives who regarded the Negro advance with foreboding—unwittingly contributed to his national and international eminence. These elements searched his books and his sermons, his words and his anger, for clues to the dreaded shape of things to come. And it was all these Americans together, the fervent and the frightened, who invested Baldwin with the authority to speak for black men everywhere.

He hurtled into this role. So total was his commitment that his family (with the notable exception of his youngest brother, David) and most of his associates regularly reminded him that his most effective battle station was the typewriter, not the platform.

"What they overlook," Baldwin snapped, "is that it was exactly *because* I kept writing that all this happened." In his view, he was part of a global "convulsion of nature" rather than an American political movement.

"I don't see any way of—of escaping your role if you *have* one—in a revolution. Y'know? It's up to you somehow to figure out how to do two things at once. It's just—kind of *difficult*. But, if you're really *unhappy* in a role, you wouldn't be able to play it. I'm very *wary*. It's very important not to begin to take your identity from what other people *say* about you or what's *written* about you.

"There's absolutely no point in pretending that, at some point in my life, I'll be able to retire into some study and not—and not be *involved*. Because the way the world goes, 'these present days' is likely to go on for the next twenty *years*. That's the way the thing breaks *down*."

But Baldwin remained addicted to despair. What was in youth his cross had become with maturity his ballast, railed against, yet irresistibly familiar. He still succumbs to it, automatically, involuntarily, sliding into hopelessness the way another man might slip into a comfortable garment. Baldwin's unhappiness as a child was unbidden, his anguish unwanted; now they are a habit he cannot break, a defense he cannot surrender.

The bleakness of his threnodies is often relieved by the lightning of his perception. After interviewing Martin Luther King, Baldwin predicted that the Negro and the white man who will emerge "out of this present struggle" will need every ounce of moral stamina they can find: "For everything is changing, from our notion of politics to our notion of ourselves, and we are certain, as we begin history's strangest metamorphosis, to undergo the torment of being forced to surrender far more than we ever realized we had accepted."

It was evidently his feeling that Dr. King had passed serenely through that cycle. "King," Baldwin wrote, and the italics are his, "really loves the people he represents and has—*therefore*—no hidden, interior need to hate the white people who oppose him."

In that illuminating sentence, Baldwin was virtually sitting in judgment on himself. For he had not resolved the subterranean conflict that can afflict maligned minorities and distort their outlook. Jimmy Baldwin's own attitude toward people—and therefore himself—continues to be streaked with a galling and most painful ambivalence.

"All I wanted *is* what I *still* want. I want to be a *great writer*. And the only way to *do* that, it seems to me, is not to complain about anything that happens to you, but to *use* whatever happens to you—from starvation to champagne . . ."

Twelve

Tyrannized by ANOTHER COUNTRY, Baldwin was still grappling with it tenaciously during the opening weeks of 1961, astonished that he hadn't "fatally miscarried" during his long pregnancy, yet convinced that the novel was far too important to be ruined by haste. He had revamped his concept of the book three times but the moment—always for him unmistakable—had not yet come when he would assume command of the material that until then seemed to command him.

Baldwin refers to ANOTHER COUNTRY as "the easiest" of his fictional works. But this is a minor lapse, swiftly amended. "That book almost *killed* me," he says. "The Rufus suicide scene—the whole section of Rufus—I must have written that about—at *least* four times." Until the final draft, the interlocking elements refused to mesh: "I never could finish that book properly—until I was in *Turkey* . . ."

In his effort to master the novel's crisscrossing relationships—racial, sensual, professional, national—Baldwin shifted the locale from a New England town to New York to Paris, before moving it back once again to New York. At one point he planned to redo the entire book, telling the story through a Negro narrator, a Southerner modeled on his old friend Beauford Delaney. On another occasion the character of Yves, a young homosexual Frenchman, was projected as the heavy who would steal the Negro heroine, Ida, from her white lover. And Ida herself, the figure with whom Baldwin was most concerned, simmering with his own rage, swathed in his own bafflement, was to have wound up as a patient in a psychotic ward, a fate reserved in the published version for a white girl.

In Manhattan, in Paris and at the MacDowell Colony in New Hampshire, Baldwin patiently erected the scaffolding for AN-OTHER COUNTRY, only to rip it down again. He was living in a monastic flat in lower Manhattan when he began to barrel along, at last making headway. But the interruptions were too frequent, the preliminary demands of the revolution too consuming. In this crisis, author William Styron and his wife offered to shelter Baldwin in their guest cottage, a separate unit adjoining their home in Roxbury, Connecticut.

The two writers had been introduced to each other at a Manhattan dinner party, where they had sung gospel songs together with such notable harmony that Baldwin, whose bookkeeping has not improved since he flunked his high school course with a 42, borrowed five dollars from Styron ("and never paid it back, come to think of it," Styron chortles). Later, James Jones brought the New Yorker and the Virginian together again in Paris, and their friendship had ripened there as they loitered in the cafés until the early hours of the morning.

"When I got back from Europe, Jimmy was floating around New York, not yet a big figure, but beginning to be harassed," Styron explains. "One day I picked him up in Manhattan and we drove up to Roxbury with a considerable amount of his baggage, and he established residence for some four or five months in the cottage. He wasn't with us consistently, but for as long as ten days or a couple of weeks at a time, from February to July 4th, I think it was.

"Jimmy is alternately wonderful and exasperating as a guest. The exasperating part is only that you can never tell when he'll come back. With most people, there's an overall law-of-average chance that one out of twenty times they won't show up for an appointment; with Jimmy, the odds are just exactly reversed. Literally nine out of ten times, he doesn't show. It's a kind of psychic quirk."

On the whole, the Styrons enjoyed Baldwin's company. They would linger after dinner, sipping their drinks, until he upended his final scotch on the rocks and walked back to the cottage, there to labor on his book most of the night.

An unabashed ham, Baldwin can be prevented only by force from reading his work aloud to a live audience. He once promised his sister Gloria he would take her out for a birthday dinner; instead he celebrated the occasion by reading to her in its entirety his lengthiest essay, then recently finished, while she nibbled hungrily at a remnant of sandwich. But the Styrons listened sympathetically as Baldwin read them chunks of his manuscript, fifteen or twenty pages at a clip.

"It was very difficult to get by listening, but he preferred reading it to my wife and me," Styron says. "And that was all right with us. I think he was proud in a way that all writers are proud when they know their work is going the way they want it to be."

Although Baldwin boasts that he is a superior cook, unexcelled at cornbread, fried chicken, spaghetti and biscuits, he rarely exhibits his culinary skill in the United States. But several times he prepared delectable spareribs for the Styrons. Mrs. Styron's reign over the kitchen was otherwise uncontested. "We managed," Styron reports with the faintest trace of smugness, "to feed Jimmy fairly well."

During his stay in Roxbury, Baldwin was persistently pursued by liberal ladies with amorous inclinations. "He'd given one lecture at Westport," Styron recalls. "Afterward, I went to the reception to bring Jimmy back up here. There was a Mrs. X: well-married she was, but quite smitten with Jimmy. He wasn't interested in her, but two or three times a week she'd drive up in her Volkswagen, with her guitar, and hang around the cottage for hours while Jimmy would work upstairs.

"It was really quite amusing because he would try to outlast her. But she would wait for an audience. And, in the late afternoon, he would come down and they'd sit and have a drink. I think she wanted to move in with him. Every time she left, he'd groan, 'Oh, God!' But he was successful in giving her the impression that he was delighted to see her."

As warm weather advanced, so did the swarm of friends, near-friends and would-be friends who had precipitated Baldwin's departure from New York. Violating the quiet of Roxbury, they closed in on their willing prey.

"There were people who would call Jimmy whom he found it irresistible to allow to intrude upon him," Styron observes. "So there were plenty of visitors who began to clutter up the place, particularly in the spring—Lucien Happersberger (whom I like very much), along with the sycophantic, nauseating group. I've never seen a guy who can attract so many people to whom I respond with a distinct plus or negative!"

Baldwin and Styron have always hit it off well, and the latter is inclined to attribute much of the quality of their understanding to his Southern birth: "I've been there, as Jimmy would put it. I've had to come a long way. I've had a long struggle with myself in terms of eliminating a lot of nasty things about race. But that's not all of it. I think there's some kind of subtle rapport we have, a mutual respect for each other's work. Which is not true of many writers, since the respect is often obscured by envy or malice."

While in the throes of creativity, Baldwin regularly progresses from one house to another, rather like a medieval king traveling through his realm, dispensing royal favor by granting honored subjects the privilege of serving as his host.

From Connecticut, Baldwin moved on to Westchester, settling down for close to two months in a wing of his publisher's spacious establishment. "He was in isolation when he started," comments Richard Baron, George Joel's successor as the head of Dial Press. "Then everyone found him."

In September, Baldwin cut out for Europe, carrying with him his novel. Before he left, however, he arranged for his youngest sister, Paula Maria, then eighteen, to join him in Paris. "He wanted to show me there was something besides Harlem," she observes.

The teen-ager arrived in Paris just as it was developing into a plastique battleground, a grim extension of the Algerian situation. Installed in a small hotel on the Left Bank, Paula Maria leaned heavily on her brother. "He was like two crutches," she says with a ghost of a smile. "I gave him a hard time. It was the first time I'd been away from my mother.

"Jimmy showed me around for two weeks. He was very patient, very gentle, very sweet. He took me to friends' homes and we sat in cafés a lot. Every morning—well, it was one or two in the afternoon, really—I'd meet him at the Deux Magots and we'd sit there, opposite the church. And every day I ordered a ham sandwich and Coca Cola. Jimmy would laugh and say, 'You're not in America any more.' He'd order coffee and drinks. What is that green drink? Pernod? That's what I think it was."

Baldwin had promised himself that, by commuting across the Atlantic, he could work several months in Europe and then spend the rest of the year in the United States, "being a public figure." But even this compromise was not feasible. He could now walk down almost any street and watch fame attend him like a courtier. He flew to Israel, where the ingathering of Jews from every corner of the globe only sharpened his sense of homelessness, and then on to Istanbul, where he was warmly welcomed by Engin Cezzar's sister and brother-in-law.

"When Jimmy went away, I was scared," Paula confesses sadly. "I learned a lot, but I don't think I was ready for Paris." Before Christmas, she bolted back to Harlem and her mother.

In Istanbul, Baldwin's perspective snapped into focus and he seized control of his book. He could then reconstruct Rufus' suicide scene, which duplicates that of Eugene Worth, Baldwin's bosom companion back in Greenwich Village, who had leaped into the Hudson River back in 1946. And Rufus, like Worth, kills himself after a disastrous love affair. Similarly each of the other characters in ANOTHER COUNTRY is a monument to some segment of the author's life.

"Once I got the suicide scene licked—that was the beginning of the book, y'know—I was able to write the *last* scene with Ida and Vivaldo, which is at the *end* of the book," Baldwin says.

On December 10, 1961, by his own account a bit hysterical, yet confident that the book had been achieved, he airmailed the manuscript to Jim Silberman at Dial ("Take it away, baby, and please let me hear from you"). He spent Christmas in Paris with Mary Painter, then recuperated from his customary postnatal depression—and a siege of bronchitis—by involving himself in a Swiss television filming of "Stranger in the Village" in Loeche-les-Bains.

In April, glutted with foreign places, he was lecturing at Monterey College in California. When the last palpitating student had departed, Baldwin realized he had fifteen unparalleled days of freedom on his calendar.

He flew East. From New York, he went on to Norwalk, Connecticut, and the residence of Robert P. Mills, then his literary agent, a skyscraping, cordial, unassuming man, fanatically dedicated to his client, with some of the cragginess of his native Montana in his face.

"Jimmy is fine as a house guest," says Mills. "The only drawback—which develops after a while—is when he begins to invite people up. He gets very restless in the country and can't sleep. At my house, if he went to bed as early as two or three A.M., he usually read. Possibly an anthology of mystery stories or William Roughhead, who is an English, quality, true-crime writer. But, if Jimmy is working, he may work all night. I'd hear the typewriter going when I left in the morning."

While in Norwalk, Baldwin plunged into the long essay he then called "Meanwhile, Down at the Levee," which was ultimately to form the major portion of THE FIRE NEXT TIME. He raced through two thirds of it in a little more than two weeks before getting hung up on the ending.

The two Mills children were overjoyed by Baldwin's visit. "Jimmy," Mills says, "is very responsive with kids." He is also unexpectedly firm with them. So permissive in other areas, Baldwin advocates that adults set well-defined limits for the young, and he himself neither spoils nor patronizes them.

"My wife and kids were away for a few days while Jimmy was staying with me," Mills says. "He told me not to worry because he would cook. He made hamburgers for us once. He burned them. He made hamburgers another time. After that, we accepted invitations for dinner or ate out."

Subsequently Sam Floyd, a young schoolteacher who had been

Baldwin's downstairs neighbor in Greenwich Village in 1958, extended his hospitality to the writer. Within hours of his arrival, Baldwin had alerted his acquaintances to his whereabouts. The phone rang all day and most of the night. His claque treated the flat on Horatio Street as an informal clubhouse. Baldwin's temper clouded. Finally he could contain his anger no longer.

"I'm leaving your house because it's become too *public,*" he informed his host, outraged.

"Jimmy not only meant it," says Floyd, still amused, "but he packed up and left."

Baldwin next moved in with Alex and Majorie Karmel, colleagues he had met in Paris almost a decade earlier. Out of the depths of some private idyll, Mrs. Karmel rhapsodized to Floyd: "Oh, how lovely it's going to be. Three writers, working in separate rooms all day, getting together in the evening to compare notes . . ."

It didn't work out quite that way. The locusts promptly descended on the Karmel household, disrupting the children's routine and exasperating the adults. The two telephones shrilled incessantly, almost always for Baldwin. "There was a party every night," Karmel reports good-naturedly. "People would start drifting in about ten: Jimmy's family, which is a sizable unit in itself; friends; others who were just interested in Jimmy because he was getting to be rather like a movie star. They never left before four in the morning. Having Jimmy at your house isn't like having a guest—it's like entertaining a caravan."

On June 25th, the official publication date of ANOTHER COUNTRY, Baldwin was submitting to a spate of interviews. The volume was being acclaimed and damned in almost equal proportions—and, at least once, by the same newspaper (THE NEW YORK TIMES rendered a verdict of "strained" in its Sunday Book Review section and, two days later, in the daily book column, described the novel as "brilliantly and fiercely told"); the reviewers' reaction to Baldwin has rarely been temperate.

Bruised and "briefly demoralized," he told Martha MacGregor of the NEW YORK POST: "No matter what the critics say, a writer knows if he's done his best. I've written things I've thought were failures. This may be a failure, but it's not a lie. The people who like the book like it very much; people who loathe it absolutely hate it . . .

"What I was trying to do was to create for the first time my own apprehension of the country and the world. I understood that if I could discharge venom, I could discharge love (they frighten me equally). When I was a little boy, I hated all white people, but in this book I got beyond the hate. I don't care what anybody says; I faced my life by that book, and it's a good book. It's as honest as I can be."

But the mixed grill of erotica in ANOTHER COUNTRY led one critic to inquire plaintively, "Does everyone in the known world lust heterosexually and homosexually for the bodies of Negroes?" The novel climaxed Baldwin's personal confusion over the relationship between sex and race. In ANOTHER COUNTRY, the boundaries between the two are curiously blurred. Baldwin, decrying America's prejudice against homosexuals as well as Negroes, hints that the nation's ultimate salvation lies in the acceptance of both minorities.

Undeniably there are powerful and beautiful passages in ANOTHER COUNTRY. Just as undeniably, the less standard varieties of sex are consistently sugared over and sentimentalized, with many —but not all—of the couplings between homosexual and heterosexual, Negro and white, in most of their possible equations, glorified as the apotheosis of love.

The reservations held by the critical brotherhood were not shared by the readers, who ardently embraced ANOTHER COUNTRY. Baldwin was driving up Park Avenue one afternoon with his publisher, his editor and his agent when a red light stopped them. A blonde girl in the next car, recognizing the author, waved a copy of the novel and called out in a honeyed drawl, "My daddy says the language is terrible, but I think the book is great!" It was a memorable encounter and Baldwin loved every fleeting second of it.

On June 28th, Dial gave a press reception for Baldwin at his favorite Harlem restaurant, Small's Paradise. "It was wild," says Baron with satisfaction. Almost every celebrity in town was included on the guest list, and a number of those who weren't crashed the party anyway. So did a brazen representative of another publishing house, who arrived with a little actress from LA DOLCE VITA on his arm. A critic who had cast a "nay" ballot, defying custom, wallowed shamelessly in Dial's hospitality. Even Irita Van Doren, the grande dame of the NEW YORK HERALD

TRIBUNE's literary section, who was invited everywhere and seen hardly anywhere, dropped by.

By some alchemy, compounded perhaps of such ingredients as Baldwin's ebullience, the Harlem background, hot jazz and the interracial interaction, the affair was a resounding success. The unbending bent, the tense relaxed, notorious squares appeared almost hip and one chronically troubled editor, abandoning himself to the gyrations of the twist, was overheard declaring breathlessly, to no one in particular, "I've never had such a good time." All the worlds of Jimmy Baldwin merged on that jubilant night into one.

"It was a fabulous party," says a participant. "I'm afraid to think why!" His enigmatic postscript conceivably proves just the point Baldwin was trying to make in his book. In any case, the party lifted him out of the doldrums. "Jimmy," Baron says, "really had a ball."

On this glad note, Baldwin set out for Africa. He had repeatedly postponed his journey there, grateful when illness intervened, fearful that he would loathe the land of his forefathers.

"My bones know, somehow," he had written Bob Mills from Israel in the fall of 1951, "something of what waits for me in Africa. That is one of the reasons I have dawdled so long—I'm afraid. And, of course, I am playing it my own way, edging myself into it: it would be nice to be able to dream about Africa, but once I have been there, I will not be able to dream any more. The truth is that there is something unutterably painful about the end of oppression—not that it *has* ended yet, on a black-white basis, I mean, but it *is* ending—and one flinches from the responsibility, which we all now face, of judging black people solely as people."

But when he finally kept his long-deferred engagement with that continent, he discovered that all his premonitions and anxieties had been baseless.

"I was afraid of *all* kinds of things," he says happily. "None of them turned out to be true. *None* of them. It was very strange. I was afraid I'd—you know, be put *down*. Because I was an *American*. I was also *afraid*, on another level, that perhaps something in *me* would put down the Africans *because* I was an American, you know.

"I didn't feel *any* of these things. It was *marvelous*. Something in me *recognized* it. Recognized it *all*. I was never uneasy in myself—in view of, you know, *them*. I saw African girls walking down the streets, in their—with their babies on their backs and their groceries on their heads. And they all looked to me, in all West Africa, whether they were English owned or French owned (ex-English, ex-French), like girls I'd seen on *Lenox Avenue*. Something about the way they *walked*, something about the way they *looked*. It was not unfamiliar. They even had a certain *style* which I recognized. From somewhere—from *Harlem*."

He was accompanied on his African initiation by his sister, Mrs. Gloria Davis, a young divorcée, pencil-slim, poised, pretty, chic. "You need someone to get you going places, to keep your appointments, you know, to—act as a buffer between you and the *world*," Baldwin says. "And also I wanted Gloria to *see* Africa. I thought it might be *fun*."

They traveled down the west coast of Africa, from Senegal to Ghana. A long-distance reproach caught up with them in Free-town, Sierra Leone, where a letter from Mills briefed them on the commitments Baldwin had left behind: books, essays, short sto-ries, three movie scripts, copy for a school for emotionally dis-turbed boys; number twenty-two on this list included "fifty commitments you've made that I don't know about," while items fifty-one through fifty-seven covered "commitments I probably do know about and have forgotten."

But Baldwin, almost euphoric with relief, was buoyantly giving himself to Africa. He and his sister were childishly gratified when Africans failed to identify them as Americans throughout the ten-week trip. "They thought Gloria and I probably came from Dahomey—from one of the colonies, one of the islands, but *not* from *America*," he says.

Baldwin had no sense of homecoming in Africa. He felt instead a great weight of responsibility: "Because—it sounds pretentious, but—whatever is going to happen in Africa, I was in one way or another involved. Or *affected* by it, certainly. But I couldn't—but I didn't feel it could happen on the basis of *color*. But Gloria and I loved Africa. I want to go back. I have a lot to learn there."

Pleased with his pleasure in Africa, he could settle down at his typewriter. He moved on to Turkey and again applied himself to the piece he had begun at Mills' house in Connecticut. Baldwin is always a little lost until he selects a working title. He may toss one off as he is crossing a street or having a drink ("It always *starts* with a title," says his brother David).

"Meanwhile, Down at the Levee" became "Down at the Cross" in Istanbul, where Baldwin wrote his third ending for the essay. This time he was satisfied. Ironically, something of the spirit of stern admonition with which Harriet Beecher Stowe concluded UNCLE TOM'S CABIN had somehow clung to Baldwin over the years and across the miles.

His supple, sinuous style has little in common with hers, of course. Yet there are haunting parallels between his final paragraphs and those of his predecessor. In his jeremiad, Baldwin warns that the intransigence of the white world may make God's vengeance inevitable, but holds out the hope that we can avert disaster if we are unfaltering in our obligation to terminate the racial nightmare. Then he draws upon the Old Testament for a dire prediction:

"If we do not dare everything, the fulfillment of that prophecy, re-created from the Bible in song by a slave, is upon us: *God gave Noah the rainbow sign, No more water, the fire next time!*"

A century earlier, in the fictionalized anti-slavery brief that was to entrance Baldwin as a child and irk him as an adult, Mrs. Stowe had also indulged in fiery metaphor. The day of judgment, she wrote, "shall burn as an oven" and the oppressors shall be broken into pieces. But there was still a period of grace in which to extend freedom and equality to the Negro:

Both North and South have been guilty before God; and the Christian church has a heavy account to answer. Not by combining together, to protect injustice and cruelty, and making a common capital of sin, is this Union to be saved,—but by repentance, justice and mercy; for not surer is the eternal law by which the millstone sinks into the ocean, than that stronger law, by which injustice and cruelty shall bring on nations the wrath of Almighty God!

Mrs. Stowe had more than evened the score. Discarded and disdained by Baldwin, she yet managed to exact from him involuntary homage. (But her final triumph still lay two years ahead, when UNCLE TOM'S CABIN was to be ranked by Baldwin—along with Dostoevsky's THE POSSESSED, CRIME AND PUNISHMENT and THE

BROTHERS KARAMAZOV, Henry James' THE PRINCESS CASAMASSIMA and THE PORTRAIT OF A LADY, Dickens' A TALE OF TWO CITIES, Ralph Ellison's INVISIBLE MAN, Richard Wright's BLACK BOY and Charles Wright's THE MESSENGER—among the ten books that had helped him break out of the ghetto.)

On October 2, 1962, Baldwin delivered his 20,000-word essay to Bob Mills in New York. Just six weeks later, retitled by the publication "Letter from a Region in My Mind," it was printed in the November 17th issue of THE NEW YORKER, blazing across eighty-five part-pages.

For this fusion of autobiography, American history and global politics into a document as personal as the blood coursing through his veins, Baldwin received $6,500—and a reputation as the most valuable literary property in the country. Almost overnight, with THE NEW YORKER's prestige undoubtedly furnishing some of the booster power, the piece rocketed into prominence; it was required reading among in-groups, and its author's name became a national byword.

The brouhaha of public acclaim invaded Baldwin's life, stamping out the last vestiges of his privacy. His professional timetable, always disorganized, collapsed. In his Manhattan walk-up, the telephone rang right around the clock. His unlisted number was changed frequently to thwart celebrity-stalkers, but Baldwin would genially supply it upon request—provided, of course, that he happened to remember it.

"Instead of people saying, 'What do you do?', they say, 'Won't you do this?'" he explained. "And you become, or you could become, a Very Important Person. And then—this is a confession —you find yourself in the position of a woman I don't know who sings a certain song in a certain choir, and the song begins: 'I said I wasn't gonna tell nobody but I couldn't keep it to myself.'"

Everyone he met, everyone he had ever met and thousands more he had never met pressed demands upon him. "If Jimmy accepted all the speaking invitations that come across his desk," said his brother David, "he'd be speaking for three years and never write. You find all sorts of people coming up to him with 'Loan me this' or 'Get me that.' People take advantage of Jimmy very often because of the kind of person he is. He can't say no."

Baldwin's inability to say no is a legend promulgated by his family and perpetuated by his associates. Like most legends, this is only partially accurate. Baldwin can and does say no, indirectly but no less effectively, through intermediaries. What scrambles his calendar is his habit of routinely, cordially and even quite sincerely consenting to all engagements proposed to him, relying upon the services of a hapless secretary or business connection to extricate him (often at the thirteenth hour) from inconvenient or undesirable arrangements.

Thus the disagreeable duty of breaking appointments to which Baldwin has almost certainly acquiesced, but cannot or will not keep, in the end falls on someone else's shoulders. And so he continues to say yes when he really means no, with only a few of his intimates capable of discerning the difference.

"The fact that I'd become famous—meant that I was everybody's *target*," Baldwin says. The occasions provoking his negative-imbedded-in-an-affirmative responses proliferated. To have a drink at the nearby White Horse Tavern or dine at the El Faro Restaurant was "suicidal," he contends, half believing it. Then, with a burst of laughter that creases his thin cheeks into vertical folds, he says:

"You know, I really am very *gullible*. If you tell me a story, I'll *listen* to it. And while I'm listening to you, I'll *believe* it. Really. It's *fantastic*. I don't care *what* the story is—*any* story, y'know, no matter *what* you're saying, it just *fascinates* me. And, of course, people find that very attractive. You know, people *love* to be listened to. And I can't *help* it! I really *do* believe it—as you're saying it. And even believe it *longer* than that, y'know. If you *insist* I *believe* it, I keep on *believing* it. It happens all the *time*. It's too bad, maybe.

"But I say no when I *have* to. If I couldn't say no, I'd be *dead*. But I don't say no until I *have* to—and I *dread* it. I need somebody to do that for me. But when the chips are down, I can say no. If it's important enough—a matter of—life—or death, I can be very *ruthless*. I have to, you know. I don't *like* to, but I *can* be."

However much he contributes to it, the chaos that besets Baldwin is genuine enough. Through it all, he has remained faithful to the credo he recommends as a practical technique for survival, hemispheric as well as personal. "Go for broke," he urges.

It is his conviction that safety is at best illusory. "If you accept the fact that you never will be safe," he told a group of lawyers at

Town Hall, "then you will be on the road to the only real safety. One day everybody in this room—me and even *you*, honey—will be dead."

"Go for broke" is at once a measure of his suffering and a means of communicating whatever wisdom he has extracted from the experience. It is never intended to invoke the more orthodox forms of heroism. "I *know* that I'm afraid," he says. "Most people, I think, *deny* it—yes, even to themselves."

Baldwin has developed a tolerance for both peril and his own rubber-legged response to it. He demonstrated that graphically in the waning hours of 1962, at the home of June Shagaloff, the strikingly handsome brunette who is the Educational Director of the National Association for the Advancement of Colored People —and the most recent recruit to the rarefied ranks of Baldwin intimates. Miss Shagaloff, whose devotion to Baldwin matches that of Mary Painter, presided over a New Year's Eve party in his honor. Shortly before midnight, Baldwin put in a call to actor Rip Torn, a Southerner.

"It was snowing," Torn recalls. "Earlier in the evening, I said to my wife [actress Geraldine Page], 'Why don't we have this New Year's just for us?' I opened a bottle of champagne and we watched television. Then the phone rang. It was Jimmy. We had promised to have at least a drink with him and he wanted us to come over right away.

"I said, 'We're not getting out of this house tonight for anyone.' And Jimmy said: 'But you don't understand. I'm going down South tomorrow. And I'm frightened.'"

Early the next morning, Torn picked up Baldwin. His terror had not abated. But, escorted to the airport in a cab by his friend and his customary retinue, comforted by some cookies Torn had thoughtfully stolen from his wife's secret hoard, fueled by a bottle of scotch, Jimmy Baldwin finally got on the plane and flew South to keep a rendezvous with James Meredith in Mississippi.

As soon as Meredith had become the first Negro to infringe on the alabaster sanctity of the University of Mississippi, braving (with the aid of United States marshals) the frothing packs of segregationists and the primitive tortures devised by some of his fellow collegians, Baldwin had fired off a telegram.

"I said he should let me know if there was anything I could do to help him," Baldwin says. "We finally got together via the phone. We wanted to meet each other. And I couldn't make it until New Year's Day. And I was scared—because I'd never been to Jackson, Mississippi, before."

By then Baldwin had been to many places "*like* that," of course. But he still mistrusted himself in the deep South: "I didn't know what I would say to any of those cops, you know. I never *had* known. It's a principal terror when I'm down there. Anything I *did* might not only endanger me but might endanger everybody else, too. Which is really kind of nerve-racking. You're frightened all the *time*—because nobody wants to die! Or to get, you know, his balls cut off. Or have an eye put out. Nobody looks forward to that."

Baldwin spent three days with Meredith. It must have been a strained interlude for both men. Certainly Baldwin's response to the situation was atypical: "He was very quiet," Meredith says now. Perhaps the writer's customary loquaciousness was tamed by fear, although it was not apparent to his host. But it is possible that Meredith himself nonplussed the New Yorker.

If a battery of scientists had fed into a computer Jimmy Baldwin's personality traits and then asked for his diametric opposite, the answer might well have been, "James H. Meredith." Baldwin's passage through life is a collision course, veering from immoderate grief to a wonderful, cockeyed gaiety.

But Meredith is capable of asserting, ". . . I have never made a mistake in my life, because I never make arbitrary or predetermined decisions." (This statement predated his Mississippi "march for freedom" in 1966, when he was wounded by a sniper.) A teetotaler and nonsmoker, he is rigid, disciplined, reserved, with a mystic belief in his "Divine Responsibility." He spent nine happy years in the Air Force and acknowledges that what he really would have preferred above all else was to have been a general. To Baldwin, who probably could not endure nine days in uniform, Meredith must have seemed like some baffling new species.

"He is one of the noblest people I have met," Baldwin says now. Meredith counters: "He watched more than he spoke, and he was very brave." Told that Baldwin was also very frightened, Meredith looks genuinely surprised. "Maybe that's why he said so little," he says finally. "But he enjoyed himself, I think, at a New Year's Day party I took him to."

There was plenty of hog jowl, black-eyed peas, cornbread, music and dancing, a pastime Baldwin indulges in with alacrity. "The best that I can say about Baldwin's dancing," Meredith noted laconically in his recent book, "is that he is game. He was a strange sight doing the New York twist at a Mississippi house party."

When the young Mississippian and his pride of marshals headed back to the campus, Baldwin rode off into the backwoods. His guide was Medgar Evers, the NAACP's chief representative in that state, who was to be slain outside his own house only a short time later. But, on that January afternoon, Evers was probing a murder that had been reported to him by letter.

"An extremely illiterate letter," Baldwin says. "About a Negro who had been shot—*and* killed—in, I think, DeKalb County. He'd been buried in November. And somebody wrote to Medgar, asking him if he could do anything about it. And Medgar drove out—you know, to find out if he *could* do anything about it. He was a great man. A *great* man. He had the calm of somebody who knows he's going to die, in a way. Who knows—not that he's going to be *shot*, but that what he's doing may cost him his life.

"That was a terrible journey. People talked to us behind locked doors, lights down—and out of the sides of their mouths. We found out what had happened. But there was nothing you could do about it. Because it was done by a private citizen, not by the sheriff, as it turned out. Medgar had hoped it *was* the sheriff—in which case, he might get the Justice Department to move.

"But the man had been killed by a white storekeeper. So far as Medgar and I could tell—the man was killed because the white storekeeper liked his wife. The man who *killed* him was quite old. The details are very hazy. I never made any notes about it. What I was interested in, really, was the climate. And Medgar. He was a *beautiful* man."

Somewhere on the backroads he transversed with Evers, Baldwin glimpsed a small church. "I was very oppressed that day by things we'd seen," he later told Kay Boyle in a televised interview. "And I was very aware that we were in the deep South and I'd been very close to my father's birthplace. And it suddenly struck me that *this* church must have been very much like the church in which my father preached before he ever came *North*.

"And I looked into the window . . . It was a *country* church. I suddenly saw that I could put that piano and that pulpit and those benches and the cross and that *peculiar, horrible* and moving painting of our Lord and Savior, Jesus Christ, *on* the stage."

In time, he did put that country church on the stage, just as he had put its Harlem counterpart into THE AMEN CORNER. For the murder committed by the white storekeeper and investigated that day in Mississippi by Evers, pieced together with elements of the Emmett Till case, were to form the plot structure of Baldwin's second play, BLUES FOR MISTER CHARLIE, dedicated: "To the memory of Medgar Evers, and his widow and his children, and to the memory of the dead children of Birmingham."

Back in Jackson after his expedition with Evers, Baldwin set off on a speaking tour for CORE. Trailed by a reporter-photographer team from LIFE, he streaked through the South. He preached from a pulpit in New Orleans, his stepfather's home town ("As soon as we are discontent with what you've told us is our place, we destroy your myth of the happy nigger, the noble savage, the shiftless, watermelon-eating darkie"). He preached in Durham, North Carolina ("I know you didn't own a plantation or rape my grandmother, but I wasn't bought at auction either—and you still treat me as if I had been").

In two days, he delivered eight talks, only five of them scheduled. On the morning he was to fly to Greensboro, North Carolina, he overslept and missed his flight. Rather than disappoint CORE's audience, he paid $680 for a chartered plane. As the two-engine craft nosed toward Greensboro, Baldwin murmured, "What's money for?"

He could afford such extravagances. The man who had known famine for more than three decades could now observe casually, "I like caviar when I'm in Portugal." Although a proviso in his contract with Dial put a $15,000 ceiling on the amount doled out to him annually, Baldwin could in a pinch draw upon a much lustier six-figure reserve that had accumulated in his account.

His income had nosed into the upper bracket very slowly, outstripped by his generosity toward his family. While he had been abroad, the Baldwins had struggled through difficult and arid years. They had dropped off the relief rolls only when the three younger boys, George, Wilmer and David (to whom Baldwin dedicated his second book of essays), could supplement their mother's scant wages with their own pay from jobs or Army service.

Strapped as they were, George, the sibling Jimmy Baldwin had most resented as a child, somehow managed to wire a few dollars to Paris whenever prolonged fasting reduced the emigré to writing home for a handout. "While Jimmy was in Europe," Paula Baldwin says, "George took care of the family."

But he was relieved of that burden as soon as the earnings of his older brother climbed above the subsistence mark. Perhaps in atonement for the past, the writer now regards his resources primarily as an emergency fund for the Baldwins. Driven by a need to guarantee their future against penury, he periodically confides to associates his anxieties about maintaining the present lofty level of his finances.

On January 31, 1963, THE FIRE NEXT TIME was released. The slender volume was saluted with booming salvos from coast to coast, with only a few of the commentators carping that the text was brilliant but muddled. For the second time within seven months, Baldwin was wedged high on the best-seller list. For forty-one consecutive weeks, THE FIRE NEXT TIME was grouped among the top five, a record virtually unprecedented for an essay.

Torn between his allegiance to the civil rights movement and his obligation to himself as an artist, Baldwin grew haggard and fretful. He lectured, appeared on television, delivered radio addresses, spoke with newspapermen. "His doctor says he's living on nervous energy," his mother said, worried. Quaffing a chalky potion prescribed by his physician, Baldwin reported glumly, "It's the only thing that keeps me *alive*." But he had embarked on his second play.

In the aftermath of ANOTHER COUNTRY, Baldwin was given to periodic reiteration of his ambition: "I intend to become a *great novelist*," he would announce. Each time he sounded as though he were intoning a vow, possibly in defiance of critical insistence that he was primarily an essayist.

"I was not—*anxious*—to give people one more occasion to say, 'Well, he can't write plays *either*,'" Baldwin says now. In the living room of his Manhattan apartment, with its shoji screen, twin brown couches, black area rug and rectangular glass coffee table, everything is still new and gleaming, as though the price tags had just been removed. Only Baldwin himself looks worn. He picks up a can of beer, stares unseeing at the two neat punctures, and then cradles it in the palm of his left hand.

"So—the way I *did* it was to blackmail myself into doing it by saying I was doing a *play*." He grimaces. "And—saying it so *often* and so *loud* that, sooner or later, somebody would say, 'Where is that goddamned play?' " He rises and paces the room, rubbing the small of his back. "It was the only way I could *do* it!

"I didn't believe I could *write* a play. I was just too *terrified* by the *form*. And I didn't dare *allow* myself to think about trying to get it done. The question was trying to get it *written*." Baldwin seats himself listlessly at the teak dining table. A lamp suspended from the ceiling sways, splashing a play of light and shadow over his face, but his eyes are inscrutable behind dark glasses.

"I'm in very bad shape," he says. "I have a cold in my back and a hangover." He tilts the can to his mouth and takes a swig. "And," he adds morosely, as though issuing a warning, "I'm in a bad mood." Then he drains the rest of the beer.

". . . There's a fantastic amount of energy on the part of people who have *never* ruled the world and that never ruled the world in the memory of anyone *living*, which is coming *into* the world. I mean the people previously subjugated—I mean Africans, I mean Latins, I mean Orientals, I mean *all* the people who, according to our peculiar theology, are not *white*. You know? Whom *we*, in the West, defined and described for so long. Who always *resented* that *definition* and that description. And are about to correct it."

Thirteen

As the freedom movement accelerated, Baldwin quickened his own tempo, spinning faster and farther, seemingly in several directions at once. "The times are catching up with me," he remarked, "and now I have to branch off and keep moving ahead. The times always catch up—if one isn't careful."

Stabbed by the fear that Negroes might suspect him of having sold out, he had a compulsion to prove his innocence. "When a Negro becomes famous, he's assumed by the bulk of those he helplessly represents to have become a whore," he said. He said it often, recoiling from the thought that he might be charged with having sacrificed his integrity to the bitch goddess, Success.

"I'd rather be eaten by dogs or put in a concentration camp than betray them in any way," he declared. "You know, the real point is that people like me and Harry Belafonte and even Martin Luther King are not Negro *leaders*. We're doing our best to find out where the people are and to follow them."

Toward this end he unleashed that "rage of the disesteemed" that was still his, that he has said will always be his, and flogged America with it. A note of desperation pervaded his preaching. Like every professional lecturer, Baldwin developed a series of set pieces that could be reshuffled to suit the occasion. But his heightened intensity surged through them all, sweeping his listeners into the turbulence that was his native habitat.

What had been essentially a warning to America gradually acquired the overtones of a threat: the conflagration promised for "next time" might consume the nation today. Goading his audiences, simultaneously goaded by them, he sometimes edged perilously close to the hate philosophy of the Black Muslims, whose segregationist doctrines he had unequivocally rejected in "Down at the Cross."

On an intellectual level, Baldwin still rejects them. But he confesses to emotional ambivalence toward the advocates of Negro supremacy. It could hardly be otherwise. To have lived a lifetime under the grotesque ground rules devised by this country's ethnic majority cannot but induce in black Americans a sudden, liberating (even if unwanted) elation at the notion that the racist principles so long operative against them can be reversed. In fantasy, at least, retribution is its own reward.

"From my own point of view," Baldwin says, "the Black Muslims are just like the white *power* structure, y'know. And I simply don't *believe* most white people when they object to what they call inverted racism. They never objected to it *before*, y'know. And they *profit* by it, y'know—[by] the other inverted racism. So I don't take their moral proclamations seriously at all.

"On the other hand, I think of the Muslim movement as being terribly, terribly *dangerous*. Dangerously frightening, from my point of view, because of what it can do to Negroes as—considered purely as people. Dangerous because—it's dangerous for *any* group of people, you know, to—believe they are superior to any other group of people. For *any* reason. And I think it's spiritually fatal, y'know. Inevitably so.

"And yet I can also see that it's the very *intransigence* of a dying structure—because the West as we know it *is* dying. There's no question about it. And this intransigence on the part of people who think of themselves as white will add fuel to the Muslim movement—and not only the Muslim movement—for generations to come.

"In fact, it is *more* than probable—that the days we're living through will turn into a *race* war—and that people will have to make *alliances on* that basis. And that they *will*, y'know. And someone like *me*, someone like *Lucien*"—Happersberger, just returning from an errand on which Baldwin had sent him, looks startled—"will *perish*. In the *middle*. Because I *can't* make my alignments on the basis of color."

But it was on the basis of his color that he was sought out by the mass media. For them, Jimmy Baldwin, with his biblical cadence and his insider's outlook, with his aptitude for expressing racial calamity in disturbingly personal terms, had become the voice of black America. To scan a newspaper or flip through a magazine or focus on a television screen was to collide with some manifestation of his hostile-loving personality.

Baldwin the revolutionary was rapidly devouring Baldwin the playwright. Stalled in an early sequence of BLUES FOR MISTER CHARLIE, he worked between speeches, in planes and buses and trains. But crumbs of time were not enough. He flew to Istanbul and there managed to complete the first act of his play.

On April 4, 1963, he won the George Polk Memorial Award for "outstanding magazine reporting." From his Turkish retreat, Baldwin signified his delight with this honor, adding in a cautious aside: "But what is it? Please don't tell them I had to ask."

By the end of that month, reverting to his limelit stance, he was again sounding the alarm throughout the United States. His eyes like a pair of giant, glowering, convex lenses, his long-lipped mouth an upside-down U, he inveighed against the bigotry that was shredding America's unity, deforming its citizens and scrapping their future.

In California, he hopped from city to city, propagating the religion of equality in high schools and colleges, asking from each platform as he had been asking all his life: "Can you hear me up there? Can you all hear me in the back?"

While he preached, Martin Luther King was shepherding the Negro children of Birmingham, in immaculate white shirts and splendidly starched dresses, through the pacific rituals of civil disobedience. Hundreds of these young warriors were arrested. Against their elders were pitted club-swinging police, lathering dogs, fire hoses and bombs. Riots were the sequel.

On May 12, 1963, from Los Angeles, Baldwin cabled Attorney General Robert F. Kennedy: THOSE WHO BEAR THE GREATEST RESPONSIBILITY FOR THE CHAOS IN BIRMINGHAM ARE NOT IN BIRMINGHAM. AMONG THOSE RESPONSIBLE ARE J. EDGAR HOOVER, SENATOR EASTLAND [of Mississippi], THE POWER STRUCTURE WHICH HAS GIVEN BULL CONNOR [the Alabama sheriff] SUCH LICENSE, AND PRESIDENT KENNEDY, WHO HAS NOT USED THE GREAT PRESTIGE OF HIS OFFICE AS THE MORAL FORUM WHICH IT CAN BE. THIS CRISIS IS NEITHER REGIONAL NOR RACIAL. IT IS A MATTER OF THE NATIONAL LIFE OR DEATH. NO TRUCE CAN BE BINDING UNTIL THE AMERICAN PEOPLE AND OUR REPRESENTATIVES ARE ABLE TO ACCEPT THE SIMPLE FACT THAT THE NEGRO IS A MAN.

Badgered by insomnia, Baldwin nevertheless whipped through a three-week tour for CORE. "Well," he said then as he often had before, "I think I paid my dues this time." Baldwin's need to pay his "club dues" (as a human being, as a Negro) is immeasurable, possibly because he has never really forgiven himself for deserting his family at nineteen.

On Wednesday, May 22nd, acceding to a request from author Kay Boyle, Baldwin was to speak at Wesleyan University in Middletown, Connecticut. Bone-weary, he taxied to Bob Mills' office in midtown Manhattan and had two dollops of scotch, each augmented by a spoonful of water (an ingredient Baldwin warily dispenses with in the company of strangers, lest the amount of dilution be increased to treacherous proportions).

Only partially resuscitated by the liquor, he set out with Mills for Norwalk in a limousine the agent had wangled. At four P.M. they arrived at Mills' home, where they found a message from Burke Marshall, chief of the Civil Rights Division of the Justice Department under Bob Kennedy, asking Baldwin to return the call.

Baldwin and Mills fortified themselves with another round of scotch before telephoning Washington. Marshall invited the writer to breakfast with the Attorney General and himself the next day. Baldwin curious, agreed to come.

The two men then drove to Middletown, an hour away, to spend the evening with Miss Boyle, a resident fellow that semester at Wesleyan's Center for Advanced Studies. The visitors, together with their hostess, a thin woman with aquamarine eyes and a high regard for Baldwin, went on to the house of Paul Horgan, novelist, historian and the Center's acting director. They dined there with several faculty members and a couple of students. Too tense and too tired to do more than trifle with his food, Baldwin drank more than he ate.

At eight-thirty, he gave his address at the college chapel. Later he kept a pledge to drop in at a fraternity house where, as it turned out, the boys were throwing a beer party. Baldwin prefers beer at the beginning of his day. Mills urged one of the undergraduates to go out and search for scotch—"for survival's sake."

Meanwhile Baldwin had been instantly engulfed by his youthful admirers. They clustered around him so thickly that he vanished from sight. All that was visible of him was one arm, flung up in mock appeal to Mills. Grasping the hand extended to him, the agent maneuvered Baldwin to the relative comfort of a seat on the stairs ("with his back to the wall").

Sipping scotch, Baldwin spoke animatedly with the students, interested in their ideas and in their reception of his. "He's very patient with kids, even when they seem obtuse," Mills says. "He has fantastic antennae which tell him if it's stupidity or ignorance."

They had a series of nightcaps at Miss Boyle's flat, where a new batch of faculty people greeted Baldwin. Before their departure at one-thirty A.M., Mills obtained a sleeping pill from Miss Boyle and fed it to his client, who dozed in the rear of the car on the way back to Norwalk.

Baldwin retired at two-thirty Thursday morning. Three hours

later, he was up—on his feet, if not entirely awake. In Mills' Renault, they sped to LaGuardia Airport. With only seconds to spare, they boarded the seven A.M. shuttle to Washington, where Kennedy's Negro chauffeur was standing by. Baldwin shook hands with him before climbing into the telephone-equipped limousine. In McLean, Virginia, at the Attorney General's Hickory Hill estate, Baldwin and Mills breakfasted with Kennedy and Marshall.

The author, who had met the Attorney General a year earlier at the White House dinner for Nobel laureates and their colleagues in the arts and sciences, had professed himself "chilled by the look in Bobby's eyes." Kennedy, handsome, virile, clever, born to wealth and security and social position, by temperament enamored of sports and challenged by mountain peaks, a prime exponent of the cult of charisma, was mantled with the authority Baldwin instinctively distrusts. Of approximately the same age, Kennedy and his guest sprang from antithetic backgrounds. Baldwin's antagonism was virtually preordained.

Now, over poached eggs and coffee, Kennedy inquired, "How important do you think the Black Muslims are?" Baldwin told him the situation of the Negroes in the North was so appalling that it made them vulnerable to Muslim propaganda ("because the extremists best articulate the Negro's pain and despair"), an appraisal that was soon to be borne out by massive riots in Northern cities.

"Who are the Negroes other Negroes listen to, do you think?" the Attorney General wanted to know. "Not politicians. I don't mean Adam Clayton Powell. Or even Martin Luther King." Baldwin reeled off a list of names. Kennedy said, "Look, I'd like to meet them." Baldwin consented to round them up.

The temptation to present the Negro's case directly to "the white power oligarchy" is sufficient explanation for Baldwin's acquiescence. But Kennedy's motivation in assigning to Baldwin the casting of the conference is somewhat dimmer. Burke Marshall now says the Kennedy administration was then consulting "as many people as possible" on constructive methods of banishing discrimination.

"Someone—Dick Gregory, maybe—suggested that Jimmy Baldwin wanted to see the Attorney General," Marshall says. "And it seemed like a good idea. He's an interesting person, anyway. So I called him."

Only Baldwin's focal position in the integration drive could have made it seem like such a good idea. He had inflamed the campus generation with his words. A 120-pound featherweight with a loping walk and a resplendent smile, he bestrode the contemporary world of protest like a colossus. One leg in the Negro community, the other planted in the white, Jimmy Baldwin could almost be classified as a national institution. To earn his commendation would be to gain a notable prize.

Marshall's recollection is that Kennedy, talking with Baldwin at McLean about Chicago's critical shortage of Negro housing, had probed for "the people who have the answers." Baldwin had mentioned his friend June Shagaloff of the NAACP and Edwin C. Berry, director of the Chicago Urban League. "Baldwin's a very intelligent, articulate, persuasive person," Marshall remarks, not irrelevantly.

Even so, that does not dispel the mystery as to why Bob Kennedy required Jimmy Baldwin's intervention to corral individuals like Miss Shagaloff and Berry, both readily available to the White House.

At Hickory Hill, the Kennedy children had not yet been served breakfast. Twice they trooped in to confer with their father. Since Baldwin hadn't eaten his bacon, the Attorney General distributed the slices to his always ravenous offspring. Baldwin, sensitive as ever to tokens of paternal affection, observed the interplay sympathetically.

After one such interruption, he put his cup on the table and remarked that President Kennedy had failed to make it plain to the country that civil rights were "a moral issue." The Attorney General assured him that the President had said precisely that in his message to Congress in January (during New York's newspaper shutdown) and offered to furnish copies of the Presidential statement from a stack in his office.

As the foursome prepared to get into Marshall's sedan for the drive to the capital, Kennedy introduced his Negro maid to Baldwin. Her eyes shone with excitement. "You'll probably want his autograph, won't you?" the Attorney General asked.

"Oh, yes!" she said, and fluttered about, hunting for paper.

"Why don't you get the copy of TIME that has Mr. Baldwin's picture on the cover?" Kennedy said helpfully. "There's one upstairs in the bedroom."

She ran up the steps and was back almost immediately with the

May 17th issue of the magazine. Baldwin graciously scrawled his signature over Boris Chaliapin's portrait of him.

A few minutes later, in the car, Kennedy proposed that they meet Friday afternoon in his Manhattan apartment (which actually belonged to his father). Mills took out a pocket pad to jot down the address. "I don't know it," Kennedy confessed. "One advantage of being an Attorney General is that you don't have to remember your address—you can call someone on the phone and ask." It was Marshall who finally supplied that nugget of information.

On the trip back to New York, Baldwin and Mills talked very little Both were subdued. "At least Bobby loves his children," Baldwin ventured. After an interval, he commented that Kennedy "really seemed interested" in the civil rights issue. Nearing New York, he consoled himself with the thought that they were drawing closer to a bar.

In Manhattan, Baldwin frantically juggled two sets of business negotiations. With Mills, he lunched at the home of an editor who was attempting to lure him away from Dial Press (another publisher with similar designs was even then flourishing as bait a $1,000,000 contract: $50,000 a year for twenty years).

Between courses Baldwin and Mills began placing calls to Lena Horne in Palm Springs, Belafonte and Rip Torn in New York, Berry in Chicago. Afterward they took a cab to the office of Robert Whitehead of the Lincoln Center Repertory Theatre. Over highballs the disposition of Baldwin's still unfinished play was heatedly contested.

Whitehead and Elia Kazan, directors of the new enterprise, wanted BLUES FOR MISTER CHARLIE for the grand première of their much trumpeted but still embryonic company. Kazan, who might be called the godfather of BLUES, was incredulous when Baldwin declined to let him produce it.

"I was committed, I thought, to the Actors Studio," Baldwin says now. "I never thought about another management, y'know, until it was really too *late*. Kazan wanted it very *badly*. And I just *could* not *see* myself in that—in that ornate—overproduced—*assembly*. It was not for *me*. I don't want to be sandwiched between S. N. Behrman and Arthur Miller, for one thing. And I didn't have confidence in Lincoln Center. And *finally*, also, they couldn't get my *actors*. I mean the actors *I* wanted—were not *at* the Center. And were not about to *go* to the Center. So that *did* it, y'know . . ."

Baldwin was determined to have Sidney Poitier and Rip Torn (a founding member of the Actors Studio Theater) as his stars. Whitehead insisted he could get both. For two and a half hours, the pros and cons seesawed back and forth. To prove his point, Whitehead even put a call through to Poitier at the Hotel Metropole in Belgrade and then handed the phone to Baldwin, who obligingly went through the motions of trying to persuade the actor to appear as the lead in a Lincoln Center BLUES.

Poitier, refusing to be stampeded, remained noncommittal. "I wish you were as well organized as Poitier is," Mills later told Baldwin. "Sidney," the author retorted, "only looks well organized when he's standing next to me."

Kazan and Whitehead guaranteed Baldwin a lot more money than he had been offered elsewhere. "But I'm afraid you want me as your 'nigger in the window,'" he said. "And I don't want to be your 'nigger in the window' . . ."

Still accompanied by Mills, Baldwin returned to his own apartment. His brother David and Freedom Rider Jerome Smith were waiting there for him. Drinking slowly and steadily from a constantly replenished double scotch on the rocks, Baldwin tidied up the arrangements for the meeting the following day.

He spoke to Lena Horne, with whom he had a slight and casual acquaintance. She had once dashed off a fan letter to him ("something I practically never do"), but even now considers him "a strange, distant, brilliant man whom I don't suppose I will ever know very well." Torn, then appearing in Eugene O'Neill's STRANGE INTERLUDE, could not be reached backstage until the final curtain descended at eleven-thirty P.M.

It is not unusual for Baldwin to maintain a virtually unbroken fast until long after dark, then impulsively convoke as many of his coterie as possible at some restaurant for a late supper. That night he cajoled Torn and his wife into coming down to Greenwich Village. With Mills, Smith and his brother, Baldwin then headed for El Faro's. Torn and Miss Page joined him there. After coffee, Torn saw his wife home and then backtracked to Baldwin's two-room flat on 18th Street, planning to review the strategy of their interchange with Kennedy.

By then music was blaring from the record player and Smith

was teaching David Baldwin how "The Fight" is danced down in New Orleans. "Jerome can outdance any of us," Torn says. Smith, twenty-five, built along the elongated and attenuated lines of an El Greco, was a swing man in the emancipation drive, often jailed, frequently beaten up, once so severely injured that his left side was paralyzed for months. His features are somber but, as he illustrated the steps of "The Fight," his face was as bright as a summer day.

Baldwin's sister Gloria had arrived with her date, Frank Karefa-Smart of Sierra Leone's United Nations delegation (now her husband). Frank Corsaro of the Actors Studio, who lived around the corner, stopped by. Corsaro, Baldwin's schoolmate at Clinton High School, had directed GIOVANNI'S ROOM for the Actors Studio and was slated to perform the same function for BLUES.

When Mills took off at four A.M. Friday to check in at a hotel for what was left of the night, the impromptu party was still going strong and Baldwin, who had slept four hours out of the past forty, gave no indication of weakening. He was unfurling the kind of two-in-one day that periodically impels his sister to demand of him with an awe that is half sardonic, half genuine, "What—are you still alive?"

On Friday afternoon Baldwin was interviewed at Sardi's West by Lewis Funke of THE NEW YORK TIMES, who was doing a piece on BLUES for the Sunday drama section. Baldwin found it difficult to swallow anything solid. Watching him toy nervously with his food, Funke said, "Relax—I'm a nice guy."

"I'm going to a secret meeting with Bobby Kennedy this afternoon," Baldwin blurted. "Right from here, in fact."

Alerted, Funke learned that Baldwin had seen the Attorney General and Marshall the day before. "Baldwin told me that Lena Horne was flying in for the conference and he named a few others who were to be present," Funke remembers.

"I said: 'This is a helluva story. Do you mind if I tell my paper? Because I will anyway.' Baldwin said, 'Not at all.' And I scooted back to THE TIMES and passed the story on to the national desk."

While Funke was tipping off his editors, Jimmy and David Baldwin, Jerome Smith and Lorraine Hansberry (whose "Raisin in the Sun" had been a smash success on stage and screen) gathered at Mills' office. A TIMES reporter, Layhmond Robinson, had already rung up the agent to ask where the talk with Kennedy was to be held. Mills refused to divulge the location.

The group then walked to the Kennedy apartment at 24 Central Park South. The Attorney General and Marshall were just striding into the building. Several of the others summoned by Baldwin were in the lobby and the elevator had to make two ascents before all the conferees could be deposited at Kennedy's door.

Baldwin had assembled a strange and disparate crew, more representative of the diverse elements in his own life than of "the Negroes other Negroes listen to." His aim, as he explained later, had been to get "as wide and even as rowdy a range of opinion as possible." Rowdy it was, but not very wide. In addition to the principals, there were thirteen participants:

David Baldwin and his girl friend, Thais Aubrey; Belafonte; Lena Horne; Miss Hansberry; Jerome Smith; Mills; Dr. Kenneth Clark, who was to interview Baldwin on television later that day; Henry Morgenthau, producer of Clark's Channel 13 program (who was actually to be on the telephone in the next room much of the time); Torn; Edward Fales, vaguely defined as Baldwin's secretary; Clarence B. Jones, Martin Luther King's associate and then Baldwin's lawyer; and Berry, the Chicago Urban League executive. Miss Shagaloff, later erroneously reported to have been present, was out of town.

The composition of this council doomed the dialogue before it got under way. For one thing Baldwin had weighted his team too heavily with theatrical figures whose real and profound despair was characterized by an emotionalism that struck the government officials as too facile. Moreover Torn, Morgenthau, Mills and Fales, who are white, were at best in an ambiguous role as spokesman for Negroes (Torn, realizing this, commented, "I don't know why I'm here—maybe because I'm a Southerner").

The minority with the requisite prestige and experience for the discussion—Clark, Berry and, to a lesser extent, Jones—was inclined to remain on the periphery, intimidated perhaps by the uninhibited rhetoric exercised by the others. Clark and Jones, incidentally, like Berry, were hardly inaccessible to the Attorney General by a more conventional route—a telephone call, say; indeed Clark was even then viewed by the White House as a valued adviser.

The two Administration men regarded many of those present as celebrities who had "made it," a condition that presumably disqualified them as Negroes. What was not clear to Kennedy and Marshall was that fame does not exempt Negroes from the endless series of humiliations that white Americans, high or low on the totem pole, never have to face.

The sixteen men and women seated themselves in a large, informal circle in the drawing room. Even footstools were requisitioned to accommodate the entire group. If there was some initial stiffness among the visitors, it was swiftly vanquished. Kennedy, who had selected a straight-back chair, removed his jacket and rolled up his sleeves.

Belafonte, a frequent guest of the Kennedys, asked about the Attorney General's wife, Ethel, who was pregnant. Kennedy quipped that the baby might usurp Belafonte's room. The singer seemed ill at ease. Some of his companions sensed that he was condemning himself for not having long ago communicated to the President's brother what he was now about to hear.

The session, scheduled from four to six P.M., was to continue for an additional forty-five minutes. But the two sides never established any real rapport. Whatever empathy existed at the beginning was dispersed long before the adjournment.

"Jimmy kind of chaired the meeting for us, as Kennedy did on his side," says Tom. "Jimmy was very quiet, very reserved."

Smith was to be described by Professor Clark as the central figure in the colloquy. But the Freedom Rider impressed Marshall as "very emotional, but very inarticulate." Still, Smith was pivotal in one respect: he was, for Marshall (and probably for Kennedy, too), "the only one who was *real*," since he alone had been at the front in the battle for integration.

That in itself defines the depth of the abyss between McLean and Harlem. Kennedy's callers were proud of Smith. They had a reverence for him. He was, as one of them said, "the soul of the meeting." But they also felt that every Negro, simply by existing, is an expert on the frustration and futility allotted him in the land of his birth. From their perspective, Baldwin could have selected an eminently qualified panel of combat veterans just by stationing himself on a street corner—any street corner, North or South—and tapping the first dozen Negroes to pass by.

The gap was never bridged. Consequently Baldwin's message (that the alienation of the Negro in the North as well as in the

South had arrived at a crucial juncture where he "won't listen any longer, no longer believes a word you say") could not be delivered or Kennedy's (that the Administration was deeply concerned with the civil rights dilemma and avid for fresh ideas on how to resolve it) received with anything approaching objectivity.

Jerome Smith had been selected to open the dialogue. "As the most important person here," Miss Hansberry said at the outset. His first words were unfortunate. "It makes me nauseous to be here," he said. He meant that it should not have been necessary to plead that the Federal Government adequately protect Negro and white civil rights crusaders against mob violence.

But his awkwardly phrased introduction was construed by Kennedy as a deliberate insult. "I'm not going to sit here and listen to that kind of talk," he snapped, arms folded across his chest.

Smith plowed on. He told of working for voter registration in the South, mentioned that his wife and children had had to be sent away to ensure their safety, touched very briefly on what had been done to him physically in and out of jail by racists. His material was ugly; he did not pretty it up. He was factual even in relating the fury that had been disbursed upon him.

It was Baldwin, says Lena Horne, "who asked the boy if, feeling the way he did, he would fight for his country." Smith said he felt no moral obligation to help liberate Cubans as long as his Government appeared unable to insure his own freedom.

This, in Clark's judgment, is where Kennedy lost touch with the group. "Oh, I can't believe that," the Attorney General declared sharply.

"Smith's statement was much broader," Burke Marshall says. "It was that 'no Negro would fight for Cuba.' The Attorney General didn't believe that. He tried to argue about it. He may have been upset because it was Cuba that was singled out and he was awfully close to many Cubans. And they're colored, not white. But the thing the Attorney General really argued [against] was that no Negro would fight for the United States—and, by implication, that no Negro would fight for the United States *ever.*"

The Attorney General, Clark was to observe later, "seemed genuinely unable to understand what Smith was trying to say." From that moment on, the discourse went downhill.

Kennedy's rejoinder to Smith provoked a rapid fire of explanation, expostulation and amplification. In the hubbub, David Baldwin seized the floor. Half standing up, he shushed Lorraine Hansberry, who sat beside him. "Wait—wait—*wait!*" he ordered. Then, carried away by anger, he shook a fist at Kennedy and exclaimed, "By God, you'd better believe it!"

"There is no need to use such language," Kennedy said austerely, responding perhaps to the spiraling militancy of the proceedings rather than the reference to Divine Providence.

But his rebuke cooled his guests, who felt that David Baldwin's outburst had been, as one of them was to put it, "the holiest invocation of the Lord's name." It was that hiatus that prompted Jimmy Baldwin to speak later of "the great gulf" between his comrades and the Attorney General.

Kennedy could not conceal his growing irritation. "I'm sure part of the reason," Marshall says, "was that there had been no suggestion that anything the President or the Attorney General had done was meaningful at all. Or even that it had been done in good faith. I think it was *that* that made Kennedy mad. It was the assumption behind everything that was said that the President and the Attorney General had been acting cynically. Which was not true, of course. So the session got kind of wild."

When the subject of civil rights as a moral issue was raised, Kennedy turned to Mills. "Didn't I give you those copies of the President's message to Congress?" the Attorney General asked.

"Yes," said Mills. "The President said there that it was a moral issue. He said it clearly and well. But—nobody here saw it. Which can only mean it didn't receive much publicity."

Kennedy, taken aback, did not reply. Some weeks later, in pushing for his civil rights legislation, the President was to reiterate his belief in the moral basis of the Negro revolution.

Baldwin had intentionally remained on the sidelines, intervening only to push a point a bit further. But, when the subject of the FBI and its relationship to the South was broached, Baldwin said: "Let me give you an example of what we're talking about, if I may intrude here. If I'm walking down Main Street in, let us say, Montgomery, Alabama, and three white men come up to me and beat me up and castrate me, the FBI might be assigned to the case. And the odds are that the FBI man who investigates the case will be one of those three who castrated me."

Kennedy balked at this. "But Mr. Attorney General," drawled

Lena Horne with her inimitable beat and timing, "you've never been a Negro being questioned by the FBI in the deep South . . . Have you?"

The Attorney General let Marshall try for that return. For Kennedy, himself involved in a behind-the-scenes tug-of-war with the FBI, aware that the President did not intend to reappoint J. Edgar Hoover and wholeheartedly in concurrence with this decision, it must have been peculiarly grating to be compelled to champion the record of Hoover's organization.

Marshall explained that the FBI's G-men were crack investigators but that "special men" were sent into situations where the FBI seemed delinquent. Clark said later, "This answer produced almost hysterical laughter."

Baldwin's faction wanted to concentrate on the predicament of Negroes in the North. Kennedy, firm in his belief that the attainment of voting rights for Negroes below the Mason-Dixon line was the crux of the civil rights crusade, kept steering the conversation south to Birmingham and Mississippi.

The proposition that the President personally escort two Negro applicants into the University of Alabama in June was summarily rejected. It would be, Kennedy said, merely an "act." Someone replied, "But that's what we want—an act." They were of course talking about two different things: the Attorney General about an exhibitionistic stunt, Baldwin's group about a gesture of affirmation to America's Negroes.

Double interpretations like that one may have induced Kenneth Clark to put himself in Kennedy's place. "Suddenly I looked at the Attorney General and understood that he did not understand us and for just a minute I felt for him," the psychologist recalled later.

"We were, after all, saying something quite un-American. We were talking against tinkering. We were saying that even the most effective political manipulation is basically unacceptable to Negroes. It didn't mean anything for him to tell us that this Administration has done more in this area than any other Administration. We were asking him to stop thinking about this as the special problem of a particular group of people and to begin to think about it as an American problem."

According to Clark, the meeting stirred in Baldwin and his confrères "an intense level of emotion. The seeming inability to communicate the passionate insistence of Mr. Baldwin that the Attorney General *had* to understand the sense of urgency of the Negro people, and the need of the Attorney General to protect the image of liberal concern within the context of political realism, had contributed to an excruciating sense of impasse." That impasse was never pierced.

There was mention of the damaging effect passive resistance might have on the character of Negro men subjected during Southern sit-ins and marches to wanton aggression. Here Miss Hansberry's restraint cracked. She cried out that the country should worry more about "the specimens of white manhood" recently photographed with their knees dug into the breast of a Negro woman who had been pinned to the ground. "I'm not worried about *Negro* men," she asserted.

"Even Lorraine Hansberry was talking about getting guns out of her basement," says Burke Marshall sadly.

Clarence Jones interjected that some of the Federal judges appointed by John F. Kennedy in the South had been disastrous. The Attorney General reminded the lawyer that at least one of the jurists cited by him had enjoyed the support of local civil rights groups.

"There was one judge they talked about," Marshall concedes, "who had *local* NAACP approval—the national NAACP was not involved, I want to emphasize—and turned out very badly."

As the session broke up, three of the conferees (Baldwin, to be sure, was not among them) went to considerable pains to explain individually to Kennedy that "they had been unable to say anything that sounded like a defense of the President," Marshall recalls dryly.

Jones took the Attorney General aside and said, "I just want to say that Dr. King deeply appreciates the way you handled the Birmingham affair." Kennedy was not appeased. "You watched these people attack me over Birmingham for forty minutes and you didn't say a word," he retorted. "There's no point in your saying this to me now."

Belafonte too managed to have a minute alone with Kennedy. "Of course you have done more for civil rights than any other Attorney General," the performer said. "Why do you say this to me?" Kennedy whipped back. "Why didn't you say this to the others?" Belafonte explained lamely that he would have been regarded by his cohorts as a traitor.

With some acerbity, Marshall comments that he has "more respect" for those who did not extend such belated apologies.

"What was impressive was the gap of ignorance between what the Federal Government had done and their knowledge of it," Marshall says. "You see, with actors, actresses—that group—they were all rich, in the first place. They were rich, and they were artists. So their emotion was a little like—not artificial, but it had that air about it. So the emotion didn't have the impact that I got—and, later, the Attorney General got—from our meetings with students, Negro and white, but mainly Negro."

By Kennedy's standards, the group was appallingly uninformed. "They didn't know anything," the Attorney General was to tell Arthur M. Scheslinger, Jr. "They don't know what the laws are—they don't know what the facts are—they don't know what we've been doing or what we're trying to do. You couldn't talk to them as you can to Roy Wilkins or Martin Luther King. They didn't want to talk that way. It was all emotion, hysteria. They stood up and orated. They cursed. Some of them wept and walked out of the room." But it was Kennedy himself who had specifically barred from the meeting men like Wilkins and King.

Before Baldwin and his friends disbanded, Mills asked Marshall how to handle the call from THE TIMES. "It doesn't make any difference," Marshall said. "Tell them anything you want to."

Baldwin and Clark, more than an hour late for the taping of their television interview, patrolled Central Park South after the meeting, hailing indifferent cabs. "What Kennedy doesn't realize," Baldwin said, "is that if I were to go up to a Harlem barber shop and say that the Attorney General was not doing a bad job on civil rights, I'd never get out of that barber shop alive."

Torn, who felt "it had been a good meeting," had left early to get to the theater. Clark was of the opinion that there had been "no villains in the room—only the past of our society." Mills alone felt that Kennedy had been "shaken" by his ordeal. "That's what we have to hope," Baldwin said.

When a taxi was eventually snared, Baldwin was so jittery that he doubted whether he was in condition to do the show. "Kenneth," he kept saying on the way to the studio, "all I need is a drink. Can't we stop at the nearest bar? I must decompress." He was not to have that chance until much later.

When Mills finally got back to his office, THE TIMES telephoned him again. "We've discovered the meeting was at Kennedy's apartment," Robinson said. He had called Ethel Kennedy at Mc-Lean to ask where the Attorney General could be reached. "He's in New York to see a few people," Mrs. Kennedy had replied, and had suggested the conference might be taking place at the Kennedy apartment. Robinson had also picked up a few more names. Mills figured he might as well furnish the others, but made it a point to omit the white participants.

On Saturday, May 25th, in the first edition, a page one headline in THE TIMES announced:

ROBERT KENNEDY CONSULTS NEGROES HERE ABOUT NORTH

JAMES BALDWIN, LORRAINE HANSBERRY AND LENA HORNE ARE AMONG THOSE WHO WARN HIM OF "EXPLOSIVE SITUATION"

Baldwin's telephone began to behave erratically that morning: "I could make calls only with the greatest difficulty because my line was loaded with clicks, growls and bleeps to such an extent, in fact, that in the course of a single telephone call, I was cut off four times—which I reported indignantly to the operator. My conclusion, not unnaturally, was that my phone was being tapped."

That conclusion was to be reinforced some time later when an old and dear friend, summoned from Europe to New York by Baldwin via his allegedly tapped telephone, was detained upon his arrival at Idlewild by two plainclothesmen. They questioned him, searched him and then released him, courteously wishing him a pleasant stay in the United States.

In the wake of THE TIMES article, Baldwin was besieged by reporters. At an informal press conference Saturday afternoon, he declared that Kennedy "now knows more about the Negro situation than he did before." But the author would not write off the experimental seminar. "I am not prepared to say it was a failure,"

Baldwin said. "It has to be looked at as the beginning of a dialogue. No one can expect that dialogue to be polite . . ."

With varying degrees of accuracy, the story was picked up by other papers over the weekend—and, in several instances, embellished upon editorially, to the marked disadvantage of the conferees, who were reported to be quarreling among themselves.

On Monday there was another development, somewhat more puzzling. Eddy Fales learned from the apartment house superintendent that two men claiming to be FBI agents had requested admittance to Baldwin's apartment in order to look through his files. The super had refused to unlock the door for them.

On Monday night, Baldwin and his embittered friends met at Belafonte's home. By then, Berry had gone back to Chicago, and two or three others were missing. There were several replacements.

Since it was taken for granted by the participants that Kennedy's office had leaked the news of the confidential conference to the press, there were some muttered indictments of the Attorney General. Baldwin, generally so inept at secrecy, refrained from admitting that he himself was the culprit who had informed THE TIMES.

The consensus that emerged almost at once was that all public declarations should be channeled through Baldwin. He was tendered a generous profusion of advice on what he "must do" politically. Mills felt certain Baldwin's health would crumble under this pressure.

"One thing I'd like to call to the attention of this group," Mills said, steaming, "is that Jimmy is a novelist, a great novelist, and will become even greater—but not if he gets so involved in politics that he cannot survive." He went on to assert forcefully that if Baldwin tried to do everything everyone was urging him to do, the burden would not only impair his career but conceivably might even kill him.

At this, there was a growl of resentment in the room and Eddy Fales said petulantly, "Oh, Bob, stop being an agent." Baldwin, who had remained silent, whirled on Fales and blazed, "That's not what Bob meant!" Mills, fuming, stalked into the kitchen, where Belafonte was filling the ice bucket. When the entertainer returned to the living room, the situation was still strained.

"Well, now," Belafonte said sunnily, his tone casual, his pace unhurried, "if we've settled the question of whether Jimmy Baldwin will live or die, should we get on with the meeting?" The almost palpable tension dissolved in laughter.

In a taxi later, Mills, up front with the driver, turned toward Baldwin in the rear and expressed regret for the inadvertent melodrama of his pronouncement. "I hope I didn't embarrass you," Mills said.

"You didn't embarrass me, baby," Baldwin assured him. "You scared the shit out of me."

On May 28th, Mills sent a letter to Marshall. "I think you should know about something rather curious which happened at James Baldwin's apartment house yesterday morning," it began. The visit of the "two FBI men" was described. "What the meaning of this may be," Mills wrote, "we find it difficult to imagine, and would be extremely grateful if you could discover for us what it was all about."

Although the details are now hazy in his mind, Marshall remembers investigating a Baldwin complaint of "FBI persecution." The former Kennedy aide says patiently: "It was not true that the FBI was persecuting Baldwin. But, in true bureaucratic fashion" —he cannot quite suppress a smile—"the FBI insisted upon seeing Baldwin and telling him so. Which, of course, only convinced him all the more that they *were* persecuting him."

More and more versions of the confrontation with Kennedy continued to appear in the dailies and in the news magazines, most of them distorted, all of them fragmentary. NEWSWEEK's postmortem summed up the conference, in the words of an unidentified participant, as "a gigantic flop." Shock tremors traveled across the country. The quake of publicity distressed the Attorney General.

"It wasn't," Marshall says carefully, "very helpful."

Yet in the causes Kennedy has endorsed and in the statements he has issued since New York elected him to the United States Senate, there have been unmistakable echoes of the dissenting report submitted to him by Baldwin and his allies back in 1963.

Much of what Senator Kennedy has said about black ghettos ("it is the inevitable erosion of the spirit which isolation has brought that we seek to counteract"), about the violence in Watts ("a revolt against official indifference"), about public housing ("a significant force in perpetuating segregation"), could have been attributed with minimal editing to Jimmy Baldwin.

The writer's more benevolent attitude toward Kennedy may reflect this. "I don't think he could possibly have been entirely impervious to all those people—Lena Horne, Lorraine Hansberry —who were so adamant and so lucid," Baldwin says now. "And really were doing their best to convey to him some of the dangers and errors in the situation.

"And who all agreed on the same points. And who obviously were speaking to him because he was the chief law officer in the United States: the man who had the power to do—to *begin* to do some things, if he would. If we could make him see them. As it turned out, we were *absolutely* right.

"We were going to tell him what would happen in the North. And, obviously, it's going to happen again. On the other hand, the structure of American political life is so complicated, so complex, that we can't blame him for everything. Because he himself, you know, couldn't overthrow the structure of Washington. But I think he could have done more than he did.

"And, of course, there's also the possibility, you know, that my *own* judgment of him is—quite wrong. Or, at least, outdated. And that he's *learned* more—since that *stormy* meeting. I feel, of course, that people after all *do* change. He has developed a great *deal* since that time. I'm told that by people I trust. I'd like to *see* him again."

Most of all, Baldwin would like to ascertain whether those bristling one hundred and sixty-five minutes exerted any affirmative effect on the White House occupant and his brother. In Bob Kennedy's opinion, the colloquy on Central Park South swayed neither the President's thinking nor his own. "No," the Senator says flatly, "it didn't influence us."

Yet it may be that Bob Kennedy would not now turn away with anger and distaste from the "rich" Negro "artists" who sought, with too much belligerence and too little diplomacy, to convey to him on that afternoon in May the volcanic mood of America's Negro community. "The great gulf" that existed then might be appreciably narrower today. But whether that overexposed undercover meeting had any positive impact on the education of Robert F. Kennedy may never be truly known.

"I think," Baldwin says devoutly, "maybe it did."

"I think, in fact, that what has to happen is that, if one can crack the power structure sufficiently to let—to allow Negroes to function as *people*, you know—*in* the society, then white people will simply begin to be accustomed to seeing Negroes around without a *broom* in their hand. Their image of Negroes will change. At that point, you know, it is conceivable that— white people will be liberated from their terrors and *whatever* it is that bothers them in relation to Negroes. But until then, you know, the first thing, I think, is simply to—to let Negroes *through*."

Fourteen

The parley with Robert Kennedy, dismissed by both sides as a debacle, pitched the writer into even greater prominence. For days he was monopolized by envoys from the news media.

With his propensity for martyrdom, Baldwin oftens seems to will defeat so that he can clamor against the lamentable unfairness of the outcome. Although BLUES FOR MISTER CHARLIE was shaping up so slowly that it began to appear it might more accurately be entitled BLUES FOR MISTER JIMMY, Baldwin had perversely undertaken still another professional obligation, further complicating the already complex patterns of his design for living.

His old classmate, Dick Avedon, had been commissioned by HARPER'S BAZAAR to shoot some portraits of the inflammatory author of THE FIRE NEXT TIME. Their reunion, releasing the floodgates of nostalgia in both, was an instant success.

Once the camerawork was out of the way, the two former Clintonites lunched together in Avedon's studio. The photographer had previously collaborated on one volume of pictures and commentary with Truman Capote, and was then in the process of assembling a second book.

"I asked Jimmy if he'd be interested in doing the text," says Avedon, who is dark, faun-like and almost as slight as Baldwin himself. "His decision was immediate. He said, 'Yes.' And he walked out. I said to myself, 'He can't possibly do this, but I'll go ahead as though he could.'"

Several months elapsed. Toward the end of May, Avedon telephoned Baldwin. "I can't move without showing you what I've done," the photographer said. Baldwin might reasonably be expected to have claimed priority for his overdue play.

"Great," he said. "Let's get out of town."

Avedon's calendar was crowded, but Baldwin and Happersberger flew to Puerto Rico on June 3rd as his harbingers. In Santurce, not far from San Juan's airport, they rented rooms at a pleasant, unpretentious inn with a lively bar and a relaxed, laissez-faire atmosphere.

"Marge Karmel had recommended the place," Baldwin says. "She thought I looked terrible and should get some rest. I'd been to Puerto Rico before. I liked the climate. I liked the people. Marge called Bill Hurst, who operates The Duffys', and said I was coming down."

Hurst, a lean, tanned six-footer who had severed his affiliations with a New York advertising agency to turn innkeeper, was charmed by Baldwin. "We became good friends and happy companions," Hurst says. He and his wife took Baldwin and Happersberger on sightseeing trips, some of them overnight.

At La Parguera, a fishing village off the southern coast of Puerto Rico, they heard that a colony of rhesus monkeys had been established the year before on La Cueva and Guayacan, two islands lying approximately three miles to the west. Here scientists were studying the social behavior of *Macaca mulatta* in a natural environment. But a telephone inquiry produced the information that the public was not admitted.

At the mention of Baldwin's name, however, the voice at the other end of the wire reversed itself. Jimmy Baldwin? The writer? It would be a pleasure to show him and his friends around the island. And so they spent an enlightening afternoon learning about the feeding, mating and fighting habits of nonhuman primates.

Avedon arrived on June 23rd. In three days, he and Baldwin blocked out their project. "It was exactly the way we used to work at school," the photographer says. "I kept thinking, 'Here we are, back in the tower.' We worked on the theme. Which was despair, dishonesty, the alienation of all things that keep people from knowing each other, that keep people from helping each other—all the things that might lead to the end of our world."

Baldwin wanted to call the book "Crime and Punishment." Avedon demurred. Baldwin, who has on occasion compared his life situation with Dostoevsky's, said, "It's a great title." But he supplied an alternative, "All Our Motives."

"Look at those eyes," Baldwin would exhort, studying the sea of photographs around him. "Look at the cruelty in that face." Then he said, "Let's call it NOTHING PERSONAL." Avedon's response was halfhearted: "I thought it was glib, Ogden Nash-ish. But Jimmy loved it, and now so do I. To him, it meant no personal examination. He said, 'Anyone who finishes this book will know what the title means.'"

During the day, Baldwin closeted himself in his room, emerging only when the sun was going down, like some nocturnal creature. "He never went swimming that I can recall," Avedon says. "I don't think I ever saw him in a bathing suit or shorts. At six sharp, he would walk into the bar. No matter who was there, *he* was there."

Avedon had learned a very fast game of double solitaire from

Mamie Eisenhower. He taught it to Baldwin while they sat in the small bar with its picturesque clientele, overhead fan, tiled floor and crosshatched open wall offering a view of the garden, all of it reminiscent of a scene glimpsed in a Bogart movie. They dined late, at a Mexican restaurant perhaps, or a steak house.

"And we'd go on all night, moving from one place to another," says Avedon. "We'd get back to the guest house at three, four, five, six in the morning. Jimmy has to be *in* the world, the way I have to be out of it. Anyway, when I left Puerto Rico, I had the form of the book. I knew what I had to do and what he had to do."

Baldwin remained behind, burrowing deeper into his lair with his play. In July he was in New York for a long weekend. Mrs. Baldwin visited him with David and three of her daughters. "We were sitting and talking," says Paula. "And Jimmy said, 'You're all coming down to Puerto Rico with me to celebrate my birthday.'" They assumed he was joking. It took a while to convince them he was not.

Baldwin's original intention had been even more elaborate. In the bar one evening, he had told Hurst he was thinking of taking his family to Paris for his birthday. "I remember showing some disappointment and asking why he couldn't bring them down here," Hurst says. "He seemed to like the idea immediately and asked if we'd have room for all of them. I said we would simply make the room."

Eventually eleven members of his family joined Baldwin on Isla Verde Road in Santurce: his mother, George, Wilmer, David, Paula, Ruth and Herbert Crumm, Elizabeth and Leroy Dingle, followed three days later by Barbara Jamison and Gloria Davis.

"I always vowed I'd never go in a plane—never, never, never," Mrs. Baldwin reports, smiling. "When James said, 'You have to get mama in a plane,' I tried every way to get out of it. I got sick right away—I was so terribly frightened."

"After that, she was surprised the ride was so smooth," Paula contributes. "I fell asleep," Mrs. Baldwin acknowledges.

"It was," says Paula, "a wonderful week."

It outstripped in every way the daydream Baldwin had nursed as a lonely boy in Harlem, when he had visualized himself driving his family in "a big Buick car" to his house in the country. "Yes," he says now, nodding. "It must have had something to do with that old dream. Although I didn't remember it at the time . . ."

For a decade, Jimmy Baldwin's first line of defense has been his family. It hovers over him like a swarm of ministering angels, loyal, complaisant, just a little nagging, until suddenly, tiring of protective custody, he slips away, as undetainable as a shadow. But, whether he is at home or abroad, his relationship to his mother, three brothers and five sisters remains singularly close, even symbiotic.

His Horatio, adviser, and ally is David. In some ways he is almost an extension of Baldwin. Not only do they look remarkably alike, but they often think alike. Both are super-intelligent, hot-tempered, emotional, with a flair for capturing stage center. David, the Army veteran, is more direct, relaxed, confident—and seemingly less ambitious, which means he can also afford to be less devious.

When Baldwin is in New York, the two are never long apart. David is sometimes attached in one capacity or another to Baldwin's enterprises. He was to be credited in the Baldwin-Avedon book with "editorial assistance," an inexact phrase for his contribution ("I opened some doors for Dick"). And, in that summer of 1963, he was preparing to embark on the acting career his celebrated brother has always wanted.

Baldwin is nourished by his family's constancy, its love, its devotion, even its dependence. He banishes lawyers, managers and agents. But the Baldwins are his permanent hearth. He gains from them the sense of continuity other men derive from their children. What the Baldwins draw from him in return is a kind of solidity. He is at once eccentric patriarch and precocious child, revered and indulged, but always the head of the clan, financially and emotionally. Displaying some of his stepfather's egotism and rigidity, he is both concerned and demanding, as only an older brother can be. "I grew up telling people what to do and spanking them, so that in some way I always will be doing that," he says.

Whatever frictions exist within the family are glossed over in public. In private, they are generally smoothed away by Mrs. Baldwin, a woman of unassailable dignity who continued to work as a domestic until 1962, when illness compelled her to yield—reluctantly—to her children's entreaties for her retirement. If old feuds are periodically revived among her offspring, she tends to align herself with the weakest, a traditional form of maternal blackmail. Once she obstinately refused to accept money from her eldest son unless he agreed to contribute a monthly stipend to a younger who was then unemployed.

Baldwin regularly incorporates his family into his visions of the future, just as he did as a youngster. "We're buying a house, you know," he explained at frequent intervals between 1963 and 1965. "For my mother and for me. So, in principle, I suppose what'll happen is that Lucien and his wife will have a floor, my mother will have a floor and I'll have a floor."

Like a child playing house, he shuffled around the occupants of this unlikely ménage, sometimes giving preference to one friend, sometimes to another, occasionally domiciling both, but always reserving one level of his fantasy for Mrs. Baldwin. When a rather shaken interviewer inquired what would make this strangely assorted household run, Baldwin replied benignly, "Love, baby—just love."

But he may be more realistic than he is willing to admit. Recently he purchased a brownstone on Manhattan's West Side. His mother currently occupies one apartment, Paula another, while a third has been designated as Baldwin's. But for the most part he has remained an absentee landlord, thereby deferring any curtailment of his freedom.

Still, Baldwin is at his best when surrounded by his kin. Their presence warms and soothes him. He genuinely enjoyed himself with them in Puerto Rico. Twenty minutes after the first contingent of Baldwins arrived, they had donned fresh attire and were speeding by car to an encampment in the Rain Forest, a mountain area dotted with waterfalls and lush with banana trees, bamboo, hibiscus and fern. "I gave a lecture there to a student group," Baldwin says. "At the very *top* of the hill."

But he managed to conserve most of his time for his family, even though a local newspaper and a radio station were hounding him for interviews. He even made a point of rising much earlier than is his custom to breakfast with the Baldwins on the patio, lingering there over his coffee until noon or later. During the afternoons, they would check in with him from time to time. "Jimmy, we're going downtown," one of the girls might say. Or Mrs. Baldwin would inform him, "We're going to the beach and sit on the dunes."

One evening he assembled them all in his room for a reading of BLUES—the first two acts and a portion of the third. David, who hoped to win a part in the Broadway production, was cast as Richard, the juvenile lead, a bitter, brash, young Negro who has become a jazz musician and a drug addict up North but finds his way back home to die in the small Southern town where he was born. Paula was Juanita, the spirited girl who loves Richard, and Mrs. Baldwin, after much coaxing, read Mother Henry, Richard's grandmother.

"My mother was shy in the beginning," says David. "She was very *good*," Baldwin comments, gratified. "She would have made an *extremely* good actress."

He himself undertook all the other roles: Meridian Henry, the minister who is Richard's father; Parnell James, the white editor who is the principal interpreter of the tensions in the play, "civilized and aristocratic to the point of impotence," personifying the playwright's concept of the white liberal; Lyle Britten, the cracker storekeeper who is the "Mister Charlie" of the title and Richard's murderer; Lyle's wife, Jo, plus fifteen minor characters, white and black. The heroic feat did not faze Baldwin at all.

"It was very hard to get into it," says Paula. "Just the four of us. We started about nine-thirty or ten. Jimmy filled in whatever part wasn't being read by one of us. David taped it. We finished about two in the morning. We did the reading because Jimmy just wanted us to hear the play. Then we spent the rest of the night talking. My mother left earlier than the rest of us. I left about seven in the morning. The others were still there."

On August 2nd, a hot, rainy day, Baldwin was thirty-nine. Age affronts him. Every birthday, broadening the span between himself and his youth, shrinking the years ahead, withers his self-image. But he was looking forward to a gala party at the home of Signorina Ana Garcia, a petite, dark-haired ballerina and choreographer. It had been arranged by the son of Governor Luis Muñoz Marin, the reticent and very serious Luis Muñoz Lee, who had been introduced to Baldwin at the Duffys' bar ("we called him Luisito").

Richard Baron, Baldwin's publisher, together with his wife, Virginia, had flown down a day or two earlier. In the evening a cavalcade of cars carried the group up into the mountains to Guaynabo, some twenty-five minutes away. The winding roads were tricky and a couple of the mainlanders lost their way. When they reached the low, rambling house, a fleet of automobiles was parked outside and some fifty to sixty guests were assembled inside.

A suckling pig, promised as the main course, was roasting. The liquor was abundant and the rain had let up. But clouds of flying termites obscured the refreshments. The New Yorkers recoiled, as though beset with a Biblical pestilence. The Puerto Ricans shrugged. "Once a year this happens," they explained. "Then the termites go away and we don't see them again." The Baldwins, not entirely reassured but supremely courteous, retreated to the porch. It was a little cooler there anyway.

Baldwin and Happersberger arrived late. They had had a minor mishap on the way. Baldwin exhibited a sizable bump on his head. He was a trifle jumpy but he soon recovered and drifted from one group to another, his attention concentrated, his smile seraphic, his liquid capacity formidable.

In due course the sacrificial pig was brought in and carved. Each slice was ceremoniously wrapped in leaves. If the taste proved something of a disappointment to a few of the New Yorkers, the Baldwins apparently were not numbered among them. "They're not very interested in food anyway," one witness reported. Dead insects were strewn everywhere, their corpses carpeting the floor without visibly depleting the number of airborne divisions.

At the peak of the evening, Muñoz Lee, brimming with good will, presented Baldwin with the rights to an acre of land and urged him to build a house there (the site was later deemed impracticable and the spur-of-the-moment transaction lapsed by mutual consent into roseate memory). Hurst says the festivities were "a delight." But, driving back to San Juan, the passengers in one vehicle were rather seriously injured. The incident lent to the celebration a touch of the macabre.

Baldwin distributed more gifts than he received that week. He had purchased a handsome stole for each of his womenfolk, black Chantilly lace for his mother, Oriental plaid silk for Paula, who had turned twenty on July 29th. "We didn't give Jimmy a present," she explains. "What we wanted, we couldn't get him in Puerto Rico: a large album for his clippings and photographs."

The Baldwins' hegira to the Caribbean cost a substantial sum.

The round-trip flight, the largest item of all, came to more than $1,740. But Jimmy Baldwin did not foot that portion of the bill: "He was going to pay for it all," Paula says, "but Dial took it over as a birthday present." The gesture may have been inspired by Baldwin's threat of secession but that did not rob it of a Medicean splendor Dial's less favored authors might well have envied.

When their holiday was at an end, Paula says, "Nobody wanted to go home." Jimmy Baldwin flew back to New York with his family, content.

But the third act of BLUES had not progressed beyond a sketch, and the commentary for NOTHING PERSONAL was only a rapidly dulling gleam in Avedon's eye. The photographer thereupon concocted what he optimistically regarded as a foolproof scheme for sealing Baldwin off from diversionary matters.

"In order to have a place for Jimmy to work in peace," Avedon says, "my wife and I had rented a boat in the Mediterranean. And"—four-beat pause—"the boat sank the day before we got there."

The first leg of their journey had carried them as far as Paris. They could hardly have been stranded in a more exposed spot. Baldwin, determined to savor the "first fruits" of his fame, promptly set out in quest of an apartment; he was prepared to pay a juicy $25,000 for the purchase of five rooms, preferably in an older building. So there he was, footloose, well-heeled, vulnerable to all the blandishments of the city of light. From Avedon's point of view, the juxtaposition was unfortunate.

"Everywhere Jimmy goes, people come over to him and he *talks* to them," Avedon says stoically. "Really talks to them. In a bar in Paris one night, the owner—an American—came over and began to defend segregation. It took only five minutes before I realized either I was going to let him have it or get out. I couldn't understand Jimmy's unending patience with this guy. They argued on and on.

"I said, 'Are you going to keep on with this?'

"Jimmy said, 'Yes.'

"So I left. The next morning, I said to him: 'How could you listen to that idiot rant on and on and on? Aren't you bored with the Negro problem?'

"And Jimmy said: 'I'm bored with being a *Negro*. But listening is the only way I learn.'"

In New York, Bayard Rustin was then mapping out the nation-wide March on Washington for Jobs and Freedom to dramatize the push for civil rights. The Americans in Paris felt left out. "Alienated," they said. William Marshall, a tall, handsome, Negro actor who had just starred in OTHELLO in Ireland, sought out Baldwin and, over a beer, explained that the American colony was anxious to show its "sympathy and solidarity" with the struggle of their brethren back home.

Baldwin must have recognized the symptoms that had afflicted him in 1957. He agreed to meet with Marshall Saturday afternoon at a small nightclub just off the Champs Élysées, The Living Room, where Art Simmons, a jazz pianist, held forth. Marshall passed the word around.

Enter a luscious, copper-skinned, American ex-stripper billed as Venus (or sometimes La Doll), gay, freckled, brainy, a singer in the early Pearl Bailey manner, who had been known as Ruth Brown back in Cleveland, Ohio. With the rugged individualism characteristic of her occupation, Venus took it upon herself to insert a classified ad in the Paris edition of the HERALD TRIBUNE. In the week-end edition of August 17-18, there were four public notices.

The first three publicized a coin-operated laundry, an American diaper service ("Stork coming? Give mom a break") and a coin-operated laundromat. The last said:

> *If you are an American and/or interested in the civil rights march in Washington, August 28,* JAMES BALD-WIN *will be at 25 rue du Colisée at 3 p.m. on Saturday, Aug. 17.*

With those five lines of agate type, Venus boldly converted an informal discussion into a public meeting. By two o'clock Saturday afternoon, the plush Right Bank jazz club was jammed with Paris-based Americans, black and white, "drawn either by sympathy for the civil rights program or by curiosity," as the TRIBUNE later reported.

Among those in the first category were Memphis Slim, Johnny Griffith, Mae Mercer, Art Simmons and, of course, Venus; Hazel

Scott was there murmuring that she had not been born in America and her passport was missing and maybe her participation was illegal.

Marshall was tapping a toe outside. "Go in and wait for us," he advised a friend, "because any minute a car should be pulling up and Jimmy Baldwin will be getting out."

That minute did not arrive for a couple of hours. By then Baldwin was no longer expected. The white Americans were a little plaintive. "We wanted to see Baldwin," they said. But they lingered. The couches in The Living Room were comfortable, the conversation was good, the company—the women in summer-weight fur jackets, the men in dark suits—attractive.

"I was sitting at the bar with a painter when Baldwin finally came in," a Trinidadian reports. "It was a dressy affair, but he was wearing a gray turtleneck sweater. Marshall whisked him to the stage. As he passed us, walking the way he does, loose in the hips, he called out to my friend, 'Hi, baby!'"

"Just because Americans are abroad doesn't mean we're not interested in the civil rights problems facing Americans," Marshall said. "We want to make contact with those at home, make some show of togetherness."

Baldwin spoke next. "I've just come back from the United States, and I may say things that sound cruel—but I don't mean them to," he declared. "The situation is no more intense in the South than in the North. The situation in the North is even more dangerous, because it is less clear. People don't want to hear the facts, but the people in the North must re-examine the whole structure of their lives.

"We here in Paris, too, are not uninvolved. We must tell our black brethren back home that we are involved in their struggle.

The American white man is provincial. The Negro is, too—his mind is ghettoized. The American Negro abroad, then, can bring another level of experience into the struggle."

Mrs. Martin Van Buren Sargent, wife of the pastor of The American Church in Paris, was one of those drawn by Venus' appeal. Deputized by her husband, Mrs. Sargent invited Baldwin to address the congregation the following morning. "Her suggestion was well received," Simmons says, "since The American Church can accommodate 650 people or more."

A committee was promptly formed. That night a proclamation

was drafted by Baldwin, Marshall, several of the musicians, a few American whites, an Italian, an Algerian and a Ceylonese lawyer who advised them on what form of protest could be legally undertaken on French soil.

"Jimmy," says Avedon, "was the symbolic—and actual—leader. And when the press came, the person they wanted to talk to was Jimmy."

"We want to serve notice we are part of this revolution in the United States," Baldwin told reporters, the immediacy of the goal flushing from his mind his resolve to isolate himself with his typewriter.

By morning, word of his scheduled appearance at The American Church had galvanized the American community. Most of the United States residents trickle out of Paris in August, surrendering the boulevards to the tourists. But that Sunday every pew was occupied. At the close of the service, Dr. Sargent announced that Baldwin would speak. After all, the minister said, the notion of human dignity is "a matter of deep concern" to all Christians.

Preaching to the attentive congregation, Baldwin urged Americans to assemble outside the church Wednesday for "a walk on the Embassy" that would terminate with the presentation of petitions to United States Ambassador Charles E. Bohlen.

"This meeting didn't begin yesterday," Baldwin said, "but one hundred years ago, with the Emancipation Proclamation."

He cited as "a terrifying comment" a George Gallup survey, printed that day on the last page of the TRIBUNE, disclosing that 56 per cent of all Americans believe that Negroes are treated the same as whites in the communities where they live.

"Wherever I've been," Baldwin said, "wherever I've been talking to well-meaning white people (and what other kind can you talk to?), they feel there's no segregation. This is committing one of the most fantastic crimes. They say, 'The Negro doesn't want to destroy the social order, just enjoy its bourgeois benefits.' But . . . there must be changes. The church itself must be changed."

The petition that had been composed only a few hours earlier, unmistakably stamped with Baldwin's hallmark, was then read aloud. It said in part:

We, the undersigned, as American citizens, hereby publicly express our support of the March on Washington Movement, which aspires not only to eradicate all racial barriers in American life but to liberate all Americans from the prison of their biases and fears.

We cannot physically participate in this March but we, like the rest of the world, have been tremendously stirred by so disciplined an exhibition of dignity and courage and persistence, and would like to associate ourselves with it.

All Americans, traveling no matter where in the world today, are in the position of ambassadors and are very often made bitterly aware of our country's reputation. It is not easy to be an American abroad, nor is it easy to make coherent to those who are not Americans the nature and the meaning of our struggle.

We are therefore forever indebted to those Americans represented by the March on Washington for giving us so stunning an example of what America aspires to become, and by helping us redefine, in the middle of this dangerous century, what is meant by American Revolution.

About ninety worshippers, including Anthony Quinn, came forward to sign this statement. "I've heard for a long time that it's the land of the free and the home of the brave," the actor said. "That's what I'm supporting."

The Sunday morning rally was filmed by a television crew and shown on the news program that night— "which started things mushrooming," Simmons says.

On August 21st, more than 500 Americans, two thirds of them white, converged on the American Embassy with declarations of support. On the Quai d'Orsay, just outside The American Church, Baldwin, sick from weariness, his stomach queasy, led eighty of his compatriots, walking two by two at well-spaced intervals to avoid the impression of a "march" (which would have required official approval), along the bank of the Seine, across the Pont de la Concorde and into the cobblestoned courtyard of the Embassy.

Photographers' bulbs flashing in his face, journalists matching their steps to his, Baldwin paced the quiet, orderly demonstration, offering the French Republic a slightly ragged preview of the March on Washington. Marshall carried the fifteen-foot scroll with the petitioners' signatures. The Sargents brought up the rear of the procession. The French gendarmes, who had frightened

Baldwin when he had initially arrived in Paris fifteen years earlier, now watched over him benevolently.

"The Embassy was a little nervous about what we would do," Simmons says. "The Ambassador suddenly found out that he was on vacation, and so the First Secretary was delegated to receive us."

Consul General Herbert Fales ushered the leaders to the office of Chargé d'Affaires Cecil Lyon. When the petition was presented to him, Lyon said, "I can understand your feelings," and pledged himself to forward the scroll to Washington.

"After numerous television interviews and much picture taking by local and foreign journalists," Simmons says, "everyone retired back to The American Church across the river for one last TV show to be taped for England, with Baldwin speaking and with Hazel Scott accompanying Mae Mercer in Freedom Songs."

Baldwin's duties as high priest were at an end.

"I am surprised not only at the number of people who supported us," he said, "but mainly at the spirit in which the whole thing was accomplished."

"From my own personal observations after sixteen years in France," Simmons concludes, "this was the first time the American community had shown any solidarity—that is, white and colored."

But two weeks had rolled by and Avedon was desperate. "I was ready to tell Jimmy that I didn't expect him to do the book with me," the photographer says. "He was being pulled in every direction at once."

The Avedons dined with Baldwin three nights before their departure. Dr. Clark and his wife, Mamie, also a Doctor of Philosophy, joined them. "We went to a restaurant next to the hotel," says Avedon. "It was our first quiet moment in two weeks. I was exhausted. Jimmy was exhausted. But the Clarks, who were passing through Paris, brought an entirely new atmosphere with them. We could just sit and talk with friends."

But Baldwin could not decelerate. "It's as if Jimmy can't drop down from the level of tension he's at," Avedon observes.

Turning to his old high school friend, Baldwin said: "You're leaving Saturday. And I haven't written anything."

"Would you like to?" Avedon asked.

"Immediately," said Baldwin.

It was ten-thirty in the evening. Avedon telephoned the wife of a physician. "Jeanette," he said, "can I come over with a friend who absolutely must be put in a guest room and left there until he's finished writing?"

"Of course."

Avedon went with Baldwin to his hotel. They picked up Baldwin's portable and some paper—nothing else, not even clothes. Then they proceeded directly to the doctor's apartment. Baldwin's eyes were so bloodshot that Avedon could not look at them without twinges of remorse.

"I'm so frightened," Baldwin said ritualistically, investing the words with the quality of incantation. Then he entered the guest room, shut the door and remained incommunicado for two full days.

"We didn't know what he was doing in there," Avedon says. "We didn't know whether he was sleeping or not. He just stayed there. I slept on the couch in the doctor's office. It was so frustrating. I would have given anything to help him. And what could I do?

"Jimmy came out and asked for breakfast. The maid brought him sandwiches. And scotch, which he never touched. I asked him about that later. He said liquor's 'impossible' when he's working."

After forty-eight hours, Baldwin emerged, much the worse for wear, but clasping five pages of copy.

"He couldn't wait to see what I thought of it—whether it would seem right," says Avedon. "He read it to me immediately. Then I read it, and read it again. I'm a slow reader. I thought what he'd written was a miracle. One sentence went on for two pages. I thought, 'This is the most beautiful sentence since Proust.' "

Those five pages were to form the first section of NOTHING PERSONAL. They went into type just as Baldwin had written them during that frenzied stint in Paris. Only one word was eventually altered: in the phrase, "eyes as sensuous and mysterious as marbles," the final noun became "jelly beans."

"Which is so much better," says Avedon. "It was a beautiful, beautiful, passionate piece of writing. It recharged me. We discussed a little bit the direction in which he would continue. We went back to the hotel and Jimmy took us to the airport."

Baldwin had not planned to return to the United States for the March on Washington. "I loathe parades," he says. "I can't bear them. The whole *parade* idea—there's something in me that profoundly disapproves of it. I don't like to be on *exhibition*, for one thing. I don't watch other people parade. If there's a parade in the city, I stay home. Or go to some *other* city. I *loathe* 'em. They're so mindless. All this—you know, sweating people . . . Alas, I'm involved in social movements, and all social movements have some of the [parade] quality. Inevitably. Irreducibly. And I suppose it's necessary . . ."

But, in the end, he couldn't stay away. On August 26th, he arrived at Idlewild Airport with the Paris scroll, retrieved from the Embassy. To a bevy of welcoming newspapermen, Baldwin predicted the March ultimately would "force the Republic to meet the challenge they should have met one hundred years ago, at the time of the Emancipation Proclamation." On August 27th, he flew to Washington.

The next day he was on the platform along with Marlon Brando, Harry Belafonte and Charlton Heston. The camera caught Brando looking into the eye of the lens, Baldwin looking at Brando, both of them smiling broadly, their faces suddenly fresh minted, younger than their years, a little dazzled by the glory of the occasion.

The hope that bloomed that August afternoon wilted on September 15th, when bombs exploded in a Birmingham Sunday School, killing four Negro children. Three days later, Baldwin, wearing a black armband, held a joint press conference with his sometime political mentor, Bayard Rustin, at the Utopia Club House in Harlem to announce a Day of Mourning for the young victims.

"Birmingham," said Baldwin, "may prove to be exactly what the Reichstag fire was for Germany."

In the course of the next hour, he gave several versions of his speech for a string of networks and radio stations. Each of his statements was different. The theme remained the same, but the violence with which he phrased it increased, as though his fury fed on his words.

"We are all responsible for Birmingham," he said. "President Kennedy—*and* his brother—and *both* political parties."

And: "I would hesitate to ask the Negroes of this country, in the face of the apathy of the Government, not to defend their wives and children."

Standing in the backyard, an area strewn with splintered glass, discarded tin cans, dead leaves, empty cartons, a broken chair and fragments of brick, Baldwin spoke into a latecomer's microphone. "If you do not let these people go," he prophesied, "there will be blood in all American streets . . ."

A voluminous woman with spectacularly fringed eyes and a dulcet voice proffered him a cardboard container of coffee. "I need scotch," Baldwin said.

A couple of weeks later, his mother accompanied him to Fire Island. There, in the summer house of Lee Strasberg, founding director of the Actors Studio, Mrs. Baldwin cooked and cleaned for her son while he drove himself to complete his recalcitrant play.

"He'd sit at the typewriter, get up and pace, put on his jacket, go out for a walk, come back and go back to his typewriter," Mrs. Baldwin says. "Then he'd work all night and go to bed when the sun was up. When I went to sleep, he would always say, 'Mama, I'm going to stay up and work a while.' Then, when I'd get up, he'd still be pounding away. I'd let him sleep until eleven or twelve."

Her efforts to flesh out his bones were valiant but futile. "I'd fix some soup and stick it under his nose," she says. "For breakfast, he had coffee and a little toast."

He seemed to subsist on music rather than calories: "The minute he'd get out of bed, he'd put records on and keep them going all day. He played spirituals just constantly. I had no idea he played them so much." They were, of course, "mood music" for BLUES, but Mrs. Baldwin, who is distressed by her son's irreligiosity, was heartened by his passion for hymns. "I thought, 'That's a sign,'" she says. Then she chuckles. "I like spirituals. Fortunately. Because Jimmy plays them very high."

More than twenty years had slid by since mother and son had spent so much time together. "I told him I was so surprised he could get up and talk to so many people," Mrs. Baldwin says. "He said, 'Mama, you have no idea how shy I still am. And how frightened.'"

When they headed back to New York, the thrifty Mrs. Baldwin was affronted by what she considered an unwarranted display of extravagance. "Why can't we take the train?" she scolded. "Why a taxi?"

"Mama," he said, "it's easier. On the train, people come up to me for autographs or bring me their troubles. And I have enough of my own."

By then Baldwin was unquestionably, to borrow Langston Hughes' description of him, "the white-haired black boy of America." Yet he was stalked by discrimination as well as autograph hounds. Locating a suitable residence in Manhattan had been a punishing experience. Vacancies had mysteriously filled as soon as real estate agents discovered the applicant was Negro. But he had finally managed to rent seven rooms in a still fashionable ("for the next five minutes") building at 470 West End Avenue, well below Harlem's southern frontier.

"I am now a famous person," Baldwin noted grimly several days later, "but let me try and get an apartment in New York . . ."

Although Lucien Happersberger was indulging in an orgy of furniture-buying, the new quarters had not yet been furnished. Michaelis, the lawyer who had been Baldwin's benefactor in Paris, was living down on Third Street in an old house whose interior he had ripped out and modernized. He vacated one floor for Baldwin and Happersberger. "Tom," Baldwin says in an excess of gratitude, "took me in off the streets."

Taut with anxiety about his play, whose third act—the trial scenes—still had to be pried loose from the straitjacket of legal procedure, Baldwin nevertheless bulleted back into the Negro revolution. Civil rights crusades once again usurped his attention.

Item from a newspaper about a memorial service in Town Hall: "James Baldwin caused a stir with a bitter indictment of American society . . ."

Item about a press conference at the Astor Hotel: "The Artists and Writers for Justice is headed by James Baldwin . . ."

Meetings, rallies and conferences demanding his presence multiplied. The opening of BLUES was indefinitely postponed. Corsaro, worried about Baldwin's long delay with the final scenes, vibrated like an overwound spring. On a midnight in October, the director telephoned Baldwin.

"He said he'd have the last scenes for me in the morning," Corsaro recalls. "I went home and found I didn't have my key and couldn't get in. I called Jimmy and asked if I could sleep there. He said, 'Of course.'

"Then Tom Michaelis got on the phone and said: 'Frank, I speak to you for your own good. If you come, he will play music and stomp up and down all night. If you want to get some rest, go to a hotel.'

"I realized I'd wanted to be there to be sure I got the last scene. I'd been waiting for it for two weeks. So I went to a hotel. At eight-thirty in the morning, I went to see Jimmy. He had stayed up all night to finish it. He said reality kept interfering with the play's completion.

"He'd finished the script at eight A.M. He was wearing one of those wonderful, flowing, African costumes"—it was Arab, really —"a linen thing, cream-colored. He looked great. He looked alive. He'd awakened everybody to see the fresh copy of the play. He said, 'My God, I have nothing to *do* this weekend!'"

Several days later, Baldwin was dressing in preparation for an address to Harlem teachers on "The Role of the Negro in the Culture and Life of the United States." He put on his coat. Standing in the middle of the room, he bit a knuckle, then plucked at his lower lip with his thumb and little finger. "I'm nervous," he said. "All those teachers . . ."

At four P.M., he was inquiring, "Can you all hear me in the back?" A few minutes later, he was saying that any Negro born in the United States and subjected to the American educational system runs the risk of becoming schizophrenic:

"He is assured by the Republic that he, his father, his mother and his ancestors were happy, shiftless, watermelon-eating darkies who loved Mr. Charlie and Miss Anne, that the value he has as a black man is proven by one thing only—his devotion to white people."

To the predominantly Negro audience, Baldwin declared that "those silent people whom white people see *every* day of their lives—I mean your porter and your maid, who never say anything more than 'Yes, Sir' and 'No, Ma'am'—they will tell you it's *raining* if *that* is what you want to hear, and they will tell you the *sun* is shining if that is what you want to hear. They really hate you—really *hate* you, because in their eyes—and they're *right*— you stand between them and life."

James Baldwin had come a long way since assuring the white

students at Kalamazoo College that no one in the world loved them more than the American Negro. His talk was enthusiastically received. During the question-and-answer period that followed, Baldwin reiterated that he had been born in Harlem, raised in Harlem and, indeed, had never really left Harlem. Then a white teacher, shy, earnest and misguided, asked, "How would you define the role of the white liberal?"

Baldwin stared at him. "I don't really want to be abusive," the author finally remarked, his teeth gleaming like chipped ice. "But what I really want to say is there is *no* role for the white liberal. He is really one of our *afflictions.*"

There was a surge of laughter and applause from his Negro listeners, their white colleagues turned to stone. The instructor who had put the question slumped in his seat, crimson with embarrassment. Baldwin went in for the kill:

"The role of the white liberal in my fight is the role of the missionaries, of 'I'm trying to help you, you poor black thing, you.' The thing is—*we're* not in trouble. *You* are. I'd like to suggest that white people turn this around and ask what *white* people can do to help *themselves.* No white liberal knows what Ray Charles is singing about. So how can you help *me?* Work with yourself!"

This hostility, intricately interwoven through the labyrinthine Baldwin personality, reveals itself from time to time, gratifying some spectators, alienating others. But what Baldwin occasionally preaches is flatly contradicted by what he practices. Even his business associates are generally white. Carried away by rhetoric, he is apt to convey a distorted message.

Later, backstage, Baldwin was petted, praised and fussed over. A Catholic priest wanted his book autographed. A librarian reminded a member of Baldwin's entourage, "Will you see he gets home?" Her solicitude suggested he was far too fragile a package to reach his destination without assistance.

A very pretty teacher and a lady reporter simultaneously attached themselves to Baldwin, clinging to him with a proprietory air. "I'm so proud of you," the teacher said. "My mother used to teach you . . ." It was actually Baldwin's nephew who had been the mother's pupil, but no one was concerned with that. Baldwin bestowed wide, vagrant smiles in the general direction of both girls. They were still with him when he departed with

Happersberger, David Baldwin and a TV man. The group strolled along 125th Street while Happersberger whistled in vain for a cab.

"Can you give me a lift downtown?" the reporter wheedled.

"Jimmy needs a drink," Happersberger said.

With practiced skill, David steered the party into a bar. The girl reporter squeezed in beside Baldwin, aggressively affectionate, hugging him, stroking his cheek, kissing him boisterously. He wore a diffused grin, half enjoying himself. Happersberger, abstracted, sat on the edge of the circle. David relayed the orders for drinks.

Ostentatiously casual, he said to Baldwin, "I hear Corsaro called you." David had just that morning read for the director, who was then conducting extensive tryouts for BLUES.

"Oh, yes," Baldwin said, his face lighting up. "I meant to tell you." He leaned over the table and kissed his brother. Relief knocked the wind out of David. "Whoosh," he said, and fell back beaming.

The waiter set before Baldwin a double scotch of Johnny Walker Red Label, both glasses tremulously full. Baldwin poured them on the rocks, adding five drops of water as though he were filling a prescription, and then stirred carefully.

The teacher acknowledged that she had just written a play that was to be produced by a little theater group. Baldwin sipped his scotch.

"My play is just being cast," he said, one playwright to another.

"We're not ready to cast yet," the teacher said.

Baldwin's brows were arched almost to his widow's peak to indicate a high degree of attention, but his eyes were not quite focused. David, in a huddle with Happersberger, was explaining how he had utilized his stagefright to heighten the intensity of his reading for Corsaro.

"I'd love you to come up to my house for a quiet evening," the teacher said to Baldwin.

"Sure," he said politely.

"Just a small group for an evening of talk . . ."

"I'd love to," Baldwin said.

His tone was noncommittal but the young teacher heard only his acquiescence. Awkward with excitement, she took a small notebook out of her purse and scribbled his name. But when

Baldwin told her his new West End Avenue address, she said accusingly, "I thought you'd never left Harlem!" Baldwin looked sheepish.

"He won't come without *me*," the reporter declared. She locked arms with Baldwin. "*Will* you?" she crooned, rubbing her cheek against his.

Baldwin blinked amiably.

"You'd better take down my address too," the reporter said. The teacher obediently complied.

Over the rim of his glass, Baldwin peered hard at David. David lowered his chin once. "All right?" Baldwin said. Their eyes met again. A message had been passed and received. A rescue operation would shortly be under way . . .

On October 18th, "An Evening With James Baldwin" was presented at Town Hall.

On October 28th, James Baldwin, Ossie Davis, Ruby Dee, Odetta, John O. Killens and Louis Lomax released a statement: "Thousands of atrocities committed against humanity and the Negro people from slavery to the present time have gone unpunished. And now we are mocking the Prince of Peace; throwing bombs in the Holy Place of God; blasting the brains of His children against the high walls of His Tabernacle in Birmingham . . ."

On November twenty-second, Baldwin was silent. In Dallas, an assassin had fired at the President of the United States.

Two days later, on Sunday, Theodore R. Kupferman, a member of the New York City Council, was ice-skating in Central Park's Wollman Rink with his small son, Teddy. "I got a message from my wife that James Baldwin was trying to reach me," says Kupferman who, at Michaelis' request, had assumed the responsibility of representing Baldwin legally, replacing Jones as the author's attorney. "I got on the phone.

"Jimmy said there was an NBC crew at the apartment. 'They want to take a statement about the assassination,' Jimmy said. He was preparing one, but he was perturbed because, under the circumstances, he didn't want to be misquoted or partially quoted."

Kupferman took his son home and hurried down to Michaelis' house. "Jimmy was working on a brilliant statement in which he compared the shooting of the President with the shooting of Medgar Evers," Kupferman says. "It has been done since, but that was the first time I ever heard the comparison made.

"Jimmy's mood was solemn. He was conscious of the fact that, as the outstanding spokesman of his race, anything he said would have special significance. Which is why he didn't want any part of it taken out of context."

Baldwin says now he was "appalled" by the assassination:

"Of course. *And* frightened. I still don't believe a lot of things in the Warren Commission report. I simply *refuse* to believe—I *will* not *believe*—I'll go to my *grave* and I will not *believe*—that in this country, at this moment in our history, that one isolated *lunatic*, y'know—shot down the President. And then was promptly shot down before he could say a *word*, by another *lunatic*. In Dallas, Texas? No, I *don't* believe it! *I—do—not—BELIEVE—it.*"

Baldwin's reaction to Kennedy's death was tempered by the conviction that Negroes had been murdered for decades in America without rippling the surface of the nation's indifference.

"You know," he says, "people have been being bombed into eternity in this country for the last few years, and absolutely *no* one seems to *care*. Nobody seemed to care about Medgar Evers' death—and the kids in Sunday School . . ."

He discussed this aspect of the tragedy with commentator Barry Gray on a WMCA radio program early in 1964.

"I think for a long time in this country, indeed until today," Baldwin said, "we supposed that only Negroes get lynched. Only black men get their heads blown off. In the climate we have created—*allowed* to be created—in Dallas, Texas, in New York City, in Birmingham, it is not just the Negroes, but every living soul.

"A country which can blow off the President's head can do anything. And if we don't do something about it right away, we may turn out to be a worse disaster for the fate of nations than Germany. I mean that from the bottom of my heart."

Gray asked if Baldwin had considered President Kennedy a friend of the Negro: "No, I did not consider him exactly a friend of the Negro. But I did consider him to be what is very rare in our political history—someone in the Twentieth Century. You could argue with him. You could talk with him. He was alive. Do you know what I mean? He could hear. He began to see.

"There was no reason whatever for President Kennedy to know more about the black Negro, the black population, than anybody else. How would he know? He was a young man who was a millionaire—was Irish. He was from Boston. How could he know how it was to grow up in a Harlem ghetto? But he could hear it. Imagine fighting with Eisenhower about it. You would have to be out of your mind to try. It is a tremendous loss."

"What I mean when I say 'white liberal' is someone who says, 'I'm with you,' you know, and 'It's *horrible* to be in Mississippi' and who moves *out* when you move *in*. And that's my experience with white liberals. And I could go *further*. What they want me to do is to accept their *weak will* for the *deed*. They want me, you know—they want me to sympathize with them because *they* suffer because *I* suffer. And they're never willing to risk themselves, their jobs, their psychiatrists, their wives or their children—or *anything!*"

Fifteen

The theater is in itself as fertile a source of drama as any of the plays framed by its proscenium arch. Jimmy Baldwin, coming to it with his histrionic equipment buffed and burnished by years of virtuoso performance, lent luster to Broadway's off-stage divertissements.

"That was," he says, detached, impersonal, as though referring to some cataclysm of nature over which he had no control, "a great storm in my life."

Much of it was of his own making but it almost ripped him apart. During the staging of BLUES FOR MISTER CHARLIE, Baldwin was fighting on two fronts: the battle for civil rights and his own civil war against the Actors Studio Theatre. There were times when he seemed to think they overlapped.

In a fit of temper, he rasped at Arthur Waxman, the Studio Theatre's general manager, "You're only doing this to me because I'm a nigger!"

"Don't," said Waxman coldly, "use that word with me."

Soothsayers all over town were shaking their heads gloomily, prognosticating that Baldwin and the Studio were too similar in several respects to be compatible.

"Well, of course," Baldwin says, alluding to the conclusion, certainly not the premise, "*everybody* could see it except *me*," and heaves a great sigh, like wind soughing through trees. "It turned out from the *very* first moment we went into rehearsals——even *before* we went into rehearsal—that the Studio and I were at *loggerheads*. Total—*total*—TOTAL opposition."

In Lee Strasberg, for two decades the Studio's centrifugal force, and Cheryl Crawford, the vice-president, Baldwin had protagonists worthy of his mettle. Indeed, he may even have been overmatched. He was an amateur—with flashes of genius, to be sure, but unseasoned—clashing with two wise and wily pros, one of them a major deity in the pantheon of Thespis.

Strasberg, short, didactic, owlish, was the father and the master, cracking his training whip over his acolytes, teaching, directing, proselytizing, prizing from them the best acting of their careers—or the worst. He was once described by Mailer as "the most boring brilliant man I've ever met." Yes, someone said, but does he promote good or evil? "Both," Mailer ruled. "To the hilt."

Crawford is a small-scaled woman in voice, gesture and proportions, torn between fiscal scruples and an unfettered love of poetry. Tailored, laconic, she is given to old-fashioned words of moderation like "nice" and "good," her accent a well-bred blend of Ohio and Smith College. But she can curse an indigo torrent in her gentle, near monotone, and her calm is not so much placid as shock-proof.

The differences between these two and Baldwin reproduced the dark mood of the play itself. Or perhaps Baldwin's touchiness was a hangover from his play. He had set down with smoking vehemence just what his characters, black and white, really think and feel and do about prejudice in the United States. His harsh conflicts, crude invective and dissonant rhythms were like a Morse code, alerting America to disaster.

Mailer had written earlier of Baldwin that he "seems incapable of saying 'Fuck you' to the reader," an alleged shortcoming that doomed him in his colleague's view to minor status. The put-down had irked Baldwin considerably. It is unlikely that this constituted cause and effect, but ANOTHER COUNTRY was generously larded with four-letter Anglo-Saxonisms, and the venerable hortative cited by Mailer almost acquires a touching innocence when compared with some of the epithets perforating BLUES FOR MISTER CHARLIE.

Most of them are employed as ammunition flung at one race by the other:

"In a play like *this*, where white actors have to say, 'You—you —dirty *nigger!*'—a play which is *directly* about racial *tensions*, after *all*—the actors have to *use* themselves to *achieve* it," Baldwin says. "And that's going to make it very *stormy* backstage for quite some *time*. Because—you can see *this* coming—they *have* to be free enough in *themselves* to *say* these things. You know? In the case of my own company, something very wonderful happened. Which I *hoped* would happen.

"After the *first hump* was *over*, they got used to saying 'motherfucker,' 'nigger' and 'black bastard.' And no—no *roofs* caved *in*." He snorts derisively. "Nobody got—nobody got a *rise* out of it, y'know. And they *themselves* discovered to their *relief*—that they didn't really *feel* that way. That they themselves did *not— hate* Negroes. A lot—a lot of this shit that goes *down* is involved with people's *fear*. If you can get past *that* . . . So we had a swinging company, I must say."

But, of course, he could not get past his own fears. Handicapped by inexperience, he was quick to interpret every criticism as an assault. Persecution lurked everywhere, like fallout. The faint traces of paranoia that materialize when Baldwin is under a constant barrage of pressure became more marked.

His suspiciousness was reinforced by Happersberger and by his family. The Baldwins have been victims so long that they have a collective distrust of strangers. "It's a part of that whole effort on the part of my family—to protect me," Baldwin says. "Gloria thinks that I'm surrounded by all *kinds* of sharks." A puff of laughter. "And I probably *am*."

He shed ten pounds from his seemingly fleshless frame. His controls buckled. He changed his agent as well as his attorney. His nights overran his days, all but extinguishing them. A reporter arriving for a noon appointment was informed by Happersberger, "Mr. Baldwin has just gone to bed and I will not wake him."

The lumbering machinery of the Studio, which pretends to democracy, hampered understanding. Baldwin's grievances had to be pondered by committees. Moreover Strasberg and Miss Crawford were still wavering about producing BLUES. They regarded the script as a work of art, full of vitality and pertinence, but obtuse, overwritten, self-indulgent.

Still undecided, Strasberg rode out to the airport to catch a plane. But, before boarding it, he called his office. "He said he felt the Studio had to produce the play, even if it lost all its money," Waxman says. "And that maybe Jimmy would do the work the play needed."

But BLUES was regarded by the executives as a prestige item rather than as a money-maker. Accordingly, it was to be given a tight-budget production, with actors reading their parts on a bare stage. And this preconception, which was to be revised but never expunged, hovered over the staging of the play, like marsh gas.

"Not unless—not unless I, you know—I'm attacked with leprosy of the *brain*," Baldwin says, laughing without mirth, "will I give another play to the Actors Studio. I don't have any *respect*—in general, for the Actors Studio method of *working*. At *all*. At—*all*. It's *appalling*."

Of the famed acting "method"—derived from the Stanislavski system, with its stress on interior perception of character—that has attracted such disciples as Rod Steiger, Kim Stanley, Marlon Brando and Marilyn Monroe, Baldwin maintains: "It has *nothing* to do with *acting*. You really run into some kind of *weird, psychotherapeutic* class up there. I never saw so many make-believe *safety* pins. And make-believe *diapers*. And sense-memory perception." He hoots. "I went out of my *mind*."

The first reading of BLUES was on Halloween. The day may have imparted some of its own sinister connotations to the proceedings. Baldwin arrived with a batch of boys ("twenty to thirty," a member of the company insists; "all Negroes") who, by accident or design, stationed themselves at the doors and the windows. At least a couple of the whites present began to understand how most American Negroes feel most of the time.

"I felt trapped," a woman confesses. "I thought I'd never get out alive."

The play ran more than five hours, just twice the length of the average Broadway production. Baldwin agreed that cuts were essential but, like most authors, considered each deletion a mutilation.

"If O'Neill could have the full STRANGE INTERLUDE produced," he said hotly, "then BLUES can run five hours."

"But you're not O'Neill," Waxman said.

The part of Lyle, the "Mister Charlie" of the title, had been written for Baldwin's friend Rip Torn. "Jimmy said he had written me a part with affection and love," the actor says. "I read it. I played the murderer. I said, 'Yeah, you son of a bitch, if this is a part with love . . .'"

But Torn was eager to do Lyle. Corsaro had misgivings; he felt Torn's stage personality was too hostile. In the director's view, BLUES was basically a whodunit with a racist setting. He preferred someone with a softer presence for Lyle, to build suspense. Strasberg sided with Torn. Baldwin blew hot, cold, hot.

But there was an even more serious area of dissension. Baldwin had his heart set on having his brother David as the juvenile lead, Richard. Corsaro, brushing David aside as a novice, wouldn't even allow him to try out for that part.

"I'd rather quit than hurt the play," David said. But Baldwin reported to the Studio as early as November that he was experiencing "a crisis of confidence" in his director. On Christmas Day, he told friends he was "in bad trouble" with the play. On January 2nd, in the Russian Tea Room, Baldwin declared that Corsaro had to go.

"I didn't think that Frank—would be *able*—to make *some* of the Negro actors *listen* to him," Baldwin says now.

He had his way. After four months, Corsaro was relieved of his assignment. His duties were assumed by Burgess Meredith, nicknamed Buzz, pale, thin, sensitive, with hair like a dandelion going to seed and a clown's star-dazed eyes.

"Buzz was in, from my view," Baldwin says, "the very *lucky* position of not *needing* the Studio at *all.* And—y'know—*loving* Lee and *knowing* him (and *Cheryl*), but not being in the least in *awe* of him, y'know. Which is *very* important . . ."

The new hand on the helm did not miraculously still the doubts ravaging the actors. "I spent a *fortune,* y'know, buying drinks for various *hysterical, demoralized* thespians," Baldwin reports with a grin. "Keeping them from quitting—and blowing up."

But David Baldwin remained a source of contention. He had been cast as Lorenzo, originally a very long part. Meredith had proved his good will by letting David read Richard, but that's as far as it went.

"BLUES was a rough experience for Jimmy—and for me, too, in a way," David says. "They wanted to fire me . . ."

The younger Baldwin was a raw actor, his training skimpy, his enunciation thick. When the Studio insisted he had to be dismissed, the playwright went into a tailspin.

"Jimmy said to me, 'This is my brother—how can I do this to my brother?'" Waxman remembers. "I told him: 'Then don't do it. I don't think David's that bad. His style is not finished, but that may be an advantage in a play of this kind.'"

David was retained but his lines were slashed.

There was still the problem of compressing the script. Baldwin's attitude exasperated Miss Crawford. "I'm very fond of Jimmy," she says. "I just wish he wasn't so scattered and disorganized—and so ready to listen to the last person he speaks to."

Her fondness didn't detract from the fervor with which she pursued her argument with Baldwin: "Over a certain intransigence, no doubt, in *me,*" he says cheerfully. "Cheryl said to me, 'If the play goes on until eleven-thirty, we'll be on double-time.' And I said: 'I *understand* that and your feeling. It's nobody's *fault,* I guess. But, on the *other* hand, I'm ready to put on a five-*hour* play. If people who live in Scarsdale want to be back *home,* I'd let 'em. Fuck *'em!* I'm not *writing* this play for people from *Scarsdale.'*"

The cast was more realistic. One by one, they took Baldwin aside for private interviews in the congenial atmosphere of

Junior's Bar. Gradually the playing time was whittled down. But each trim shortened Baldwin's fuse.

"There was a very bad rehearsal one day," his friend, Bob Cordier, recalls. "Jimmy said, 'Let's get out.' Both of us were worn out. We'd been there day and night. We went to El Faro's. A girl and a boy were at the next table."

"Are you James Baldwin?" the girl asked. "I'm a great fan of yours."

Baldwin's cordiality was unaffected. While they chatted, the boy sulked. Somehow the girl dropped a contact lens. Baldwin scrambled about on his hands and knees, searching for it. Increasingly sullen, the boy started to needle the writer. He took it for a while. Then his patience snapped.

In pure Hollywood Western, he thundered, "Ride into the sunset!"

The tough guy backed down at once. "I'm just trying to talk to you," he said placatingly.

Cowboy Jim Baldwin pointed an unrelenting forefinger at the door. "Ride into the sunset," he repeated, hissing like a cobra.

Cordier was entranced. "It was like seeing a man get 247 bullets pumped into his belly," he says gleefully. "It was the first time I've ever seen Jimmy mean. He should be mean more often. He acts like a combat general with Lucien and Mary and June Shagaloff, but not where he should."

To help the actors interpret his characters, Baldwin wrote a fourteen-page, single-spaced analysis of "The Blues People." Circulated in mimeographed form, it seems to have shed more light on the playwright than on the play.

Richard, his creator explained, "might be able to forgive white people if he were able to forgive himself." Only five words are underlined in this section: "His father has betrayed him." And of Pete, a young student, Baldwin observed: "He is strange—perhaps—in that he is unable to question his manhood, no matter how viciously it is assaulted."

After a brief flurry of popularity, this document became something of a collector's item.

Throughout rehearsals, the subject of coffins kept cropping up in eerie fashion. The casket was a prop for Richard, the youth who is killed. The first one was constructed by the stagehands. It was rejected. The second was bought from the man who supplies cheap boxes for Potter's Field, the burial ground for New York City's unclaimed dead. Baldwin rejected that one, explaining that a Negro family would get the most expensive coffin it could for a son. The third was purchased from an undertaker—and "looked wrong." It was rebuilt by the stagehands.

"And that's the coffin we finally used in the play," Waxman says.

It was a fitting leitmotif, since Baldwin envisioned the opening night as his funeral. He was convinced he would be crucified by the reviewers. During rehearsals, he would periodically lurch out of the men's room, wan and trembling, to report that he had just vomited. "I'm deathly sick," he murmured feebly.

"Oh, it's so awful," he groaned at a run-through. "It's going to be a terrible failure. I'm going to *die*—I'm just going to die . . ."

"I don't know what made me do it," says Nan Lanier, a pleasant-faced woman, breezy and direct, then Waxman's assistant, "but I finally turned to Baldwin and said: 'Jimmy, it's the worst piece of trash ever written. I don't know why you wrote it. I can't bear the play.'

"He began to laugh and, for the first time, he didn't throw up. After that, every time he started to go on that way, I used to tell him, 'It's terrible—I don't know why you ever did it.' He would gradually brighten and that gray look of his would disappear."

During those weeks of exigency, he had two comrades: Cordier was on the payroll as Musical Coordinator, Jerome Smith as Special Consultant. Baldwin was rarely seen without one or both of them. Cordier, who had directed plays and films in Paris, knew his way around the theater; his confidence made him a kind of stabilizer—imperfect, to be sure—for Baldwin (one of the first copies of BLUES to come off the press was to be inscribed, "For Bobby, without whom this journey could never have been achieved").

"The three people who were always on time for rehearsals," says Cordier, stocky, blue-eyed, with a thick mop of curly hair, "were Jimmy, Buzz Meredith and myself."

Baldwin's pristine punctuality didn't extend beyond the theater. "For every time I saw Jimmy," says Miss Crawford, "there were five times he didn't keep his appointment with me."

Then there was the night he arranged to have Waxman and Torn meet him at his apartment at eleven P.M. to discuss a snag in the production. Waxman rang the bell sharp on the hour and was admitted. "But neither Rip nor Jimmy was there," he says. At midnight, Torn telephoned: "He told me I'd better go home because Jimmy was still holding forth at a restaurant. I said, 'Okay, but call me any time up to three A.M.' I didn't hear from Rip again until nine A.M. He said he'd finally heard from Jimmy at seven in the morning. We scheduled another conference."

Lucien Happersberger, on whom Baldwin had conferred the title of "my international manager," frequently monitored rehearsals. The covertly attentive company, rife with gossip, watched the handsome Swiss court Diana Sands, the Juanita, a deliciously pert young woman who is one of the finest actresses in America. There was speculation that Baldwin had sanctioned this match. Some claimed he was actively encouraging Happersberger's suit, a plumeless Cyrano opposite his long-time friend's Christian.

The wrangling with the Studio continued. Baldwin reeled through long days in the theater, longer nights of cutting, tightening, revising. At a preview, he was sitting in the last row of the orchestra with Cordier and Smith. Suddenly the Musical Coordinator and the Special Consultant raced down to Row Q, thumped Burgess Meredith on the shoulder and whispered frantically in his ear. Craning his head toward the rear, Meredith glimpsed Baldwin stretched out in the aisle, flat on his back. He was rushed to the lavatory, where he once again upchucked.

"Of course, the *great* dread I had—was that people would simply get up and go *out*," Baldwin admits. "That the illusion wouldn't *hold*. I really was *terrified* of that."

So, to a lesser extent, was Meredith. BLUES was impressionistic in form, flowing backward and forward in time. "Quite a new style," the director commented. But he found the structure cumbersome and confusing in operation.

"Three or four days before the opening," David Baldwin says, "they told Jimmy they wanted to redo the play—have it follow the time sequence instead of moving back and forth. That would have destroyed the effect Jimmy wanted. They said the audience would be confused by the jumps. I said if the audience was confused, they shouldn't come to the theater. Jimmy finally said he didn't want it redone."

"I have to trust to my judgment," the playwright declared.

"Meredith announced he wanted 'all the brothers and sisters to keep away from the theater,'" David Baldwin says, frowning. "Well, the only brother there was me and the only sister was Gloria, who is Jimmy's secretary and so had a right to be there. Burgess just didn't have the guts to say it directly to me, that's all."

The dramatist, his family's caretaker, had established a trust fund for the Baldwins with a portion of his royalties from BLUES. Two days before the première, he was in a restaurant, a tranquilizing scotch-on-the-rocks in his hand, an untouched steak Tartare before him.

"There's a lot riding on this show," he said. "Those actors over there are depending on it, I'm putting part of the proceeds in trust for my nieces and nephews, and I put a lot of blood into it, baby—a lot of blood." He drank the scotch but shoved away the plate of meat.

BLUES FOR MISTER CHARLIE opened at the ANTA Theater on the night of April 23, 1964. It was, Baldwin says, the first time he really heard his play. "I was a *wreck*," he says. "I was working—I really worked *around* the *clock*. Right up to the wire."

With Mary Painter beside him to comfort and sustain him, he listened to Diana Sands' rhapsodic monologue commemorating her love for Richard, a stunning passage, yet somehow—like the romantic revelations of other Baldwin heroines—more passionately maternal than sensual.

"And the *house* came—*fall*-ing *down*," he says. "The house came *fall*-ing down. Wow! *That* was something. It made me *shiver*."

Punctuating the play are several other set-pieces, savage, wounding, Greek tragedy with a syncopated beat. But around them is the inchoate jungle of Baldwin's emotion, with only an occasional shaft of light to illuminate the darkness.

After the third act curtain, Baldwin was pushed out on the stage. He thanked Meredith, he thanked the cast. A spectator in the second row, young, lovely, flushed with enthusiasm, leaned over and handed him a crimson rose. He bowed and smiled, a little high on liquor, a little higher on applause, weak with relief, looking tiny and uncoordinated, like a partially unstrung puppet, as he bowed again, stretched out both arms as though to encompass the audience and then tottered into the wings.

"I was standing backstage when Jimmy came in with his retinue," Mrs. Lanier says. "He kissed me and gave me the rose."

There was a party at Lee Strasberg's apartment. A temporary truce had been declared, "We *all* were there," Baldwin says. "I was *tired*. And I was *scared*. I was *terribly* scared. Somebody came over to me and said, 'Well, that's two out of three.' The opening night reviews, you know. And I didn't know what he *meant*."

Sam Floyd, Baldwin's former neighbor, was in the library with Miss Painter. "We were quietly talking," Floyd says. "Jimmy came in. He'd read the reviews by then. He said wearily, 'Well, it's done.' And kind of collapsed. He was sitting on the floor, his arm on Mary's knee. And then he said, 'I'd like to go home.' And David got a taxi and took him home."

The reviews were mixed. "James Baldwin has written a play with fires of fury in its belly, tears of anguish in its eyes and a roar of protest in its throat," Howard Taubman wrote in THE TIMES. But the other dailies were more guarded.

The blazing hatred racism kindles in Negroes, whether accurately gauged or overstated by Baldwin, confounded the integrated audiences and, in a sense, resegregated them: most of the Negroes responded to the murderous lines with the laughter of recognition and catharsis, but many of the whites reacted with unsheathed antagonism.

Baldwin's intentions were widely misunderstood. He had quite deliberately denied Richard a lovable, laudable, all-American-boy personality, siring in the interests of "balance" a taunting, derisive nonhero, who brags about his virility. But Richard was generally interpreted as Baldwin's mouthpiece.

Even the conscientiously hip Greenwich Village weekly, THE VILLAGE VOICE, protested: "I can't think of any motive but psychic sadism for Baldwin's harping on the traditional theme of Negro sexual prowess versus the white man's limited potency. It simply seems unfair."

It seemed unfair to Baldwin, too. "It was very important for *me*, y'know, to have Richard Henry as *offensive* and *brash and* stupid as he *is*," he says. "Sure, he had no right to talk to anybody like *that*. I know *that*. But do you have the right to *shoot* him? *That's* the question."

The failure to make this point transparently clear to onlookers may have been Baldwin's. But it could also be that white America, having brainwashed itself into believing that the Negro really is intellectually inferior and sexually superior, was willing to accept as fact the Richard's braggadocio.

Curiously, New Yorkers drew the line at Baldwin's Southern whites, who were condemned as cruel parodies. But white supremacists performing their off-color rites in and out of Southern courtrooms are, of course, only too apt to behave like parodies. "There's nothing in my *text*—nearly as vindictive and *horrible* as things I've seen," Baldwin says, "and nothing as *grotesque* and *outrageous*."

"All my Southern friends understood the play much better than the people in New York," says Mrs. Lanier, who was born in New Orleans and raised in Mississippi.

One magazine, THE REPORTER, refused to print the decisively pro-BLUES verdict of its drama critic, a Methodist minister, who was so incensed by this act of censorship that he resigned. All of this strengthened Baldwin's instinct for martyrdom.

On May 23rd, the Actors Studio posted a one-week closing notice on ANTA's backstage bulletin board. Baldwin was then out on Fire Island, again at work on NOTHING PERSONAL.

"I came back and met with the brass of the Studio," he says. "And by *this* time, of course, any *attempt* to be *polite* or *friendly* —had long ago been given *up* by *me*. The only way I could *talk* to them was—was to *sound* the way I don't *like* to sound. I had to *sound* that way—like *dictatorial* and—*unreasonable*.

"I accused them of professional incompetence—that they were a derelict management. And that they would *close* that *show*— over my *dead body*—or *theirs*. They thought I was *crazy*. And I walked *out*. I didn't know *what* I was going to *do*. But I knew I was going to pull the closing notice *down*.

"And I don't know how we *did* it. We *mobilized* my apartment and—turned it into a *factory*. There were no posters for BLUES. Nothing! People would have had to be telepathic to *know* we were *in* New York. I made the *first* posters *myself*. I put out *leaflets*. I got signs *painted*. I got—two sound trucks. People thought Jimmy *Baldwin* had gone *mad*—up here on"—he bursts into laughter—"West End Avenue!"

In this crisis, three white Southerners allied themselves with Baldwin: Mrs. Lanier; her husband, a Floridian, the Reverend

Sidney Lanier, an Episcopal minister; and Mary Lee Settle, a novelist from Virginia.

"Isn't it strange," Baldwin said to the clergyman, "that the only white people helping me at this point are not Northern liberals but three reconstructed Southerners?"

Mrs. Lanier persuaded a couple of friends to sponsor an advertisement in two morning papers. Miss Settle wrote the copy: "Once in a very great while, a play transcends its form and becomes an experience—as real, as imposing, as true as experience itself . . ."

There followed, like a roll call of Baldwin's associates, a list of seventy-three signatories, including the Laniers, Marlon Brando, Lorraine Hansberry, Lena Horne, Sidney Poitier, Harry Belafonte, Richard Avedon, June Shagaloff, Sammy Davis, Jr., Tom Michaelis and James Forman. By far the most significant names were those of the Reverend and Mrs. Robert L. Pierson and Mr. and Mrs. William J. Strawbridge, since Ann Pierson and Mary Strawbridge happen to be Rockefellers, daughters of New York's governor. But none of the amateur fund raisers seems to have realized the connection.

The ad appeared on May 28th. That evening the Piersons and the Strawbridges encountered Father Lanier during the second-act intermission. Father Pierson, a boyishly handsome Episcopal priest with the look of a Viking, devoutly committed to integration, had been jailed as a Freedom Rider for six days in 1961 (along with fourteen other clergymen, eleven white, three Negro), in Jackson, Mississippi. Now, in the ANTA lobby, he inquired of his colleague, "What can we do to help?" But Lanier, who thought of Pierson simply as a fellow minister, muffed that opportunity.

After the final curtain, Mrs. Lanier gathered the cast and an assortment of visitors on stage, where she delivered what she describes as a "Joan of Arc" pep talk. "If any of you know anybody with money who would help us," she said, "please let me know. All we need is $10,000."

A small voice said, "We'll give it."

Mrs. Lanier moistened her lips. "What did you say?"

"We'll give it," the voice said again. It issued from a tall, slender, unassuming, young woman. "I'll give $5,000 and my sister will give $5,000," she said.

Waxman nudged Mrs. Lanier. "Get their names," he urged.

"Who are you?" Mrs. Lanier asked Ann Clark Rockefeller Pierson of Scarsdale.

The offer of succor from donors he had previously derided as suburban Philistines ("I'm not writing this play for people from *Scarsdale*") sent Baldwin into a paroxysm of joy. "There were fifteen minutes of chaos," says Mrs. Lanier. "Jimmy hugged and kissed everybody. For five or six weeks, the play made money. It was very exciting."

Shortly after this reprieve, the company decided to express its appreciation to Baldwin and Meredith. Two Paul Revere bowls were presented, one to the playwright, one to the director.

"Pat Hingle, who played Parnell, made a little speech to Jimmy," Mrs. Lanier recalls. "'There's one member of the cast who was so touched by your work that she has this certificate for you,' Pat said, and then he read what was on the certificate.

"It went something like: 'This entitles James Baldwin at every other Wednesday matinee to play my role, which he likes so much, as the Second Girl in Blacktown.' We all laughed and Jimmy cracked up. He thought it was very funny."

Not long after, dining with Meredith and Mrs. Lanier at Gallagher's, Baldwin scrawled his name on a napkin to signify that the director had his permission to shift the scenes of the play into chronological order, without flashbacks.

"It was really much better that way," Mrs. Lanier says. "But Jimmy never saw BLUES after the sequence was changed."

BLUES FOR MISTER CHARLIE survived for four months. When Cheryl Crawford returned from her vacation in August, she demanded of Waxman: "How dare you keep that play open? I told you to close it."

"They closed BLUES FOR MISTER CHARLIE on the 29th of August," Baldwin says. "I'm very bitter. If they had not told me they were reopening at another theater—if it hadn't been for that, I *would* have been here in *New York*. But I was in Istanbul—just starting work on my new novel . . ."

He had left for the United States early in June with his sister Gloria, who had never before accompanied him to Europe. "Well, Gloria wanted to get me out of town," Baldwin says. But Nan Lanier felt he had abandoned his play.

"There were daily crises," she says. "I acted as a filter. I'd call

Burgess in Hollywood, Jimmy in Finland. Jimmy wouldn't come back to this country. He didn't cooperate at all in helping us keep the play open. His personal fight with the Studio was more important than the play to Jimmy.

"I broke my back working on BLUES. I collapsed of exhaustion in the middle of the season and had to go to the hospital. But Jimmy doesn't see me any more. I don't know why. I may never know why. But I think it's because he feels guilty about letting the show down—about running off to Europe and not coming back when we needed him to help us fight for BLUES."

There were others who attributed Baldwin's flight to empathetic premarital jitters stirred by the approaching nuptials of his international manager. Lucien Happersberger and Diana Sands were married that summer. "Jimmy," says one of the bride's associates, "never even sent a telegram."

In Finland, his first port of call, Baldwin had participated in an international writers' seminar. Dick Avedon flew to Helsinki for an emergency conference with his collaborator, wiring him to leave word at the airport where they could meet. When the plane landed, the photographer was notified that Baldwin was waiting for him at the hotel. He found Baldwin in the bar with some acquaintances.

"Hello, baby," he said radiantly. "We're going to the country for the weekend."

Avedon, uncompromising, insisted they must talk business first. Baldwin's brows soared but he led his friend into the next room. They had their consultation. From time to time someone would walk in and plead, "It's late, Jimmy—let's go." Baldwin waved them all away, without speaking. Finally the two old schoolmates arrived at a satisfactory agreement.

"And then we did go away for the weekend," says Avedon. "A German, a couple of Finns, an Englishman, an American."

"And Gloria," Baldwin contributes.

"About four men and four women," Avedon says.

"One of the girls at the conference, a little blonde, invited us all to her home, outside Helsinki," Baldwin remembers. "Her parents were there, very warm and hospitable. They served the meals themselves and made us feel thoroughly at home."

Baldwin had brought along with him a record of the music composed for BLUES FOR MISTER CHARLIE. He played it, Avedon reports, "all night—and we danced to it." It was a merry party. They were still dancing when morning came.

At the breakfast table, the two New Yorkers were asked how they had met. They unfolded the story of their years at De Witt Clinton. Baldwin triumphantly climaxed the tale by quoting a poem by Avedon published in The Magpie back in the days when he was New York's high school poet laureate. Reeling off the ten lines of "Spring at Coventry" without a break, Baldwin recited:

> *I shall watch for Spring this year*
> *With cautious eyes,*
> *With fingers reaching*
> *Where no vine lies,*
> *With a hand searching*
> *Where no bud falls,*
> *And a heart calling . . .*
> *I shall watch for Spring this year*
> *With a heart calling*
> *Where no bird calls.*

"Word for word," marvels Avedon, who has trouble recalling even the title of his youthful opus.

"Dick was astounded," Baldwin says with his eye-crinkling grin. "And not entirely *pleased*. It was a very leisurely weekend We'd get up at various times. And bump into each other near the wood-burning sauna on the lake. Oh, a *wonderful* lake. And a wonderful *week*end."

Later that summer, in Istanbul, a sightseeing bus filled with American social workers careened through a main thoroughfare. Suddenly there issued from the women tourists peering through the windows at the Moslem street scene a cacophony of shrieks.

"What is it?" demanded James Dumpson, then New York City's Welfare Commissioner. "I thought," he says now, "that there had been an accident. They squealed, 'Jimmy Baldwin—it's Jimmy Baldwin.' I didn't believe it. But I looked. And there he was. I stopped the bus and chased after him. But he was lost in the crowd."

At cocktail time that day, as sunset was gilding the fabled skyline and the last rays of the afternoon ricocheted from ar-rowed minarets to bubbled mosques, Dumpson strolled through the lobby of the Hotel Divan. "Look," someone said. "There's Jimmy Baldwin."

As familiar with Istanbul's oases as with Manhattan's, the writer was having a drink on the terrace.

"He was very gracious," Dumpson says. "I think he's one of the most gracious people I know. I'd never met him before and I was a little embarrassed when every member of the group I was shepherding stopped at the table to speak to me—hoping, of course, for an introduction."

Baldwin invited the Commissioner to dinner. "He said he was going to cook Southern fried chicken for his friends in Istanbul," Dumpson says. "But, when I got back to the hotel from the affair I had to attend, it was too late to join him. I was sorry to miss it."

At the end of November, Baldwin was balancing a coffee cup in the principal's office at Benjamin Franklin High School in Manhattan, very Ivy League in dark suit, dark tie and white shirt. He had just addressed a vociferously appreciative Junior Assembly (due at 9:30 A.M., he had arrived at 10:13 with his sister Gloria, his publisher, his publisher's wife, his editor and Bob Cordier) and was now carefully and courteously replying to the questions of a trio of flurried journalists from The Ben Jay Flash, the student publication.

"What made BLUES such a hit?" one of the boys asked.

"Was it?" Baldwin countered. Then he drew hard on his cigarette and delivered a straight answer. "Well," said Jimmy Baldwin, "I wanted to *upset* people—and I did."

"The only reason anyone tries to become an artist is because life is more important than art. Therefore no general, no statesman, no priest and no saint can bear witness to the human condition as the artist must. And if that is so, in order to love life, to act on it, every baby born, every woman, every man, all over the world, is sacred. And that means, in order to deal with *that*, which means *yourself*, one must be obscene —a strange word—and irreverent. One must be aware of the possibilities of the human spirit and, by watching, tell what we could—if we only dared—become."

Sixteen

James Baldwin now belongs to The Establishment he continues to profane. Rich, famous, sometimes snarling, sometimes beguiling, with a flat in Istanbul, a new apartment in Paris ("behind the

Bastille, naturally") and a newer house in New York, he is an essayist, novelist and playwright esteemed on at least four continents, an American relatively secure in the literary firmament (yet sweating to stay there), the Negro author younger Negro authors must measure themselves against and—yes—occasionally try to put down.

He is a distillation of the nation's experience as well as his own. Talking of whites and Negroes, writing about them, he wavers between the first person plural and the third. But his duality reflects his country's. Growing up in a culture that is neither all white nor all black, he assimilated both parts.

"The trouble with America," he says, "is that it *is* integrated —although no one will admit it." The integration is incomplete and incongruous, producing a kind of schizophrenia rather than a fusion, in Baldwin as in the rest of us. "This is no longer a white world or a black world," he says, adding *sotto voce*, "I'm not sure I've learned it yet." Of one thing he is sure: "If we do not manage to live together, we won't manage to live at all."

A master of communication, he deliberately jabs at the masochism latent in white Americans. To those Caucasians who would deny contributing in any way toward the destruction of his race, reminding him they were never slave owners, Baldwin lashes back, "I wasn't there *eye*-ther," and then administers shock treatment. "If I can pay for my present," he demands, "why can't you pay for your past?" But, saying it, he knows (and has written that he knows) that in the end each human being pays for his past, that no one of us goes scot free.

Since 1964, Baldwin has spent more time out of the United States than in it. He flew to Alabama in 1965 for the last day of the great march on Montgomery, walking hand in hand with Joan Baez, the folk singer. But it is impossible for him to man America's civil rights barricades from Stockholm or Jerusalem, from Istanbul or Paris. "I am a *writer*," he says defiantly, and now he does not postscript as he once did that there is no way of escaping your role in a revolution.

". . . It demands a great deal of time to write," Baldwin has said. "It demands a great deal of stepping out of a social situation in order to deal with it. And all the time you're out of it, you can't help feeling a little guilty that you are not, as it were, on the firing line, tearing down the slums and doing all these obviously needed things, which in fact other people can do better than you because it is still terribly true that a writer is extremely rare."

Weary unto death of the racial issue, he cannot forget it. He was in London when Malcolm X was murdered in Harlem. "You did it!" Baldwin screamed at white correspondents. "It is because of you—the men who created this white supremacy—that this man is dead. You are not guilty—but you did it!"

Inevitably, as the penalty of his success, he is castigated by many white Americans as an extremist and flailed by more radical Negroes as a moderate. A pamphlet published by a black nationalist satirized him with such viciousness that it made him weep. Yet at that very moment shoplifting drug addicts, desperate for a quick sale to finance their next fix, were hawking his books in Harlem's bars, perhaps the ultimate tribute to his popularity.

Baldwin's sensitivity extends to people, to moods, rarely to things. Visiting an English professor and his wife with Mary Painter several years ago, he glanced around him at the ample library and the mingling of plants, paintings, Oriental rugs and Danish furniture. "'This is the way I want to live when I grow up,' he said. It was a graceful compliment, but less than heartfelt. Grant Baldwin his typewriter, his recordings, cigarettes, beer, scotch and plenty of ice, and few men are as truly indifferent to their living quarters as he is.

The bleak and shabby pads he once occupied in Greenwich Village were probably more to his taste than the lavish, four-telephone, partially decorator-designed residence he leased on West End Avenue from late in 1963 until early in 1966. He called the apartment, the largest he had ever had, "the barn." The disparaging reference was apt. Only the foyer and the living room, with their melange of high-style colors (the ceiling and one wall tawny orange, another wall battleship gray, the rest stark white), and the office his sister shared with whichever of his young male assistants happened to be in residence, had any degree of warmth. The other rooms were almost bare, as though Baldwin had lost interest. Paying for three abodes, he remains essentially a nomad, rootless, dispossessed. In the very multiplicity of his homes, he succeeds in having none.

A decade ago, when he still knew what it was to be broke, Baldwin listed as his influences "the King James Bible, the rhetoric of the store-front church, something ironic and violent and perpetually understated in Negro speech—and something of Dickens' love of bravura." But now, in his ascendancy, he speaks of himself as "a street boy" and, basking in that fancy, traces his derivation to somewhat lowlier sources. Wearing a suit tailored for him by a Fifth Avenue firm recommended to his secretary by the British consulate in New York, Baldwin recently stood before an SRO audience in a school auditorium, the keynote speaker at a conference on "The Negro Writer's Vision of America," and, arms spread-eagled, declared:

"My models—my private models—are not Hemingway, not Faulkner, not Dos Passos, or indeed any American writer. I model myself on jazz musicians, dancers, a couple of whores and a few junkies . . ."

Later, exhibiting his fade-in, fade-out reliability, Baldwin attended a faculty reception, departing at one A.M., retiring at nine the following morning. That evening, without notice, he failed to show up for the second session of the conference. From ticket holders deprived of their star came a persistant obligato: "Where's Baldwin?" But no one there knew.

Baldwin is ostentatiously inept at handling money but it has the power to make him spiteful or loving. Ungrudging to the adherents of his various apostasies, he will blithely empty his wallet to assist a girl in Majorca with aspirations for the ballet or a youth in Manhattan with unfulfilled promise as a novelist. He is a soft touch for the most inept of hard luck stories. Acquaintances have sponged on him shamelessly for months at a time (one of them demonstrated his gratitude by absconding with most of his patron's wardrobe; Baldwin is hurt but, on the whole, philosophical about such heresies).

When William Hanley's SLOW DANCE ON THE KILLING GROUND opened on Broadway, Baldwin staged a party for the small cast, an act of largesse that set him back $500. It is not unusual for him to run up a $100 bill when supping with four or five friends. On one such occasion he informed Cordier, whose income was probably shorter than his own by a couple of digits, "You and I will pay." "No," said Cordier genially, "*you* will pay."

For venison prepared by a superb cook, Baldwin has gladly traveled ninety miles. But in New York he inclines toward "soul food"—chitterlings, barbecued ribs, fried chicken, pigs' feet.

When dining with fat-cat representatives of fat-cat organizations, however, he develops an insatiable appetite for luxury.

Given an opportunity, he will unhesitatingly indicate his preference for one or the other of Manhattan's notoriously expensive restaurants, then proceed to order such items as Russian caviar and vintage champagne. His appearance there is often the signal for the arrival of two, three or more members of the army of yea-sayers, fear-chasers and night-watchers he once dubbed his "menagerie." The uninvited guests promptly attach themselves to his party, no matter how arctic a greeting is tendered them by the host.

"Jimmy keeps watching you out of the corners of his eyes," one such victim reflected recently, "and I sometimes get the feeling he's using these people—his hangers-on—to test you."

But Baldwin tests everybody, endlessly probing for the chink of prejudice that will corroborate his fears and confirm his suspicions. Once he finds it, or thinks that he has, he swiftly exacts revenge for the spasms of pain thereby inflicted upon him. This circuit feeds back to him ever more reason for anguish. It spurts from him like semen. Verbalizing his grief in some way relieves it. "Jimmy," his quondam schoolmate, Art Moore, says with gentle irony, "puts the accent on suffering."

Baldwin habitually views himself as a figure of Dostoevskian tragedy. It is a concept that seems to comfort him. But if the chasms of his sorrow are fathomless, the peaks of his joy are correspondingly lofty. On his dark journeys around the globe, there are luminous intervals, a moment or an hour or a day, when life is not altogether minatory. He can be the beau of the ball, effervescent, his eyes and his lips and his perceptions synchronized, his irregular features glowing with affection.

He is better-looking than he was. Now that he has crossed to the far side of forty, his face looks lived in. His present age becomes him more than youth did. Baldwin will never be handsome but sometimes he seems beautiful. Laughter washes over him easily, pleating his cheeks, liberating his big, irregularly-spaced, white teeth, until his face is a mask of mirth. "When you say something Jimmy thinks is funny," publicity woman Andrea Smargon says of him, "his laughter is so delicious that it's impossible not to be suffused with a glow of pleasure at creating this delight in him." Rewarded with that kind of spontaneity, his friends—and sometimes even his foes—bask in it.

But his charm can freeze over, his welcome sprout thistles, his generosity transform itself with spine-jolting abruptness into malice. Langston Hughes' admirers have never forgiven Baldwin for his flagrantly patronizing review of the older writer's poems. "Every time I read Langston Hughes," Baldwin wrote in THE NEW YORK TIMES in 1959, "I am amazed all over again by his genuine gifts—and depressed that he has done so little with them."

The late Lorraine Hansberry argued that Baldwin was inimical not only to white middle-class liberals but also to black. "Jimmy can be just as mean to them," she said. "Look how he treats Langston. Jimmy talks like nobody else does in public. He talks the way Negroes talk among themselves after they've left a dinner party of mixed white and Negro. No matter how free you think you are, Jimmy makes you feel you've still got a little bit of Uncle Tom left in you."

If so, Hughes must be a notable exception. Rotund, benevolent, urbane, with a sharp pen and a mild tongue, the creator of the inimitable Jesse B. Simple was unruffled by Baldwin's critical onslaught. Unlike Richard Wright, Hughes even managed to derive some satisfaction from the incident.

"For a year after that review," he says with unmistakable relish, "every time I got a begging letter from people who wanted me to send their daughters through school or from Africans who wanted to come to the United States, I would reply: 'My income is very limited. I suggest you write to some of the best-selling writers, like James Baldwin.'

"And I went around town telling everybody about it. Someone told Jimmy. I heard he was not amused. But"—Hughes' cherubic innocence is neutralized by the contentment purring in his voice —"I think he must have been. After all," the poet concludes suavely, "Jimmy has a sense of humor."

Obviously circumstances can numb it. When his sister Paula and her escort inadvertently kept him waiting at El Faro's one night, Baldwin saw nothing remotely comical in that twist. Spluttering with indignation, he refused to sit down with them and swept out in a huff. He is now more strident than he once was, and more sulphurous. He is quicker to blame others for his own failings.

To be a Negro artist in the United States remains for Jimmy Baldwin "a very frightening assignment," magnifying the risks and the doubts that put scare on every writer's soul. "If I spend weeks and months avoiding my typewriter (and I do), sharpening pencils, trying to avoid going where I know I've got to go," he has said, "then one has got to use this to learn humility. After all, there is a kind of saving egotism about the artist's condition, which is this: I know that if I survive it, when the tears have stopped flowing or when the blood has dried, when the storm has settled, I do have a typewriter which is my torment but is also my work. If I can survive it, I can always go back there, and if I've not turned into a total liar, then I can use it and prepare myself in this way for the next inevitable and possibly fatal disaster."

He edges up to his typewriter cautiously, observing an elaborate purification ritual. "Jimmy has a very definite habit," says one witness. "When he's going to start writing, he goes into the kitchen and washes everything in sight—meticulously, like a first-class maid. He goes right through the whole house, scrubbing and cleaning everything. And the last thing he cleans is his desk. Then he starts to work."

What he produces in the next few years, he has told associates, will be crucial to his career. It is with this in mind that he has removed himself, at least temporarily, from political activity. But the turbulence of the life he leads has until now diverted much of his energy from his writing. If he could disentangle himself from the debris of his day-to-day collisions, he might bring to his fiction in particular the deliberation and the discipline that have sometimes been missing, lacunae that have delayed realization of his full power as a novelist. Fury has too often stripped his art of control; the flame might burn brighter if it threw off less heat.

His next book, currently entitled TELL ME HOW LONG THE TRAIN'S BEEN GONE, could mark his breakthrough into creative maturity. But any major work of his is bound to generate excitement, and his essays have already won him a permanent place in American letters. Whatever happens, Baldwin will be remembered as the writer who forced upon the consciousness of white America the terror and the wrath of being Negro in the United States.

Imperious, narcissistic, heterodox, incessantly and painfully aware, Baldwin is still pursued by the demons that harrassed him

245

in his youth. He detects conspiracy in adversity and feels himself a stranger everywhere, not least of all within himself. Garroted by insecurity and private remorse, he has kept his integrity undefiled. The about-faces he executes from time to time are born of febrile conviction, never of opportunism. Basically he is tough and game and resilient. Always afraid, and always conscious that he is afraid, he doesn't permit his fear to alter his direction. It may be that in the end he is less afraid than most of us.

Yawning before him twenty-four hours a day is the trap Americans set for celebrities of every magnitude: the hungry attention that baits them into detours and tricks them into excess, until they finally confuse their flatulence with pronouncements of cosmic stature.

"It's very important not to take yourself too *seriously,*" Baldwin says. In black velveteen overshirt and charcoal slacks, he looks like an animated splinter. Suddenly, he squats, his eyes wine-dark, his elbows resting on his thighs, a cigarette in one hand, a drink in the other, casual, comfortable, as though prepared to hold that muscle-straining pose throughout eternity. Smoke wreathes his brow in a lopsided halo.

"It's very important to understand that you're not a great man because other people *say* you're a great man. Y'know? It has made it more difficult for me to keep my *head.* But I *have* kept my head. And I *will.* As it turns out, I was right all *along.* I didn't want any of this shit. I didn't *want* a Cadillac. And now," says Jimmy Baldwin, "I've had the Cadillac and I *know.* Those grapes *are* sour."

Bibliographic Notes

Only the sources that provided quotations or background material have been listed here. Where books and periodicals are adequately identified in the body of the text, I have not duplicated them.

CHAPTER ONE

Note 1. James Baldwin's statement, "The really terrible thing . . . ," is from his essay, "My Dungeon Shook," in THE FIRE NEXT TIME, Dial Press, 1963.

CHAPTER TWO

Note 2. The quoted excerpts about "one's ghastly inadequacy" and the "light on a high, dark, mountain road" are from NOTHING PERSONAL, by Richard Avedon and James Baldwin, Atheneum Publishers, 1964.

CHAPTER THREE

Note 3. Some of the information in this chapter is based on the television documentary, "James Baldwin's Harlem", narrated by James Baldwin, produced by Arthur Barron, presented by Metropolitan Broadcasting Television, a division of Metromedia, Inc., Channel 5, New York City, June 1, 1964.

Note 4. Baldwin's query, "How is it possible for the child to grow up if the child is not loved?" is from NOTHING PERSONAL. *See Note 2.*

Note 5. The excerpt that begins, "Children can survive without money or security or things," *Ibid.*

Note 6. Baldwin's "melancholy conviction" that he has "scarcely ever had enough to eat" is from the Autobiographical Notes in his NOTES OF A NATIVE SON, Dial Press, 1963.

Note 7. Baldwin's reference to his mother's "exasperating and mysterious habit of having babies," *Ibid.*

Note 8. Baldwin criticized UNCLE TOM'S CABIN in two essays, "Everybody's Protest Novel" and "Many Thousands Gone" in NOTES OF A NATIVE SON. *See Note 6.*

Note 9. The description of Baldwin's attitude toward his pain and heartbreak is based on his own words in an article by Jane Howard, "Doom and Glory of Knowing Who You Are," LIFE, May 24, 1963.

Note 10. Baldwin quoted his childhood description of his teacher as "a little bit colored and a little bit white" in "James Baldwin Talks with Kenneth B. Clark," a television program, published in THE NEGRO PROTEST, Beacon Press, 1963.

Note 11. Baldwin's comment that his principal proved to him he didn't have to be "entirely defined" by his circumstances, *Ibid.*

Note 12. Baldwin cited his mother's description of Orilla Miller as "a christian" in his essay, "Notes of a Native Son," in the book of the same name. *See Note 6.*

Note 13. Mrs. Ayer's recollection that Baldwin's mother had "the gift of using language beautifully" is from "Notes on My Native Son" by Gertrude Elise Ayer, in HARLEM, A COMMUNITY IN TRANSITION, edited by John Henrik Clarke, The Citadel Press, 1964.

Note 14. Baldwin's memories of his mother's job as a domestic and of waiting for her at the subway are from Bryant Rollins' series on Baldwin in THE BOSTON GLOBE, April 14 through April 21, 1963.

Note 15. The picture of Mrs. Baldwin brushing and vaselining her children's hair, greasing their faces and limbs, "mercilessly" scrubbing and polishing them, is from Baldwin's essay, "East River, Downtown," in the collection NOBODY KNOWS MY NAME, Dial Press, 1961.

Note 16. Baldwin wrote about the hill in Central Park is his autobiographical novel, GO TELL IT ON THE MOUNTAIN, Dial, 1963, and later established this as an authentic detail from his own life.

Note 17. Baldwin cited the policeman's query, "Why don't you niggers stay uptown . . . ?" in his essay, "Down at the Cross," in THE FIRE NEXT TIME. *See Note 1.*

Note 18. The description of the policeman frisking Baldwin, *Ibid.*

CHAPTER SIX

Note 19. Baldwin's essay, "Down at the Cross" (see Note 17) and the television documentary (see Note 3) furnished some of the details in this section.

Note 20. The paragraph on Baldwin's reaction to De Witt Clinton High School ("I wasn't a bad student . . .") is taken from "Liberalism and the Negro, a Round-Table Discussion," COMMENTARY, March, 1964.

Note 21. The paragraph beginning "I assumed that no one had ever been born who was only five-feet-six-inches tall . . ." is from "The Artist's Struggle for Identity" by James Baldwin, LIBERATION, March, 1963.

Note 22 Baldwin described himself as "rather atypical" in his high school days in an interview with William Schecter, THE CLINTON NEWS, February 8, 1963.

Note 23. Baldwin commented on American history books and their effect on him in his address to the Cambridge Union Society of Cambridge University in February, 1965. It was printed in *The New York Times Magazine* on March 7, 1965.

Note 24. Baldwin's "worst discovery," that he believed what white America said of him, was defined in his speech to the National Lawyers Guild at Town Hall, on October 18, 1963.

Note 25. For the references to "Faith, Hope and Charity" and "Blindness, Loneliness and Terror" in connection with the church, *see Note 17.*

Note 26. David Baldwin's question to Jimmy ("You'd rather write than preach, wouldn't you?") and the boy's answer are from Baldwin's essay, "Notes of a Native Son," from the book of the same name. *See Note 6.*

Note 27. Baldwin's boyhood poem, "To Her," was published in THE MAGPIE, Volume XXV, Number 1, Winter, 1941.

Note 28. Baldwin's remembrance of his last sermon, "Set Thy House in Order," and of his agony in facing the fact that he didn't believe any more are from the series in THE BOSTON GLOBE. *See Note 14.*

CHAPTER SEVEN

Note 29. The material in this chapter is based in part on the essay, "Notes of a Native Son." *See Note 6.*

Note 30. Baldwin talked about his father's lapse of memory in the subway in the television documentary cited in *Note 3*.

Note 31 Baldwin wrote of the homicidal resentment aroused in him in New Jersey as "a kind of blind fever" and compared it to "some dread, chronic disease" in NOTES OF A NATIVE SON. *See Note 6.*

Note 32. The paragraphs beginning, "There is not a Negro alive who does not have this rage in his blood . . ." and "I do not know why, after a year of such rebuffs, I so completely failed to anticipate his answer . . . ," *Ibid.*

Note 33. It was in his television interview with Kenneth Clark that Baldwin declared, "By the time I was seventeen, you'd done everything that you could do to me." *See Note 10.*

Note 34. Baldwin recalled pressing pennies on his eyes "to make them go back" in a taped interview with Eve Auchincloss and Nancy Lynch, "Disturber of the Peace: James Baldwin," in MADEMOISELLE, May 1963.

Note 35. Baldwin referred to Richard Wright as "my witness, and alas! my father," in the essay, "Alas, Poor Richard," in NOBODY KNOWS MY NAME. *See Note 15.*

Note 36 It was in "Down at the Cross" that Baldwin said Elijah Muhammad reminded him "of my father and me as we might have been if we had been friends." *See Note 1.*

Note 37. The paragraph beginning, "He was righteous in the pulpit and a monster in the house . . . ," is from the MADEMOISELLE interview. *See Note 34.*

CHAPTER EIGHT

Note 38. For the source of Baldwin's reference to himself as "broke, naturally, shabby, hungry and scared," *see Note 35.*

Note 39 Richard Wright's greeting to Baldwin, "Hey, boy!" *Ibid.*

Note 40. Baldwin's comment that he is "not a writer" but "a rewriter," is from "A Talk With James Baldwin," by Martha MacGregor in THE NEW YORK POST, October 2, 1962

Note 41. Baldwin told about the people who advised him, "You can't write all the time, Jimmy—relax," in LIBERATION *See Note 21.*

Note 42. Baldwin's references to "trying not to act like a nigger" and what "acting like a nigger meant" to him, as well as "hated white people from the bottom of my heart" and "hated black people for being so common," are from the MADEMOISELLE interview. *See Note 34*

Note 43. Baldwin said the color of his skin "automatically" made him an expert on "the Negro problem" in his introduction to NOTES OF A NATIVE SON. *See Note 6.*

Note 44. Baldwin's feeling that white America's concept of the Negro male is "terrifying" and that he is a "phallic symbol" are from MADEMOISELLE. *See Note 34.*

Note 45. Baldwin's short story, "The Previous Condition," is included in the volume GOING TO MEET THE MAN, Dial Press, 1965

Note 46. The details about Baldwin's friend, Eugene Worth, are from "The New Lost Generation" by Baldwin, ESQUIRE, July, 1961.

Note 47. The paragraph beginning, "I could not be certain whether I was really rich or really poor," is from Baldwin's essay, "Notes for a Hypothetical Novel," in NOBODY KNOWS MY NAME. *See Note 15.*

CHAPTER NINE

Note 48 Baldwin mentioned his meeting with Richard Wright in Paris in "Alas, Poor Richard." *See Note 35.*

Note 49. Baldwin's early years in Paris are described in his essay, "Equal in Paris." *See Note 6.*

Note 50. For the affair of the stolen bedsheet, *Ibid*

Note 51. Baldwin suggested that

the price an American Negro pays for "acceptance" is "a profound, almost ineradicable self-hatred" in "Alas, Poor Richard," Part III. *See Note 35.*

Note 52. For the source of the paragraph beginning, "What was most difficult was the fact that I was forced to admit something I had always hidden from myself . . . ," see *Note 6.*

Note 53. Baldwin recalls hoping— "sad and incomprehensible as it now sounds"—to be patted on the head for originality by Richard Wright in "Alas, Poor Richard." *See Note 34.*

Note 54. "The man I fought so hard and who meant so much to me is gone." *Ibid.*

Note 55. In his book, REMEMBER TO REMEMBER, Henry Miller erroneously spelled Beauford Delaney's name "DeLaney."

Note 56. Baldwin said he wrote THE AMEN CORNER to explain "what those brothers and sisters were like when they weren't wearing their long white robes" in an interview with Nat Hentoff, THE NEW YORK TIMES, April 11, 1965.

Note 57. Baldwin was even "more scared" to write the play. *Ibid.*

Note 58. The description of the villagers in Loeche-les-Bains is from Baldwin's essay, "Stranger in the Village." *See Note 6.*

Note 59. The paragraph beginning ". . . The question of who I was was not solved because I had removed myself from the social forces which menaced me . . ." is from Baldwin's Introduction to NOBODY KNOWS MY NAME. *See Note 15.*

Note 60. For the sentence beginning, "Out of their hymns and dances come Beethoven and Bach . . ." and the following sentence, *see Note 58.*

Note 61. For the description of "that peculiar, intent, paranoiac malevolence" Baldwin saw in the eyes of Swiss villagers, *Ibid.*

Note 62. The phrase "the rage of the disesteemed" and the paragraph beginning, "No road whatever will lead Americans to the simplicity of this European village . . . ," *Ibid.*

Note 63. Baldwin said love, murder or disaster come "out of the same depths" in a televised interview with Kay Boyle, Channel 13, New York City, printed in PLAYBOY, December, 1964.

Note 64. Baldwin set down his aims in writing ("to begin to understand and accept the world and my own place in it") in a questionnaire he filled out for Dial Press on April 7, 1956.

Note 65. The book Baldwin removed from a shelf while discussing his review of Gide's MADELEINE was NOBODY KNOWS MY NAME, paperback edition, Dell Publishing Company, 1963.

Note 66. Baldwin told Kay Boyle it was "an unbearable experience" for him to listen to the overlong speeches in THE AMEN CORNER. *See Note 63.*

Note 67. The magazine for which Baldwin conducted the guided tour around his psyche was MADEMOISELLE. *See Note 34.*

Note 68. The description of the Baldwin-Mailer encounter as "the toughest kid on the block was meeting the toughest kid on the block" is from Baldwin's essay, "The Black Boy Looks at the White Boy." *See Note 15.*

Note 69. "Norman and I are alike in this, that we both tend to suspect others of putting us down . . ." *Ibid.*

Note 70. The clash between Baldwin and Mailer in Chicago in 1962 was recorded by Leonard Schecter in the "Working Press" column of THE NEW YORK POST, September 25, 1962.

CHAPTER ELEVEN

Note 71. It would be "more honorable" to go to Little Rock than to try to explain it in Europe, Baldwin noted in "The Discovery of What It Means To Be an American." *See Note 15.*

Note 72. Baldwin's interview with Negro children who were defying white mobs to enter "desegregrated" schools appeared in his essay, "A Fly in the Buttermilk." *See Note 15.*

Note 73. Elia Kazan's suggestion that the Emmett Till case would make a great movie was described by Baldwin as "a germ of a play" in the introduction to BLUES FOR MISTER CHARLIE, Dial Press, 1964.

Note 74. "I guess it's obvious that I'm afraid the dead boy will be me," from the article, "James Baldwin, an Original," by Gloria Steinem, VOGUE, July, 1964. Baldwin made the same point in his interview with Kay Boyle, but later deleted it from the printed version.

Note 75 For "The people who are in one's life or merely continually in one's presence reveal a great deal about one's needs and terrors," *see Note 68.*

Note 76. Baldwin told Bryant Rollins that "The Negro press has been unfriendly . . . because I come from the streets" and that "Those Negro leaders and white liberals who wanted me to return to America in 1957 now want to pay my fare back to Europe." *See Note 14.*

Note 77. Baldwin's address at Kalamazoo College has been included in the volume, NOBODY KNOWS MY NAME, under the title "In Search of a Majority."

Note 78. Baldwin's article in MADEMOISELLE was entitled "They Can't Turn Back," in the August, 1960 issue.

Note 79. Baldwin's piece, "The Dangerous Road Before Martin Luther King" appeared in HARPER'S MAGAZINE, February, 1961.

CHAPTER TWELVE

Note 80. It was John Ciardi in THE SATURDAY REVIEW, January 11,

1964, who inquired: "Does everyone in the known world lust . . . for the bodies of Negroes?"

Note 81. The excerpt from Baldwin's letter to Robert Mills beginning "My bones know . . . what waits for me in Africa," is from "Letters from a Journey" in HARPER'S MAGAZINE, May, 1963.

Note 82. Baldwin confessed that he had become "a Very Important Person" in LIBERATION *See Note 21.*

Note 83. James Meredith declared he had never made a mistake in his life in his book, THREE YEARS IN MISSISSIPPI, Indiana University Press, 1966. His comment on Baldwin "doing the New York twist" is from the same source.

CHAPTER THIRTEEN

Note 84. Baldwin's comments in the first three paragraphs of this chapter are from an article by Nat Henthoff, "It's Terrifying," THE NEW YORK HERALD TRIBUNE, June 16, 1963.

Note 85 Lena Horne characterized Baldwin as "a strange, distant, brilliant man" in LENA, by Lena Horne and Richard Schickel, Doubleday & Company, 1965.

Note 86. Baldwin's motives (to get "as wide and even as rowdy a range of opinion as possible") in assembling his friends for the meeting with Robert Kennedy was cited in NEWSWEEK, June 2, 1963.

Note 87. Professor Clark's comments on Jerome Smith and on several other aspects of the meeting with Kennedy are from James A. Wechsler's column, "RFK & Baldwin," in THE NEW YORK POST, May 28, 1963.

Note 88. The comment attributed to a member of Baldwin's faction, "That's what we want—an act," is from "Kennedy and Baldwin" in THE NEW REPUBLIC, June 15, 1963.

Note 89. Clark's summation, beginning, "Suddenly I looked at the Attorney General and understood

that he did not understand us . . ."
Ibid.

Note 90. Attorney General Kennedy's exchanges with the three belated apologists are from A THOUSAND DAYS by Arthur M. Schlesinger, Jr., Houghton Mifflin Company, The Riverside Press, 1965.

Note 91. Kennedy's comment to Schlesinger about Baldwin and his cohorts ("They didn't know anything . . ."), *Ibid.*

Note 92. Baldwin's statement at his press conference ("I am not prepared to say it was a failure . . .") was reported by Sue Solet, "N.Y. Negroes and Bobby—/Both Shocked," THE NEW YORK HERALD TRIBUNE, May 26, 1963.

Note 93. Senator Robert F. Kennedy talked about the black ghettos, the violence in Watts and public housing in his speech to the Entertainment Division of the Federation of Jewish Philanthropies, January 20, 1966.

Note 94. "Kenneth, all I need is a drink . . . I must decompress," from Kenneth Clark's introduction to his televised talk with Baldwin in THE NEGRO PROTEST, Beacon Press, 1963.

CHAPTER FOURTEEN
Note 95. Baldwin told Gloria Steinem that he had "a lot riding" on BLUES FOR MISTER CHARLIE. *See Note 73.*

Note 96. Richard Avedon's "Spring at Coventry" was printed in THE MAGPIE, Spring, 1941.

CHAPTER FIFTEEN
Note 97. The quotation that introduces this chapter, beginning "The only reason anyone tries to become an artist . . ." is from a speech Baldwin delivered at a conference on The Negro Writer's Vision of America at the New School for Social Research in New York City, April 23, 1965.

Note 98. In his short story, "This Morning, This Evening, So Soon," included in the volume GOING TO MEET THE MAN, Baldwin wrote: "I've never understood why, if I have to pay for the history written in the color of my skin, *you* should get off scot-free!" He answered himself in the person of a Frenchman: "You think that I—we—are not paying for our history?"

Note 99. For the paragraph beginning, "It demands a great deal of time to write . . . ," *see Note 21.*

Note 100. The pamphlet that made Baldwin cry was *Color Us Cullid* by Cecil Elombe Brath, Standard Publishing Company, 1963.

Note 101. Baldwin first listed his literary influences in his introduction to NOTES OF A NATIVE SON. The more flamboyant version was unveiled at the New School for Social Research in response to a question from the audience. *See Note 97.*

Note 102. Lorraine Hansberry's comment on the way Baldwin treated Langston Hughes was in the article, "Everybody Knows His Name," by Marvin Elkoff, ESQUIRE, August, 1964.

Note 103. For the source of Baldwin's statement on being a Negro artist in the United States ("If I spend weeks and months avoiding my typewriter . . ."), *see Note 21.*

CPSIA information can be obtained
at www.ICGtesting.com
Printed in the USA
LVHW021756240920
667016LV00014B/1299